THE TATAR YOKE

THE TATAR YOKE

Charles J. Halperin

Slavica Publishers, Inc.

Slavica publishes a wide variety of textbooks and scholarly books on the languages, people, literatures, cultures, history, etc. of the USSR and Eastern Europe. For a complete catalog of books and journals from Slavica, with prices and ordering information, write to:

Slavica Publishers, Inc.
PO Box 14388
Columbus, Ohio 43214

ISBN: 0-89357-161-X

This book was published in 1986.

Text set by Gail Lewis.

Printed in the United States of America.

Dedicatio

In Memorium, Michael Cherniavsky

(1923–1973)

CONTENTS

Acknowledgments

I am indebted to the International Research and Exchanges Board and the Russian Institute of Columbia University for financial assistance in the completion of this monograph.

I also wish to express my sincerest appreciation to Walter Michener for his assistance.

Introduction

Once, while analyzing the contributions to early Muscovite ideology of a variety of Old Russian literary works, I made an interesting discovery. All scholarship on the subject notwithstanding, the works recounting the Battle of Kulikovo Field (in which, in 1380, Grand Prince Dmitrii Donskoi of Moscow defeated Emir Mamai of the Golden Horde) did not celebrate the occasion as Russia's liberation from the Tatar Yoke. The sources hailed the military victory without mentioning its consequences for the suzerainty of Russia. I also encountered a further curiosity in the course of my research. The Russian chronicles often defended Muscovite political actions in terms of Chingisid legitimacy. They appeared both to endorse and exploit the principle that only Chingis Khan's direct descendants were entitled to the throne of the Golden Horde.[1] This latter observation was simply an extension of Michael Cherniavsky's insight concerning the Russian sources' use of the same word, *tsar'*, to translate both the Byzantine *basileus* and the Mongol *khan*. Cherniavsky pointed out that this was ideologically significant, since the term *tsar'* implicitly accorded Russia's Mongol ruler the same legitimacy as the Byzantine emperor.[2]

This research suggested that close textual reading would reveal two things. First, it would show that students of the Mongol period have allowed anachronistic modern concepts to embellish their reading of the medieval sources, an example being the widespread assumption that the Kulikovo Cycle applauds the demise of the Tatar Yoke. Second, it would reveal that at the same time scholars have overlooked much information that the sources do contain concerning Russia's relationship with the Mongols, such as the implications of Muscovite respect for the Chingisid principle. It seemed necessary to reassess the entire corpus of medieval Russian source material on the Tatars with greater concern for literal meaning, but also with increased sensitivity to the kind of information about Russo-Tatar relations that was masked behind the relentlessly religious and patriotic stance of the contemporary literature.

These concerns animated some of my subsequent research. I found proof of a detailed appreciation of Chingisid genealogy in a provincial Rostov monastery.[3] Travelers' descriptions of sixteenth-century Muscovy as "Asiatic" I dismissed as prejudiced.[4] I began to focus on the problem of Russia and the Mongols. Not only did accounts of the events of 1380 not proclaim Russia's freedom, but the tales of the Tatar conquest turned out not to express the concept of conquest. This was difficult to reconcile with Russia's later ideological exaltation of the conquering Chingisid dynasty.[5] I found suggestive the complicated pattern of interaction between the Inner Asian Turkic Bulgars and the Slavic population of the Balkans during the First Bulgarian Empire.[6] And I started to argue against a Europocentric approach to the Mongol period of Russian history as a whole.[7] At this point I resolved to undertake a comprehensive analysis of the Mongol problem.

My object in this book is to analyze precisely how the medieval Russian sources present the Tatars. My methodology is *explication de texte*, neither novel nor controversial. There are, however, two absolute prerequisites to a meaningful interpretation of a text. We must study the origin, evolution, and reliability of the text itself, and we must explore the political, economic, social, and cultural contexts which give meaning to the intellectual content. The former task is rightfully the province of textology. Soviet scholars in particular have devoted their considerable energies and erudition to tracing the literary histories of those medieval Russian chronicles and monuments of Old Russian literature which are the source base for any analysis of Russo-Tatar relations. There is a continuing debate within Soviet scholarship concerning the methodological legacy of A. A. Shakhmatov, whose comparative method demanded the examination of all manuscripts, variants, and redactions of each text.[8] Even Shakhmatov's followers concede, however, that when only one manuscript exists or when, in spite of the so-called "open tradition" of Old Russian literature,[9] a text is unvarying, internal criticism is the only possible approach. The weakness of Soviet scholarship in this area derives not from this limitation of the Shakhmatov method but rather from the conceptual framework which all Soviet literary specialists and historians bring to bear upon the issue of Russo-Tatar relations. Soviet authors are superlative technicians in tracing the history of a text and superior detectives in ascertaining its institutional, political, and ideological biases. Yet they all proceed from the assumption that the medieval sources present Russo-Tatar relations in terms of conquest and liberation and that they portray the Tatars with unremitting hostility as national oppressors. This approach is patriotic and nationalistic and has something to be said for it, but it distorts the real import of the texts. Its premises result in a series of unwarranted presumptions about what the texts say, and in blindness to what they can reveal. It must be added that this conceptual framework, which was inherited from Imperial Russian scholarship, is largely shared by western scholars and not a uniquely Soviet failing. The present monograph will take full advantage of the enormous contributions Soviet scholars have made to the study of medieval Russian historical and literary texts, while taking issue with Soviet interpretations of their political and ideological content.

It is also necessary, of course, to study the perceptions and conceptions of the Tatars contained in the medieval texts within a broader historical context. Yet Russian intellectual history during the Mongol period has often been studied in a vacuum. To rectify this I have attempted to survey the Mongol impact on Russian history in a separate monograph, the results of which are briefly presented in the first chapter of the present volume.[10] Placing the Russian experience with the Tatars within the comparative frameworks of both the medieval ethno-religious frontier[11] and the Mongol Empire[12] has permitted a more balanced appraisal of the Mongol influence on Russian history. Russian historiographic presentation of the Mongol problem also demanded investigation. This too I have dealt with separately.[13]

It has been suggested that there was in Old Russian literature a "literary etiquette," a set of literary, aesthetic, and moral norms governing the presentation of certain subjects.[14] In the case of Russo-Tatar relations, this dictated, for example, that in descriptions of battles between Russians and Tatars, the Russians should always be outnumbered.[15] These unspoken guidelines in the medieval sources are in fact far more pervasive and complex than anyone has appreciated. They form part of a broad cultural pattern of the medieval ethno-religious frontier which I have called the ideology of silence. (The essence of this intellectual stance is that the enemy must be either execrated or ignored.) This monograph should provide considerable data, much of it unexpected, for the construction of a more nuanced analysis of the literary etiquette determining the treatment of Russo-Tatar relations in the medieval sources.

The present work is an attempt to present a chronological exploration of this treatment. (The only two previous attempts have been brief articles, superficial, out-dated, and flawed by uncritical approaches to the sources.)[16] Thematic problems or texts which do not fit into this sequential framework I have dealt with elsewhere.[17] Following an introductory chapter which gives a general picture of Russo-Tatar relations, I shall analyze, text by text, the presentation of the Mongols in the medieval Russian sources, beginning with the first Russian encounter with the Tatars in 1223 and ending with the "formal" liberation of Russia in 1480. The order is determined by the events described rather than by the texts, which were often written much later.

The simplistic picture of Russo-Tatar relations in existing historiography is a distortion. Scrupulous attention to the real content of the sources reveals a complex and often contradictory set of attitudes. To observe that the Russian bookmen were hostile to the Tatars is scarcely to scratch the surface. In the analyses that follow we shall see, among other things: how Russian attitudes toward Tatars varied from region to region and from epoch to epoch; how the bookmen went to great lengths to discriminate between the image of the khan and the image of the Tatars in general; how political events were translated into religious terms so they could be reconciled with the Orthodox Christian Weltanschauung; and how Russian intellectuals avoided the concepts of conquest and liberation in discussing Russia's relationship with the Mongols. The variegated mosaic that emerges comes far closer to suggesting the nature of medieval Russian attitudes toward their conquerors than modern concepts of patriotism and national liberation imposed on medieval writers by modern readers.

Chapter I

Russia and the Golden Horde

The phrase "the Tatar Yoke," universally applied to the 240 years of Mongol rule in Russia, conjures up images of barbaric Asiatic nomads engaged in cruel oppression and parasitic exploitation. This congeries of images resonates with the whole mythology, part of European tradition since classical times, of "barbarians" who are simultaneously dangerous and inferior.[1] The consensus of traditional Russian historiography, both Imperial and Soviet, is entirely consistent with this simplistic vision. Some scholars have presumed that the Mongols exerted no influence on Russian history, others that their influence was purely deleterious. The general assumptions are that the Mongols wrecked the economy with their destruction of life and property and merciless extraction of revenue and troops; that their interference in the Russian principalities' political affairs lowered political morality and fostered disunity; and that since the Mongols remained on the steppe, converted to Islam, and assimilated with the indigenous nomads rather than settling among the sedentary Christian Russians, no cultural exchanges took place.[2] Critics seeking to explain failings of subsequent Russian or Soviet society often pointed to the Mongols. The Mongols had isolated Russia from Europe, cutting it off from the benefits of the Renaissance and the Reformation. Mongol economic exploitation had left Russia permanently backward and technologically stagnant. Worst of all, by reducing the Russian people to abject servility to absolute power, the Mongols created an "Asiatic" political culture preventing Russia from ever following the European path to democracy and industrial capitalism. The result was the survival of a Russian autocracy after the Tatars were overthrown and the eventual replacement of that regime by another equally repressive, namely the Bolsheviks. The immoral and deceitful policies, both foreign and domestic, of Imperial and Soviet regimes are simply the legacy of the medieval Mongols.[3] The most elaborate formulation of this line of argument is the theory of "oriental despotism." This was an infection the Mongols contracted when they conquered China, and which was transmitted to Russia via the Golden Horde.[4] The most metaphysical variant of this approach is that of the famous Eurasian school. Its adherents, believing autocracy congenital to the "Turanian" soul, did not disapprove of undemocratic forms of government and saw the Mongol period as the key to Russia's manifest destiny. Geopolitical determinism dictated that the Russians, who were neither Europeans nor Asiatics, but Eurasians, would recreate the empire of Chingis Khan moving eastward just as the ancient conqueror had created it moving westward.[5] The later works of George Vernadsky took a different approach. He saw autocracy as necessary to overthrow the Mongols but did not believe that this temporary need had forever dashed Russian democratic aspirations. This is a departure from Eurasianist dogma.[6]

The conception that the Mongols permanently altered Russian history for the worse is expressed in the famous nineteenth-century aphorism, "Scratch a Russian, find a Tatar!" In effect this is a double ethnic slur, attacking one hated people as resembling an even more hated people. The presumption in any case is that Russians act the way they do because they are no longer Europeans; centuries of rule by Asiatics have turned the Russians, too, into barbarians.

The tenacious assumption that Mongol rule cannot have been anything other than destructive has roots which are at best Europocentric, at worst racist. It reduces to a belief that Europeans are politically and morally (and, indeed, in every other way) superior to Asians, a belief which the history of medieval and modern European states does not substantiate. The Mongols were enormously destructive as they carved out their empires, but so too were Alexander, Julius Caesar, and Napoleon. Compared to their sedentary neighbors the Mongols were not more cruel, merely more proficient in military matters. Ethnic stereotypes do not help clarify the significance of the Mongols for Russian history. The atrocities of Attila the Hun, Chingis Khan, or Tamerlane do not constitute a picture of their influence, any more than the dynastic feuds and degenerate courts of Rome and Byzantium illustrate the impact of those empires.

A balanced approach to the Mongols' impact on Russian history must accept as its premise the fact that no relationship lasting almost two and a half centuries can either be dismissed as unimportant or assumed to have been uniformly deleterious. We can assume that Mongol influence was not the same in all areas of Russian life, and that it varied over the years from region to region.   We can assert that the Mongols must always be taken into account when studying Russian history of the thirteenth, fourteenth, and fifteenth centuries.   This may seem a modest stipulation, but the Imperial Russian historians Sergei M. Soloviev and Vasilii O. Kliuchevskii dismissed the Mongol factor so completely that no Mongol period appears in their great schemas of the periods of Russian history.   Mongol influence was too powerful and pervasive for this attitude to be perpetuated either explicitly or implicitly.

That the history of the term "the Tatar Yoke" is unknown is indicative of the neglect in Russian historiography of the historical problem of Mongol influence.   Yet the phrase does not antedate the seventeenth century, and to presume that it reflects the vision of Russians during the Mongol period or to apply the concept in the analysis of the medieval Russian sources is to risk anachronism. The impact of the Mongols on Russian history must be studied not by beginning with the premise of Russian demonology and seeking its origins, but by looking at Russo-Tatar relations between 1223 and 1480 closely and without preconceptions.   To understand them we must penetrate the medieval Russian sources by trying to comprehend them literally on their own terms to see what they actually say.   Discussing medieval Russian attitudes with anachronistic terms like "the Tatar Yoke" can only lead to distortion.   The present monograph will try to restore the integrity of the medieval Russian sources as the essential groundwork for a more accurate conception of the Mongols' role in Russian history.

Examination of the full spectrum of Russo-Tatar relations suggests that we may profitably analyze them under the rubric of the medieval ethno-religious frontier.   This concept encompasses the many societies during the Middle Ages, many of them conquest societies, that lay along the fluctuating frontiers separating the warring worlds of Christianity and Islam.   In these societies peoples of profoundly inimical religions and cultures were forced to live in close proximity.   For example, in thirteenth-century Valencia in Spain the Catholic conquerors ruled a population of Moorish Muslims;[7] the Orthodox Christians of the Byzantine Empire interacted extensively with Muslims both within and without their borders from the birth of Islam until the fall of Constantinople to the Ottomans and of course long after;[8] and the French crusaders who founded the Kingdom of Jerusalem had to contend with both Muslim and Orthodox Christian subjects.[9]   In all such societies, though mutual hostility was an ideological imperative (since extermination of the infidel was a religious duty and the justification of the original campaigns), a wide variety of peaceful interactions inevitably arose.   Christians and Muslims had no choice but to learn each others' languages and cultures; commercial and military cooperation alike proved profitable; and conquerors often found it expedient to adopt some of the institutions and even customs of their subjects.   Even in China at the far end of the continent the situation was analogous, though the religions and cultures were different.   China, where Confucian literati/bureaucrats were confronted with shamanist Inner Asian pastoral nomads, provided the model for Lattimore's articulation of the theory that the frontier was not a boundary but a zone across which people, ideas, and institutions flowed in both directions.[10]

Russia during the Middle Ages was such a frontier society, at the interface of Christendom and pagan and Muslim Asia.   Indeed, as the Eurasianists well appreciated, the East Slavs were compelled to live and fight with Inner Asian nomads during most of their history, from the earliest Kievan times through the Mongol period and the Muscovite era which followed.   Relations between the East Slavs and the peoples of the steppe conformed throughout to the pattern of mixed prejudice and pragmatism characteristic of the frontier.   From this perspective, the Mongol period emerges as merely the most intensive and dramatic portion of the continuum of interaction between the East Slavs and their steppe-dwelling neighbors.

The Mongol Empire, like all previous Inner Asian empires, expanded along the great Eurasian caravan routes.   With the wealth that came from protecting and taxing international commerce, the Mongols ran a complex and sophisticated political entity with a bureaucracy capable of the phenomenal achievement of conducting a census of all of its holdings from China to Central Asia to Russia to Persia.   Following the fragmentation of the empire, the various successor states went their own ways as each adapted to indigenous conditions.   In China and Persia the Yüan and Ilkhanid dynasties lived among their subjects and developed a commonality of interests with them.   In China, for example, the Mongols carefully fostered local economic development and legal reform.[11]   Furthermore, in China and Persia alike the Mongol overlords adopted local religions and were inevitably drawn into native sectarianism between Buddhists, Taoists, Confucianists, and Muslims in the one case and between Sunni Muslims, Shiite Muslims, Orthodox Christians, and Jews in the other. This involvement weakened a position already made tenuous by the lack in either country of extensive pastures. Without grasslands the pastoral nomadic life which produced the skilled and tireless mounted archer was not possible. Indeed, it was not even possible to support the vast numbers of horses Mongol armies needed to function. As a result of these problems Mongol rule in both China and Persia proved relatively fragile. Both dynasties were overthrown about a century after the original Mongol conquests.

China and Persia were wealthy lands and desirable prizes, and the Mongols resorted to direct occupation because they had no other means to control them. Russia was a different matter. With the steppe the true heartland of the Golden Horde, Russia was in every sense peripheral. The primary focus of the Horde's foreign policy was its alliance with the Mamelukes of Egypt against the Ilkhanids of Persia, who controlled the coveted rich pastures and caravan routes of Azerbaidjan.[12] Not only could Russia not match the wealth of other Mongol holdings, but the enormous pastures of the Pontic and Caspian steppe allowed the bulk of the Golden Horde's Mongols to remain a formidable nomadic army within easy striking distance of the Russian forests. The Mongols did assimilate an indigenous population, but of Turkic-speaking nomads whose culture was similar to their own. Drawing its profits from the caravan routes and its subsistence from the steppe, the Golden Horde stayed closest to the traditions of the original Mongol Empire and proved the most durable of its successor states. While the Battle of Kulikovo attests the vigor of Russian opposition, Mongol rule in Russia endured more than twice as long as in China and Persia because it was indirect.[13] (Ironically, it was common in traditional Russian historiography to speak of the brevity of Mongol rule. This was made easier by officially terminating it with Donskoi's victory at Kulikovo in 1380 and ignoring Khan Tokhtamysh's sack of Moscow two years later and the additional century of Mongol domination that followed.)

Whereas Mongol conquerors elsewhere eventually acquired some of the characteristics of the civilizations they had subjugated, with the Golden Horde, who controlled Russia from a distance, this did not happen. It does not follow, however, that remote rule kept Russian civilization free of Mongol influence. Indeed, given that remote rule greatly prolonged the period of Mongol hegemony, it may well have resulted in a greater Mongol influence than would otherwise have been the case. The Mongol influence on Russian history was, in fact, considerable, and in many ways analogous to the influence of the Moors on Catholic Valencia, the Muslims on French Jerusalem, and the Byzantines on Muslim Arabs and Turkic peoples. As elsewhere along the ethno-religious frontier, this impact varied in different spheres of life and at different times.

In the economic realm, the costs of the conquest and the heavy tribute extracted thereafter must have been stupendous. The Mongols razed many of Russia's cities during the campaigns of 1237-1240 and destroyed much of the agricultural infrastructure necessary to sustain urban life. Further, Mongol raids continued during the thirteenth century, systematically weakening the economic resources of Vladimir-Suzdalia, and in the fourteenth, of those of Riazan', Tver', and Nizhnii Novgorod. On top of the tribute, Russians were required to pay the expenses of the resident Mongol administrators, the *baskaki*, and of the *posoly*, the Mongol envoys. Cities and princes frequently required ransoming, and large bribes were often necessary to lubricate dealings with the Horde. Loss of manpower also affected the economy, for the loss of life during the conquest and subsequent raids was great, and the Mongols continued to indulge in desultory slave-raiding and forcible recruiting. In addition, many of Russia's skilled builders and craftsmen were removed to the steppe to help construct the new Mongol cities. We can only say that the total costs of Mongol rule are beyond calculation.[14]

Devastation and exploitation, however, are far from being the whole story of the Mongols' impact on the Russian economy. The Mongols also provided the means for new economic life. Cowrie shells, boxwood combs, and other oriental goods found in rural as well as urban sites throughout Russia show that Russia, too, benefited from the international commerce the Mongols fostered for their own profit. While the Horde did reroute the fur trade to the detriment of Novgorod, that city's continued prosperity was surely linked to the Golden Horde's protection of Hanseatic merchants.[15] In any case the new fur route resulted in new wealth for other centers such as Moscow and Ustiug.[16] Though it took half a century, the Russian economy did recover. Urban development and church construction as well as literary production (which also requires economic surplus) increased markedly in the second half of the fourteenth century. It is a peculiarity that the Russian peasants, always presumed to live in isolated, autarkic villages with subsistence-level natural economies, were able to pay the Mongol tribute in silver. How the economic surplus necessary for this arose is unknown, but the medieval Russian economy was apparently more advanced, and certainly more resilient, than has been supposed. Despite the severity of the economic drain imposed by the Mongols, the Russian economy rebuilt, surely as a result of the Golden Horde's concern for international commerce. Commerce was more profitable than any other sector of the economy, and the cities that swelled during the economic revival were those along the thriving continental caravan routes.[17]

Though the Mongols played an active role in Russian politics, they did so without displacing the political infrastructure of the Russian principalities. They occasionally executed Russian princes but always replaced them with members of the legitimate Riurikid clan. Indeed, succession to the grand princely throne of Vladimir proceeded according to Russian custom during the thirteenth century. However, the emergence in the fourteenth century of regional power centers like Moscow and Tver' in Vladimir-Suzdalia forced a change in Mongol policy. The Mongols responded to this potential threat by throwing their weight behind certain principalities to try to prevent too great a concentration of Russian strength. The outcome of the struggle for supremacy in the Volga River-Oka River mesopotamia and the role of Tatar manipulation in the rise to preeminence of Moscow has long been the subject of great controversy.[18] Part of the acrimony arises from an emotional reaction against the possibility that Moscow could receive political and military assistance from the Mongols without being "tainted." Actually, of course, military alliances between deadly ethnic and religious foes were commonplace throughout the medieval ethno-religious frontier. Catholic Spaniards allied themselves with one group of Moors against another; in Palestine the Knights Templar were at one time allied with the heretical Shiite Muslim sect, the Assassins; and in China divide-and-conquer was the tactic for dealing with Uralo-Altaic peoples since time immemorial. In the early fourteenth century Moscow collaborated with the Golden Horde, which obliged with destructive raids on Moscow's rival, Tver'. In the third quarter of that same century the two cities reversed their positions, as Moscow rebelled against the

Horde, and Tver' sought and received help from the Tatars. As it happened the Horde was in the midst of civil war and could not muster the force necessary to tip the balance in favor of Tver'. Moscow emerged unchallenged as hereditary possessor of the grand princely throne of Vladimir. It must be noted that there was no great difference in the Tatar policies of Moscow and Tver'—each collaborated or rebelled as it seemed advantageous. Moscow's timing was better.

Moscow's success and expansion must have rested on more than Mongol political and military assistance, however, otherwise the Muscovite annexations would have collapsed when the Tatars withdrew their support. Moscow's competitive edge arose in part from the fact that it continued to extract tribute at the high levels the Mongols had originally imposed. This revenue and the damage the Tatars had done to the economies of Moscow's rivals during the Muscovite-Tatar alliance secured Moscow's economic position. The Horde was never able to undermine its power base, even with the sack of the city and plunder of Muscovite territory in 1382.[19]

In addition, Moscow was able to control and exploit its new acquisitions as a result of adopting much of the Mongols' administrative apparatus. The Mongols' success in creating and administrating a great empire shows that these institutions were worthy of imitation. It was commonplace along the medieval ethno-religious frontier for the conquering elite to retain to some degree the administrative and fiscal systems of their large subject populations: hence the survival of Moorish taxes, administrative divisions, offices, and coins in Catholic Valencia; of Muslim taxes in French Jerusalem; of Byzantine taxes, bureaucracies, and provincial boundaries in the Umayyad Arab and early Ottoman Turkic Empires. In Russia the Mongols superimposed Mongol taxes on top of the indigenous taxes. Of the resulting system, the Muscovites retained what seemed best. They also borrowed the Mongol customs tax, the office of the customs tax collector, and the stamp signifying that the tax had been paid. (All were denoted by the word *tamga*, from whence derives the Russian word *tamozhnia*, customs house.) The Mongols had developed the *yam*, or postal system, into the fastest overland communications network Eurasia had ever seen.[20] It proved adaptable and efficient even in the immensity of China.[21] Muscovy needed a postal system within its own growing dominions and created one on the Mongol model.

Muscovy was indebted to the Golden Horde in other ways as

well.   Militarily, the Moscovites imitated the organization of the Mongol field army into five divisions—advance guard, main regiment, left and right flanks, and rear guard—and adopted Mongol armament.   In diplomacy, Muscovite procedures and etiquette derived from the elaborate and eclectic practices of the Golden Horde.[22]   Muscovite bureaucratic organization, and conceivably the diplomatics of bureaucratic paper, may be traced to Mongol precedents,[23] and indeed, Mongol institutional models were pervasive in the Muscovite bureaucracy.

Though Muscovite borrowing of Mongol political institutions was extensive, it was still selective.   The Muscovites never borrowed the Mongol census, probably because it was beyond their administrative capabilities.   Interestingly, all the institutions Muscovy borrowed from the Mongols were those in use before the Horde's conversion to Islam, i.e., those of the earlier Mongol Empire.   Following Khan Uzbek's conversion in the fourteenth century, the Golden Horde borrowed the *diwan* administrative system, the most sophisticated in the Muslim world and already in use in Egypt, Persia, and Central Asia.   The *diwan* system was inseparable from the Muslim faith and consequently, despite its utility and efficiency, tabu for Christian Russia.   In any case, Moscow's use of Tatar institutions was provisional.   Under Peter the Great all the Tatar models, along with a number of others that no longer met Russian needs, were discarded.   They were replaced with models from the West.

The Muscovite autocracy that emerged after Mongol power had finally been broken was neither an imitation of nor a response to Mongol rule.   A number of charges indict the Mongols as the cause of Russia's subsequent history of autocratic rule.   One is that they destroyed the *veche*, the "democratic" town meeting that was part of the Kievan legacy.   In fact, the *veche* survived, at least in Novgorod, a city quite subservient to Mongol rule which paid the tribute and other taxes and when necessary solicited Tatar military aid (no doubt with bribes).[24]   Besides, the democratic nature of the *veche* is very much open to question.   Historians have also accused the Mongols of promoting autocratic rule by reducing the Russian people to abject servility.   Actually, active and violent opposition to Tatar oppression never ceased.   A series of urban uprisings, in the northeast in 1261,[25] in Tver' in 1327,[26] and of course in Moscow in the later fourteenth century, attest to this. Russian acquiescence to Mongol rule was transient and insincere in both cities and the countryside. The ideology and forms of Muscovite autocracy were in fact largely of Byzantine rather than Tatar provenance (despite Russia's opportunistic use of the Chingisid principle). Nor did autocracy arise from the need to overthrow the Golden Horde; it did not emerge until after the Horde had already collapsed. Autocracy was the norm in early modern Europe, and Muscovy did not require a Mongol model to join in this widespread phenomenon.

Though Russians and Tatars met most often on the field of battle, they also engaged in a variety of peaceful interactions with major social consequences for Russia. One of these was Christian Russia's intimate acquaintance with infidel Mongol society. The medieval Russian sources are replete with the names of Mongol khans, princes, officials, envoys, and commanders, all impeccably transcribed. Far from being part of an alien, faceless horde, these Tatars were clearly well known as individuals to both the Russian bookmen and their audiences. In addition, thousands of Russians visited the Golden Horde, where Russian princes, nobles, warriors, merchants, clergy, and slaves were ubiquitous.[27] For these Russians dealing directly with their Tatar overlords, a thorough knowledge of Mongol customs, etiquette, and language was a *sine qua non* for success or even survival. The Russians were acquainted with Turkic languages since Kievan times, and Turkic of some sort must have been the *lingua franca*. References to translators in the sources are few and far between, and bilingualism was apparently too commonplace to elicit mention. Though religious barriers eventually became insuperable, intermarriage between the two royal clans—the Riurikids and the Chingisids—was not unknown. While the Mongols were tolerant of all faiths, the Russians were not, and Chingisid princesses married to Russian princes would have had to convert. Similarly, while many Russians became adept in Mongol social graces, Orthodox Christianity seems to have efficiently excluded any Mongol customs from Russian society.

Even in warfare Russo-Tatar relations involved more than fighting. A shared martial ethos of chivalry among medieval warrior aristocracies transcended political and cultural barriers all the way from Spain to the Great Wall of China (only the Chinese glorified intellectual and artistic achievements above military prowess). This rapport between valiant enemies surfaces in the *Povest' o razorenii Riazani Batyem*[28] in Batu's treatment of the dying hero, Evpatii, and in the epic *Zadonshchina* in the hostile warriors' mutual glory-seeking and compassion.[29]

The dearth of Mongol cultural traits in Russian culture has seemed to some to confirm their belief that the Mongols simply had little culture to offer. Of course this is untrue. The Golden Horde had its own uniform, albeit derivative, archaeological culture and also a "high" culture that arrived with Islam. Sarai was a city of paved streets, mosques, meddresses, caravansarais, and palaces. Literature in Chagatai Turkic can be dated to the fifteenth century. Russian culture remained impervious to the influences of Mongol high culture because it was tainted with Islam and hence tabu. Indeed peoples all along the medieval ethno-religious frontier resisted the transmission of elements of "high" culture because of its unmistakable religious character. (However, it was always convenient and symbolically pleasing to convert mosques into churches or churches into mosques.) Though a certain number of infidel texts did find their way into Old Russian literature, they did so through sanitized intermediate translations, and the Russians were unaware of their real origin. (Even the story of Buddha was reworked into a Christian fable.)[30] It is worth noting that the Russians excluded cultural elements from Catholic Europe as rigorously as those from the Muslim Tatars; hence it is unlikely that the Renaissance would have affected Russia even if the Mongols had never arrived.[31]

It is one of the ironies of the Mongol period that Russian culture flourished under infidel domination. The khans of the Golden Horde endowed the Russian Orthodox Church with fiscal and judicial immunities. The Church, as a consequence, grew wealthy enough to sponsor in the fourteenth and fifteenth centuries impressive achievements in church construction, icon and fresco painting, and literature. Russian culture recovered along with the economy, and renewed inspiration from Byzantium sparked a period of great cultural productivity and fascinating innovation.[32]

The preceding brief sketch, with its diplomacy and alliances, vigorous commerce, bilingualism, intimate social relations (including marriage), Russian familiarity with Tatar geography, society, customs, and politics, should suffice to show that Russo-Tatar relations encompassed a broad variety of pragmatic, friendly relations. Yet despite this, the medieval Russian sources present the Mongols with relentless hostility as hated infidels. This was

not inappropriate, given that there were indeed plenty of instances
of warfare, destruction, looting, and extortion to warrant such
antagonism. Russia was a conquered society, and military clashes
set the stage for Russo-Tatar relations. Nonetheless the absence of
any discussion of the many peaceful interactions is puzzling. It is
also typical of the entire medieval ethno-religious frontier.

Throughout the frontier, hostile peoples, either across borders
or within conquest societies, cooperated freely, but under duress.
The status quo persisted only because each side lacked the means
to destroy the other. When one side did muster sufficient
strength, peaceful coexistence usually ended (as with the
annihilation of the Baltic Slavs in the German *Drang nach Osten*,
the expulsion of the Moors from Spain, and the attempt by early
modern Muscovy to turn Kazan', the annexed capital of a Muslim
khanate, into a Christian city). In the meantime, however, the
realities of life required extensive cooperation as both sides bided
their time. This cooperation was in flagrant violation of the
ideological underpinnings of both Christian and Muslim society.
Many frontier societies had been created by wars undertaken in the
name of conversion or extermination and the mere failure to do
battle was itself a strain on the ideologies of these exclusivist
religions. Peaceful cooperation, with its tacit acknowledgement of
the possible legitimacy of the enemy's faith, could not possibly be
reconciled with the religious foundations of these societies. Any
theory justifying such behavior would have called into question the
claims to exclusive religious truth of one's own society and polity.
Medieval ideologues avoided the ideological problems posed by
pragmatic relations by pretending that these relations did not exist,
a strategy we may refer to as the ideology of silence.

This phenomenon was not restricted to the West, and in
various forms was found from Spain to China. The bookmen of
Kievan *Rus'*, as the result of centuries of mingled conflict and
cooperation with steppe nomads, were already adept practitioners
when the Mongols arrived. Yet the Mongols presented a problem
new to the East Slavs. The nomads of the Kievan era had
inflicted crushing defeats and pillaged Russian cities, even Kiev, but
they had never attempted to establish political control. No
Russian city had ever, in this sense, been conquered. When the
Mongol juggernaut swiftly reduced Russia to a minor province of a
vast pagan empire, the Russian bookmen, the articulators of
Russian ideology, simply could not accomodate the fact within their

religious world-view. Other peoples whom the Mongols had conquered had endured alien dynasties in the past and had evolved the religious and philosophical means to explain them. In China, for example, the Mongol takeover became merely another shift in the Mandate of Heaven; in Persia it just fit into the cyclical theory of empire. To the West, Muslims and Christians alike had long interpreted military victories and setbacks as signs of their god's pleasure or displeasure with his people. Such, too, was the practice in Kievan *Rus'*. But whereas other peoples simply accepted conquest as an extreme case of divine annoyance with the chosen people, Russian intellectuals demurred. Russia's complete defeat meant that either the Christian god was not omnipotent or that He had ordained Russia's subjugation. Rather than grapple with this, medieval Russian writers avoided confronting the fact of conquest at all.

Two aspects of the Russian position made this peculiar response feasible. The first was that the Mongols never occupied and garrisoned the Russian forests, and the Russian were not faced with daily reminders of their own status. The second was that the bookmen already had, as part of the Kievan legacy, a vocabulary and conceptual framework for dealing with warfare with steppe peoples in which sovereignty was not at issue. They had only to treat interaction with the Mongols as they had treated interaction with so many similar peoples in the past. Describing the campaigns of 1237-1240 and their aftermath with a lexicon free of any connotations of conquest allowed Russian intellectuals to avoid the thorny ideological problems posed by their subjugation. This was their unique elaboration of the ideology of silence. They had long been accustomed to glossing over the awkward fact of peaceful cooperation with steppe nomads. Now they continued to omit from the record such dealings with the Mongols and in addition omitted to note that Russia had been conquered.

None of this is to say that the Russian sources fail to record graphically the events of the conquest. They simply do so using words like *pleniti* (plunder) which implied that these were raids of the old tradition. They also deal gingerly with the consequences of the Tatar victory. They refer to the Mongol census-takers, tax-collectors, and administrators in the Russian forest zone rarely and without explanation. They record the journeys of Russian princes to the Horde to receive grants (*yarliki*) to remain on their thrones without saying why these were necessary. All political

events are translated into religious terms, such that Mikhail of
Chernigov's execution for rebellion appears as a simple religious
martyrdom.   In keeping with tradition, Mongol victories were God's
punishment for the sins of Orthodox Christian Russia, and Russian
victories, such as those of 1380 and 1480, His reward for improved
behavior.   Especially interesting in the Russian accounts of these
latter events is that the bookmen, having never acknowledged
Russia's conquest, could not now hail its liberation.

Glaring inconsistencies between the *realia* of life under Mongol
rule and the literary poses demanded by Russian religious ideology
made the stance of Russian ideologues especially awkward.   For
example, Orthodox Christianity expected unceasing warfare with
infidels, yet the Russian Orthodox Church itself was dependent on
the khans of the Golden Horde for its many privileges and
prospered as never before under Mongol patronage.   In a similar
conundrum, the Russians manipulated the Chingisid principle to
justify Russian actions *vis-a-vis* certain Tatar warlords like Mamai
and even went so far, after the fall of the Golden Horde, as to
present the Muscovite tsars as the successors and inheritors of the
Tatar khans, invoking Chingisid legitimacy on their own behalf.[33]
Russian ideologues thus found themselves in the position of exalting
the principle of Chingisid dynastic succession with reference to
Russia without acknowledging that Russia had been conquered.
Inevitably the complex and contradictory realities of Russo-Tatar
relations created the equally convoluted intellectual attitudes that
lie just beneath the surface of the medieval Russian sources.   It is
to the pursuit of this subtext, through critical analysis of each
work, that the present monograph is devoted.[34]

Chapter II:

The Era of Batu

The East Slavs' first encounter with the Mongols was fortuitous but hardly fortunate. A Mongol scouting expedition ten thousand strong, actually a reconaissance in force, rode north from the Caucasus and smashed a combined army of Russians and Polovtsy at the Battle on the River Kalka in 1223. The Russian chronicles contain a "tale" (*povest'*) about the battle which was altered by later scribes, copyists, and redactors and has come down to us in several variants.[1] Of these, the fullest and most reliable is that in the Novgorodian First Chronicle. Given that the tale must have originated in the south, probably Kiev, and that no Novgorodians participated in the battle, this is somewhat ironic. The versions preserved in the Laurentian Chronicle from the northeast and in the Hypatian Chronicle from the southwest differ largely in focusing on rivalries among the Russian princes which are not germain to our interests here. The core narrative is less adulterated than one might expect, and neither the lexicon nor the assumptions of the unknown author have received the attention they deserve.

The Novgorodian First Chronicle account[2] begins by noting that "A group of pagans appeared . . . and no one knew who they were or where they came from, or what their language is, or what tribe (*plemeni*) they belong to, or what their religion (*vera*) is. Some say they are Tatars, and others call them Taurmeny, and others Pechenegs." Perhaps they are the people of Gog and Magog, of whom Methodius of Patara wrote, once locked behind the mountains by Alexander the Great. "We heard that they had plundered (*plenili*) the Ossetians (*Iasy*), the Georgians (*Obezi*), the Kasogians and the Polovtsy, which is God's punishment of the Polovtsy for having shed much Christian blood and done much harm to the Russian Land . . . The Polovtsy Daniil Kobiakovich and Yurii had been killed (by the Tatars), and Kotian, father–in–law (*test'*) of Mstislav, came to Kiev with many gifts, including horses, camels, buffaloes and girls, saying: "Today they (the Tatars) take our land, and they will come to take yours tomorrow.'" The Russian princes agree to an alliance with the Polovtsy, fearing that the Mongols will only grow stronger if they meet no resistance. At this point, however, envoys arrive from the Tatars as well and make the following speech: "We hear that you are coming against us, having listened to the Polovtsy, and we have no designs on your land (*ne zaiakhom*) nor your cities, nor your villages, and we are not marching against you. We come only at God's will against our slaves (*kholopy*) and our cattle-herders (*koniusy*), the pagan Polovtsy. And you should make peace with us; if they (the Polovtsy) run to you, you can defeat them and have their goods. Because we have heard that they have done much evil to you, for which we will defeat them." The Russian princes, suspecting a trick, put the Tatar envoys to death, whereupon a second Tatar embassy arrives with this message: "If you have listened to the Polovtsy and killed our envoys (*posoly*) and come against us, then you will see [what will happen], and we have not occupied your lands (*ne zaiakhom nichim*) and God will be just as all know (*da vsem est' bog i pravda*) [God is just to all]." A Tatar advance guard is defeated and flees to a Polovtsian burial mound (*kurgan*) where they hide one Gemiabeg by burying him alive. The Polovtsy manage to find and kill him anyway. In the main encounter, Yarun and his Polovtsy panic, disrupting the Russian lines in their wild retreat. Though Mstislav holds an earthen defense works, the Tatars destroy the main Russo-Polovtsy force and leave the two commanders (*voevody*) Ch'gyrkan and Teshiukan behind to mop up. Ploskynia and the *brodniki* (freebooters) guarantee the Russian princes' safety in return for their surrender, but the Russians are betrayed and crushed under the boards of a Tatar banquet. Thus God punished the Russians for their sins. The Tatars depart, leaving the chronicler to conclude: "We do not know from whence they came or where they went again. God knows whence they came against us for our sins."

The highly abbreviated account in the Laurentian Chronicle contains no changes that concern us here.[3] The Hypatian Chronicle is more satisfactory and adds two details of considerable note. The first of these is that Bastii, a Polovtsy, converted to Orthodox Christianity (perhaps as part of the Russo-Polovtsian alliance),[4] and the second is that Chingis Khan (*Chanogiz' kan'*) was killed when the Tatars fought the Tanguts.[5] This last comment is of prime importance. The original account of the events of 1223 must have been written before news of Chingis Khan's death in 1227 reached Russia. How the Hypatian chronicler found out about it and where he thought the land of the Tanguts was must remain mysteries. He does, for the sake of consistency, omit the sentence about not knowing where the Tatars went after the battle; obviously they left for the territory of the Tanguts.

The Tale of the Battle on the River Kalka contains more than meets the eye. Although the chronicler claims not to know who the Mongols were, he does know what kind of people they are: pastoral nomads like the Pechenegs, Taurmeny, and various others long familiar to Kievan *Rus'*. He calls them Tatars, the same name used in the Chinese, Arabo-Persian, and Latin sources.[6] He also knows that the Tatars had defeated various people of the Caucasus and a group of Polovtsy, the news Kotian[7] brought to Kiev. While the chronicler asserts his ignorance of the Mongols' language, negotiations nevertheless take place, though no translators are mentioned. Since the Mongols and the Russians had never seen each other before, they must have communicated in some form of Turkic, possibly Kipchak;[8] the Mongol confederacy contained vast numbers of Turkic-speaking Inner Asian nomads. The chronicler is also well enough informed to give the names of several Tatar commanders, though he gives them the Russian title *voevody*. The unknown Tatars have quickly become more familiar.

Before reaching Russia, the Mongols had faced an alliance of Alans (Ossetians) and Polovtsy north of the Caucasus. They had played a divide-and-conquer game, appealing to the Polovtsy as fellow nomads to abandon the Alans. The Polovtsy complied, allowing the Mongols to annihilate the Alans at their leisure before turning on their brother nomads. The Tatar offer to spare Russia if allowed to have their way with the Polovtsy may well have been the same ploy. The Tatars were doubtless informed, through their superior intelligence-gathering network, of the long-standing enmity between the Russians and their steppe neighbors. On the other hand, the offer may actually have been genuine. Chingis Khan's divine mandate from Tengri, the Great Blue Sky, was to rule all who lived in felt tents, and indeed, in his will Chingis left to his sons only groups of nomads and their lands. Within the terms of the mandate the Polovtsy would have been fair game, but certainly not the Russians, who, unlike the Alans, did not even live in an area of strategic importance. In any case, the Russians guaranteed disaster by executing the Mongol envoys.

Tatar political messages were always elliptically phrased, and those of the envoys in this tale are no exception.[9] (Mongol diplomatic correspondence and imperial charters are laconic almost to the point of being unintelligible.)[10] The chronicle's rendition of the Mongol statements may, therefore, be accurate. The scribes, after all, were accustomed to recording oral political communications among the Russian princes.[11] Moreover, the Tatar attitudes ring true. The Mongols' self-confidence was legendary, but they made it a practice never to predict victory and were content, as they said, to let God settle the matter. The second Tatar embassy's words to this effect do seem to be somewhat garbled syntactically but were clear enough for a mid-fifteenth-century chronicler/compiler to alter the message to: "*my na vas ne posiagili, a vy na nas idete; to sudite Bog mezhiu vami i nami*" (*we are not advancing on you, but you are coming against us; let God judge between you and us*).[12]

The author of the tale is not generous with the Polovtsy. Making the best of a bad situation, he manages to see the hand of God in the Mongol rout of the Polovtsy, punishment for their many crimes against the Russian Land. (Similarly, Juwaini attributed Mongol destruction of the heretical and previously unassailable cult of Assassins to the will of Allah.)[13] He also contrives to blame the Russian defeat on Polovtsian cowardice and panic. A chronicler in the sixteenth century went so far as to cast doubt on the Polovtsy's sincerity in making an alliance. In this version Mstislav argues for the alliance by warning that the Polovtsy are otherwise likely to betray the Russians and join the Tatars.[14] Mstislav's concluding remark that it is better to fight the Tatars on Polovtsian territory than on Russian proves that this is an anachronistic interpolation. What actually happened in 1223 was that the Tatars lured the Russo-Polovtsian army deep into the steppe away from Russian supply lines, then trapped and annihilated it. The Russians might have done better to remain in the forests. In any case there was no chance the Polovtsy would have made common cause with the Mongols, having already been humiliated in battle and deceived in negotiation.

Several episodes in the narrative remain unclear, notably the intriguing story of Gemiabeg. Nor is it well established who the *brodniki* were. They are usually considered steppe freebooters, proto-Cossacks of mixed Slavic and nomadic blood, but references to them are few and far between. They are known to have assisted Oleg of Riazan' in his attack on Lopastna in 1353, but this does not settle the question of their identity.[15]   Despite the vagueness of certain details, however, the general tone of the Tale of the Battle on the River Kalka is most informative.

Throughout both the Christian and Muslim worlds, the first appearance of the Mongol juggernaut raised apocalyptic fears,[16] hence the Kievan chronicler's mention of the peoples of Gog and Magog, who, according to the apocrypha of Methodius of Patara, were to be unleashed at the end of time.   This is surely a profoundly pessimistic interpretation of the Mongol danger, despite Budnovits' search for an optimistic reaction to the events of 1223. Before the Mongol campaigns against Europe itself, Catholic accounts of the Tatar advance, based on rumors of the destruction of Muslims in Khwarizm and Persia, tried to see in the Mongols the forces of the legendary Christian king of the East, Prester John.   The Prester John legend was certainly known in medieval Russia, though perhaps not until somewhat later.[17]   However, as Bezzola recognizes, the Russians and Byzantines alike were far too familiar with pastoral nomads to mistake the Tatar hordes for an avenging Christian army.

Though the Kievan chronicler saw the hand of God in the Tatar victory, he was under no delusions concerning the Mongols themselves.   Though the language of the tale is not elaborate (rich rhetorical prose did not enter Old Russian literature until at least the fourteenth century) and is even slim on diatribe,[18] the Mongols are clearly cruel, deceitful, and destructive infidels.   Such creatures could only have overcome Christians if God was using them to punish Russian sins.   The alternative conclusion—that God was unable to prevent the Mongol victory—was unthinkable.   This sort of reasoning was of course widespread.   It explains why Juwaini sees the power of Allah, rather than of Tengri, behind the Tatar elimination of the Assassins and the stance of Byzantine intellectuals contemplating the inexorable advance of the Ottomans.[19]   A corollary of the Russian assumption was that once Russia had redeemed itself in the eyes of God, glorious triumphs on the field of battle would follow.

The "Tale of the Battle on the River Kalka" remained largely stable in the Old Russian chronicle tradition. Had any writer tried to retell the story after the Mongol conquest, certain elements—the musings about the Tatars' identity, the prayer that they not return—would have been left out. Why the Novgorodian chronicle should preserve the best version of a tale that originated in the south is unknown.[20]   One early sixteenth-century chronicler, in the *Vologodsko-Permskaia letopis'*, interpolates the trite observation that the *Rus'* had never known such a defeat since the beginning of the Russian land.[21]   Anyone familiar with medieval Russian chronicle-writing would expect the mid-sixteenth-century Nikon Chronicle to take the greatest liberties with the text, and indeed it does.   Considerable detail is omitted and replaced with inaccurate, misleading, moralizing padding.   The numbers involved are inflated to grandiose proportions, and, with typical delicacy, the "girls" are deleted from the list of Kotian's gifts to Mstislav.   The final line of this embellished tale is illustrative of the didacticism of the whole and also of a retrospective vision that appeared only some time after the overthrow of the Mongols in 1480.   The Nikon chronicler calls the battle of 1223 the first "campaign" (*nakhozhdenie*) of the Tatars against *Rus'*.   This is the term invariably applied to Mongol expeditions into the Russian forest zone from 1237 on.   As rapidly as the Tatars came, so did they also leave, but they would return, to do evil like demons.[22]   This is a historical perspective, albeit couched in religious garb; it has no parallels in earlier variants of the tale.

The account of the Battle on the River Kalka shows the response of the articulate elite of Kievan society to their first encounter with the Tatars.   Even while recording an event that rang of the apocalypse, the various chroniclers took care to settle old scores with the Polovtsy and to make savage attacks on rival Russian princes.   How the commoners felt about the incident, those who did not march into the steppe to die, we shall never know. The Mongols defeated the Russians in a single battle, then departed.   They did not in any sense "conquer" Russia and indeed barely intruded on Russian soil.   The Russians described the Tatars' action with the verb *pleniti*, which I have translated as "plunder."   Intriguingly, medieval Russian writers continued to use this verb when, in 1237, the Mongols returned and proceeded with the conquest of Russia.

The Mongols had originally intended to follow the scouting expedition that wrought such havoc on the River Kalka with a full-scale invasion.   Temporary difficulties in subduing the eastern Kipchaks (Polovtsy)[23] caused them to postpone this plan for a time.   Though the Russians were not aware of what was transpiring in the land of the eastern Kipchaks, they should not have been surprised when the Mongols reappeared fourteen years later. The chronicles record the Tatar conquest of the Volga Bolgars in 1235-1236, and the Russians may have been privy to intelligence from a mysterious Catholic monk, Julian, who travelled to the Tatars and reputedly reported their intentions to the East European princes and the Pope. Nevertheless, the Russian princes made no preparations for defense. Russian generals preferred fall campaigns;[24] the Mongol campaigns in the winter of 1237-1238 caught them completely off-guard.

The events of the winter are not open to question: Mongol armies swept through northeastern Russia crushing all opposition and razing the cities in their path. More complicated is the question of the origin and relationships of the three oldest chronicle accounts of these events, the Laurentian, Hypatian, and Novgorodian First Chronicles. The Laurentian account[25] records that the Tatars "took" (*vziasha*) Riazan', and "plundered" (*plenovakhu*) and "made war on" (*voevali*) the surrounding territory. Vainly attempting to save his city, Filipp Nianka, *voevoda* of Moscow, found martyrdom for his faith. The heart of the story is an eye-witness description of the siege of Vladimir. In the city's final moments one of the princes prophesies martyrdom: "Brothers, it is better for us to die in front of the Golden Gates for the Holy Virgin and the true Christian faith than to be in their (the Tatars') will (*volia*)." The tale goes on to describe the looting of the city and to list the ecclesiastics who perished. In a variant of a familiar phrase in Old Russian literature, the chronicler asserts that the Tatars "did more evil to the Suzdalian Land than since its baptism (*kreshchenie*)."[26] The accursed *krovopiitsy* (literally: blood-spillers) plunder (*poplenishi*) throughout the northeast. Prince Vasil'ko Konstantinovich, refusing to do the Tatar "will" (*volia*), i.e., enter their service or convert to their religion, is martyred for insulting their "infidel, godless, accursed Tatar customs (*obychai*)." Grand Prince Yaroslav, in a eulogy for his brother Yurii, killed at the battle on the River Sit', invokes the Heavenly Kingdom and the crown of martyrdom of those who resisted the evil-doing Tatars.

The Hypatian account[27] adds several new twists. It identifies the commander of the army attacking Riazan' as Burundai. As the princes prepare to die in the final assault on Vladimir, they say they would rather die than become the "servitors" (*poruchniki*)[28] of the Tatars. Prince Yurii, surrounded at the river Sit', tries unsuccessfully to bribe his way out. The Tatars "plunder" (*pleni*) the Suzdalian Land. In the south, the city of Kozel'sk resists Batu's army with unexpected fury. Among the Mongol casualties are three sons of *temniki* (commanders of ten thousand), and Batu in his rage orders the city obliterated.

The Novgorodian account[29] concentrates on Riazan' rather than Vladimir. Before the attack, the Tatars send two men and a witch (*charodeika*) to Riazan', demanding surrender and a tithe (*desiatina*) by the Tatars. Mongol contingents ride to Torzhok, Novgorod's border city, and to within one hundred *versts* of Novgorod itself before turning back.

The Laurentian chronicle ends *sub anno* 1305. In 1377, at the behest of Prince Dmitrii Konstantinovich of Suzdal' and Bishop Dionysii, it was recopied by the Suzdalian monk Lavrentii, from whom it derives its name. Some have claimed that Lavrentii, working only three years before the victory at Kulikovo, rewrote the narrative of the campaign of 1237-1238, creating a new redaction in keeping with the "anti-Tatar ideology" of his time.[30] However, this contention is not convincing. Lavrentii copied the text of the Laurentian Chronicle accurately from the no longer extant "compilation" (*svod*) of 1305, which appears to have been the chronicle of a grand prince of Tver'.[31] Even so, the tale could have been written any time between 1238 and 1304. The origins of the thirteenth-century Russian chronicles are quite obscure, and different scholars have dated the tale of the Mongol conquest of Vladimir-Suzdalia to 1239, the 1240s, the 1280s, and even to 1305. Clearly it is based on sources from Vladimir, and it may have been written in Rostov, probably soon after the campaign.[32]

The Hypatian account very likely derives from the Laurentian or from a common source contemporaneous with the events, adding the slander of Prince Yurii (a reflection of princely rivalries) and the story of the heroic defense of Kozel'sk.[33] The Novgorodian account is entirely separate and obviously related to the "Tale of the Destruction of Riazan' by Batu" (*Povest' o razorenii Riazani Batyem*); thus its sources were from Riazan' and Novgorod, rather than Vladimir or Rostov.[34]

Certain scholars, such as Fennell and Budovnits, have considered the Laurentian Chronicle pro-Tatar, a reflection of the accommodationist politics of the northeastern Russian princes, because it is not as anti-Tatar as they expect.[35] However, whatever its failings—and it is repetitious, padded, and contradictory—the Laurentian Chronicle is innocent of this indictment. The vain, heroic defense of Kozel'sk is absent not because it was omitted to soften the anti-Tatar animus for the Vladimir-Suzdalian audience, but because the episode was written only later for inclusion in the Hypatian account. The Laurentian Chronicle may not lay on the anti-Tatar epithets as thickly as the Novgorod-Riazan' account, but the fact remains that there is little ambiguity in its graphic description of the sack of Vladimir and repeated invocations of martyrdom. The Russian defeat was God's will, but this does not exonerate the Tatars. The Vasil'ko episode is an interpolation[36] added several decades later by a scribe working for Vasil'ko's widow, and actually serves to confirm that the original text was written soon after the events it describes. The Mongols were tolerant of all religions and would never have tried to force anyone to convert. In any case it would have been impossible for a Russian, not being a member of any Uralo-Altaic clan or tribe, to "convert" to the mixture of ancestor worship, shamanism, and polytheism characteristic of Mongol religious practices. The penalty might well have been death, however, for refusing to surrender or insulting the Tatar religion.

Both the provenance and the contents of the narrative in the Novgorod First Chronicle are problematic. There is no textological explanation for the use of sources from Riazan' rather than Vladimir; it may merely reflect Novgorod's preferences among the feuding Russian principalities. Both the Novgorod First Chronicle and the extant text of the "Tale of the Destruction of Riazan' by Batu" date from the fourteenth century. The Novgorod account, however, contains a peculiar detail apparently from a *later* version of the Riazan' tale than the one which has survived. This is the mention of the mysterious Tatar "witch" and her demand for a tithe.[37] Like all pagan Inner Asian nomads, the Mongols had shamans, but there is no evidence that they were ever female. Any female Tatar under such circumstances might have struck male Russians as a witch,[38] of course, but in fact there is virtually no possibility that the Mongols would send a woman as an envoy to Riazan'. *Khatuns*, the wives or widows of khans, were influential in politics and diplomacy in the Mongol Empire, but no woman of such eminence would have been sent as a messenger to a hostile city. The demand for a tithe is equally improbable. It presupposes a census, which the Russians, never having done it

before, were incapable of. The Mongols were in the middle of a
tightly-scheduled campaign and simply did not have the time to
conduct one. Furthermore, when the Mongols captured a city they
usually conscripted laborers and drafted all of the artisans. There
is every indication that the episode of the witch and the tithe is a
fantasy, invented by a scribe after the Mongols really had
conducted a census (*chislo*) of northeastern Russia, and intended
somehow further to defame the Tatars.

There is a less tangible but more pervasive problem with the
interpretation of *all* the accounts of the events of 1237-1238.
Where is the mention of the conquest of northeastern *Rus'* and the
onset of Mongol hegemony? The tales of the invasion record that
the Tatars "took" (*vziati*) and "plundered" (*pleniti*) the Russian
principalities. Neither verb in any way connotes that the Mongols
held on to what they had taken or that what had transpired
differed other than in degree from a Polovtsian raid. The
chronicles tell of princes who chose death rather than falling into
the "will" of the Tatars, without discussing the consequences for
those who did not. Even the later chroniclers call Batu's invasion
a "campaign" (*nakhozhdenie*) and no more. Describing the
survivors, the *Troitskaia letopis'* says, "And there was great joy to
the Christians, whom God had saved with his strong hand from
the godless Tatars."[39] The death and destruction of the conquest
were awesome, and though a number of cities managed to avoid
being sacked,[40] this was probably because they surrendered. "Great
joy" seems inappropriate. While the Mongols did not leave
garrisons or any administrative apparatus in the Russian cities still
standing, their right and ability to do so were firmly established.

The aversion of medieval Russians to political theory and
theoretical treatises is well known. Nonetheless it is remarkable
that the tales of the campaign of 1237-1238 fail to mention its
most profound consequence, the establishment of Mongol rule. The
narratives seem almost to demand a concluding phrase to the effect
that it was after these events that the Mongols began to "rule"
(*vladeti*) *Rus'* or that it was because of this military disaster that
Rus' was now "subject" (*pokorenie*) to Tatar authority. Yet
nothing of this sort appears. The later one dates these chronicle
accounts, the more incongruous this lacuna appears. For not long
after the conquest the manifestations of Tatar suzerainty started
becoming obvious. Russian princes began their journeys into the
steppe for permission to remain on their thrones; the Mongols

stationed resident administrators within the Russian forest zone, conducted a census, and began extracting a heavy tribute. Yet the chronicle accounts never allude to the connection between this state of affairs and the military actions they describe. Nor was such an explanation ever appended in later texts. Very late versions, from the fifteenth and sixteenth centuries, assert rather metaphorically that the Russians became "enslaved" (*rabota*) as a result of the winter campaign, which at least shows some historical perspective, though belated and distorted.[41]

Russian chroniclers continued to use the same two verbs, "take" (a city), and "plunder," to describe Tatar actions in Russia for the following 240 years of Mongol domination. With the conquest of Russia a *fait accompli*, it is evident that neither verb implies a conquest. The East Slavic intellectual and historiographic tradition had no prior experience of foreign conquest, let alone by infidel nomads. It was not that Russian bookmen lacked the vocabulary to describe the new state of affairs, but that they lacked the philosophy to confront it. Following, intellectually, the path of least resistance, the bookmen fell back upon the lexicon of Kievan relations with steppe peoples to describe a very different phenomenon, the Mongol conquest of Russia. And rather than dwelling upon or even acknowledging the political consequences of the Tatar invasions, the writers of all the accounts of 1237–1238 sought refuge in religious ideology. Any Christian who fell in battle with the Tatars became a religious martyr; the looting of any monastery was attributed not to avarice but to religious spite. Seeing defeat in battle as the will of their own god allowed the bookmen to deal with the religious issues; the religious cast of their narratives helped them to side-step the political ones. Thus through the use of a vocabulary and religious frame of reference that did not address political reality, the Russian writers avoided the ideological problems inherent in their new situation. The apocalyptic mood of 1223 is conspicuously absent from accounts of the conquest of northeastern *Rus'*. What appears instead is a uniquely Russian variation on the ideology of silence.

The Mongol attack upon Riazan' in the thirteenth century became the subject of a separate literary work, the *Povest' o razorenii Riazani Batyem* (Tale of the Destruction of Razan by Batu), whose heterogeneous contents and late manuscript tradition have aroused confusion and controversy over its dating and significance.[42] Batu arrives at the gates of Riazan' and demands a tithe. The city sends Prince Fedor Iur'evich, bearing gifts, to dissuade him from "making war on" (*voevati*) the "Riazanian Land" (*Riazanskaia zemlia*). The cruel and merciless Batu is nonetheless determined to attack the Russian Land. However, when the Tatar leader learns from Riazani nobles (*vel'mozhi*) that Fedor's wife is of the Byzantine imperial family and very beautiful, he asks Fedor for her. Fedor exclaims that Christians do not give their wives to an "unclean tsar" (*nechestivovomu tsariu*) for "rape" (*blud*). He is promptly executed. His father, Yurii, hearing the news weeps and declares, "It would be better to purchase death than life at the cost of living in the infidel's will (variant: faith) (*Lutche name smertiiu nezheli zhivote kupiti, nezheli v poganoi vole* (var. *byti*)." Yurii and the Riazani princes can scarcely contain their impatience to drink the last cup of death in battle with the Tatars, one against a thousand, two against five thousand, for their patrimony (*otchina*) and the Faith.

In the ensuing battle the Tatars capture Prince Oleg Ingvarevich, whose beauty (*krasna*) and bravery (*khrabr'*) impress Batu. But when Batu offers to heal his wounds and take him into his service, Oleg curses the Tatar as a "godless enemy of Christianity." Batu has him dismembered.

With the Riazani resistance overwhelmed, Batu "takes" (*vziat'*) Riazan' and proceeds to move against Vladimir and Suzdal' to "plunder" (*pleniti*) or "destroy" and "ravage" (*potrebiti, iskoreniti*) the Russian Land. Suddenly, however, to avenge the sack of Riazan', the Riazani noble (*vel'mozh*) Evpatii and a small retinue launch a ferocious suicide attack in the Suzdalian Land.[45] The sheer fury of the attack frightens Batu, who questions several of Evpatii's men, whom the Tatars have managed to wound and capture. They tell Batu they have come to honor him, and the cleverness of this reply (*mudrii otvet*) further amazes the Tatar. He order his brother-in-law Khostovrul *bogatyr'* to capture Evpatii alive,[46] but the Russian cuts him in half. Finally catapults are brought to bear on the hero, and a stone from one of them brings him down.[47] Batu assembles his nobles (*mirzas*) and officials (*sanchakbei*),[48] all impressed by the bravery, strength, and daring of Evpatii and his men, and declares that although he has fought many hordes (*ordy*), he has never seen such fighters. That the hero may die honorably of his wounds, Batu allows him to be borne from the field of battle (doubtless by surviving members of

Evpatii's retinue, spared for the task).

Meanwhile Prince Ingvar Ingvarevich returns to his patrimony (*otchina*) and sees the extent of the "plundering" (*plenenie*) of *tsar'* Batu, the "unclean lawbreaker" (*nechestivii zakonoprestupnik*), in Riazan'. Ingvar purifies the city, lamenting the martyrdom of his brother Riazani princes, who died fighting the "Hagarenes" (*agariane*) and enemies of the "clan of Ishmael" (*Izmaitel'ska roda*). He buries the fallen princes, recalling that they also fought for the holy churches and the Orthodox faith against the pagan Polovtsy. Lovingly they had "taken many of the sons and brothers of the unbelieving tsars to themselves and turned them to the true faith" (*mnogikh ot nevernykh tsarei detei ikh i brat'iu k sobe priimasta, i na veru istinnuiu obrashchasta*). Ingvar restores the churches and city walls of Riazan', repeoples the city, and revives the principality. The text concludes: "And there was great joy among the Christians, those whom God had with his strong hand saved from the godless, evil (*zlovernago*) *tsar'* Batyia." Mikhail Vsevolodovich of Pronsk, a regional capital in the Riazan' principality, then takes over his father's patrimony in Riazan'.

Likhachev notes that among the princes who die martyrs' deaths in the "Tale of the Destruction of Riazan' by Batu" are princes known to have died in 1208 and 1228, as well as Oleg Krasnii, who was captured in the campaign of 1237-1238, released in 1252, and died peacefully in 1258. The tale confuses Oleg's death with the martyrdom of Roman Ol'govich of Riazan' in 1270. These are not mistakes a contemporary writer would make. Likhachev's attempts to date the existence of the full tale textologically by showing its influence on various literary works written in the first half of the fifteenth century have not proven entirely convincing.[49] Nonetheless, there is no question but that the extant version of the tale is not unadulterated thirteenth-century narrative. The portrayal of the Tatars as Muslims supports Likhachev's proposal that the extant text took shape in the fourteenth century. Though internecine feuds were legion among the Riazan' princes, this account presents them as one big happy family. It also whitewashes the princes' relationship with their *boyare*, claiming that the Riazan' nobles loved all their princes. Ironically, as Likhachev shrewdly points out, the tale undercuts its own assertion through the episode in which one of the Riazan' nobles betrays Fedor's wife to Batu.[50] The Fedor episode is also interesting in that it brings our attention to inconsistencies in

Batu's behavior in the course of the tale as a whole. Naturally his demand for Fedor's wife reveals him as a cruel and lecherous barbarian, but these characteristics did not prevent him, in the Evpatii incident, from displaying considerable chivalric courtesy. Yet Batu executes Fedor for his bravery, just as he dishonorably killed Oleg and Vasil'ko, whose courage in battle had impressed him. The more respectable Batu of the Evpatii section of the tale may reflect the folkloric origin of this particular story,[51] and is a good example of the rather diverse nature of the entire tale.

Indeed, the tale is such a composite that its contents are often confused and occasionally defy explication. (The relationship between the "Tale of the Destruction of Riazan' by Batu" and the account of the same winter in the Novgorod First Chronicle, each of which allude to a tithe, is a matter of contention.)[52] An example is the reference to Polovtsian royalty welcomed by Riazan' princes and converted to Christianity, the relevance of which escapes me.[53] The tale is also especially inconsistent in two respects. First, its patriotic orientation is most ambiguous. Its provincial emphasis on the Riazan' Land, the bravery of Riazan' warriors, and the unity of Riazan' princes must not be overlooked. The overlap in the narration among the Riazan', Suzdalian, and Russian "Lands" suggests an origin between the mid-thirteenth and mid-fourteenth centuries, a transitional period in which the concept of the Russian Land was evolving. Only in the extremely late strel'tsy (musketeer) redaction from the seventeenth century is an attempt made to smooth the contradictions. The Riazan' Land, it says, is a "small part" (mala chast') of the Russian Land. Yet another sentence asserts that one can cross the boundary of the Riazan' Land headed "to Rus'."[54] The second suite of inconsistencies are in the variation of tone betwen pessimism and optimism. It would be fatuous to try to situate the tale on a scale between the two,[55] but it is worth noting the extremes. The Tatars wreak fearful havoc, and the many martyrs, though glorious, are necessarily dead. The "great joy" of the unmartyred survivors (similar to that in the Troitskaia letopis' sub anno 1238), suggests on the other hand that it was just as well to be spared.

The actual course of events in the "Tale of the Destruction of Riazan' by Batu" requires careful scrutiny. Batu demands a tithe from Riazan' and is refused, the Riazan' princes preferring death to being in the "will" of the Tatars. They die in battle, and Riazan' and the other cities of Vladimir-Suzdalia are taken and plundered.

Both history and the internal logic of the tale require that, just as those who chose death escaped being in the "will" of the Tatars, those who chose life, i.e., the survivors, did not. However, the tale mentions nothing of the kind. The otherwise unattested Prince Ingvar Ingvarevich rebuilds Riazan' and everyone lives happily ever after. Presumably Riazan' was subjected to exploitative Tatar rule following the Mongol campaign of 1237-1238, but instead of saying so, this tale echoes the silence of the contemporary thirteenth-century chronicle accounts and does not articulate any consciousness of a change in Russia's political status. The seventeenth-century redactions of the tale, however, do employ a lexicon of suzerainty. In the Expanded Sub-Redaction, Prince Yurii prays God not to let the Russian Land be "ruled" (*vladeti*) by the accursed pagans. He and his followers would rather die than be "subjected" (*pokornym*) to the Mongol *tsar'*.[56] In the Rhetorical Redaction, Batu promises to let Oleg "govern" (*gospodstvovati*) Russia if he will adhere to the faith of Mohammed the prophet.[57] These slight variations in later versions of the text show how readily a single sentence or even a change of verb brings to the tale an appreciation of political theory, transforming the invasion into an event pregnant with consequences for political sovereignty. The ease with which such implications might have been incorporated into the earliest redactions of the tale shows how carefully they were excluded. Whenever the "Tale of the Destruction of Riazan' by Batu" was written—any time between the fourteenth and the early sixteenth centuries—its "author" faithfully adhered to the ideology of silence to avoid confronting the intellectual problem of Mongol rule. In this respect, above all, the tale reflects the intellectual posture of the Russian articulate elite at the time of Batu's 1237-1238 invasion.[58]

In 1240 Batu's army attacked the city of Kiev and the south as part of a campaign that continued with devastating effect in Poland, Bohemia, Hungary, and Austria. Though this was of little concern to the chroniclers of the northeast (the Laurentian Chronicle allots four lines to the "taking" of Kiev),[59] it is of great interest to us. Of all the contemporary chronicles, the full "Tale of the Sack of Kiev by Batu," replete with military vocabulary from the Slavic translation of Josephus Flavius,[60] is found only in that of Galicia-Volhynia.

According to this narration,[61] Mengu Kan first scouted the city and admired its beauty at the close of the 1237 campaign. In 1240 the Tatars filled the Russian Land with the sound of their wagons, camels, horses, and musical instruments and with the wailing of refugees. The Kievans take captive a Tatar notable with the somewhat Persian name of Tovrul. Tovrul lists the Tatar leaders: Urdu, Baidar, Birui, Kaidan, Bechak, Mengu, Kuyuk, who became *kan* on the death of the *kan*, and, from a different clan (*rod*), first *voevoda* Sebediai *bogatyr'* and Burundai *bogatyr'*, who took the Bolgar and Suzdalian Lands. The Kievan commander was Dmitr' (Dmitro) the *tysiatskii* (chiliarch or thousand-man, head of the militia). Dmitro's defense is so courageous and skillful that after the battle Batu spares his life. The wounded Kievan leader persuades Batu to invade Hungary, and the Tatars depart to do so. One could see, the author remarks, "the Russian Land perishing from the unclean" (*vidi bo zemliu gibnushchuiu Rus'kuiu ot nechestivago*). After three years of campaigning, Batu recrosses the Danube and returns to the steppe.

The graphic description of the siege of Kiev and the extended list of Tatar generals suggest the first-hand report of an eye-witness, probably someone in the service of Dmitro, whom Grand Prince Daniil Romanovich of Galicia-Volhynia had appointed.[62] The allusion to Batu's three years in Central and Eastern Europe could be a later accretion and certainly constitutes the *terminus ad quem* for dating the tale. The description of the Dnepr' river valley as the Russian Land and of the northeast as the Suzdalian Land is also consistent with this assumption about the tale's date.

The enumeration of Tatar commanders deserves greater and more critical attention than it has received. First of all, it is not implausible that the Kievans could capture one of the besieging Tatars from inside the city. No translator is mentioned, so we must infer, as always, that some form of Turkic served as a *lingua franca*. Torvul's list is accurate on the whole, even if Batu's name is, perhaps by chance, omitted. Three of Chingis Khan's sons have sons present: Ugedei's sons Guyuk and Kadan, and Ugedei's grandson Kaidu; Tolui's son Mongke; and of Juchi's sons, Baidan, Bori, and the implied Batu. (Bechak is unidentified, as are the Boktur' and Bastyr' who are interpolated in the version of the tale in the mid-fifteenth-century Tverian Chronicle.)[63] Guyuk did indeed become khan after Ugedei's death, though he died two years later in 1248, probably poisoned at Batu's instigation. The tale uses the Turco-Mongol form *kan* rather than the Russian translation *tsar'* used in later writings. This is offset, however, by the use of the Russian title *voevoda* for the non-Chingisid generals Subudai and Burundai, both of whom figured prominently in Russo-Tatar relations. Though the vagaries of Slavic transliteration of Inner Asian names always make for some confusion, there is a gross error usually perpetuated in this list which should not remain unrectified. The list is generally punctuated so that the phrase "from a different clan" is applied to Guyuk, implying that he is not the son of Ugedei, his father, nor of the imperial Chigisid clan. Russian deference to Chingisids and to Mongol aristocratic sensitivities was necessarily great at this time; no bookman of Kiev or Galicia-Volhynia could conceivably have made such a mistake. The phrase "from a different clan" clearly refers to the famous generals Subudai and Burundai, whose non-Chingisid descent was a well known fact in the Mongol Empire. Repunctuation of the sentence renders it historically accurate in every way, and this emendation of the "Tale of the Sack of Kiev by Batu" must be seriously considered.[64]

On the eve of the Mongol invasion of the south, the overlord of Kiev, Mikhail of Chernigov, had fled. Prince Daniil of Galicia-Volhynia immediately seized Kiev for himself, the Riurikid princes continuing to play their political games in spite of the coming holocaust.[65] Daniil, however, was not prepared to weather the Tatar assault on Kiev either,[66] and Kiev was left to face the Tatars with only *tysiatskii* Dmitro for a leader. Dmitro certainly rose to the occasion, though his deportment does arouse some skepticism. His bravery impresses Batu, who decides to spare and honor him; this is the Batu of the Evpatii episode in the "Tale of the Destruction of Riazan' by Batu." Indeed Dmitro has earned such capital with the Tatar leader that he is able to persuade him to leave Kiev and invade Europe! This is ignorant exaggeration. A Mongol council, or *kuriltai*, had made the decision to invade Europe before the invasion of Russia even began. Not even Batu had the authority to undertake such an endeavor by himself. Nonetheless the incident manages to give Dmitro, in defeat, some credit for ridding the land of Tatars.

The implication, of course, is that Dmitro's cleverness saved Kiev from further problems with the Tatars. Their departure is described with no hint that they ever returned to Kiev. The tale depicts catastrophic destruction as the city is "taken" and "plundered," but never acknowledges conquest or any subsequent alteration of the political situation. Thus the tale of 1240 resembles the other "conquest tales" we have examined in that it is not a tale of conquest at all.

The tale was not altered in this respect for some time. It was not included in the *Troitskaia letopis'* of 1408, which followed the Laurentian Chronicle in announcing rather than discussing the events of 1240. In the middle of the fifteenth century, however, the tale found its way into the chronicle tradition of the northeast. Here, in the Tverian Chronicle, it came under the influence of the *vita* of Mikhail of Chernigov. Now Mikhail flees Kiev because he has ordered the execution of deceitful Tatar envoys who had asked for his surrender. This is why Daniil of Galicia-Volhynia is able to occupy the city, however briefly.[67] The full tale of the sack of Kiev appears to have been included in the "compilation" (*svod*) of 1448, though without significant rewriting.[68] Only in the sixteenth-century Nikon Chronicle does anything like a recognition of the political consequences of the events of 1240 appear, with typical Nikon literary ornateness and bombast.[69] The Nikon chronicler transforms Mengu kan's appreciation of the beauty of Kiev into a direct speech in which he offers the city an explicit choice. "In truth this is a marvelous place, and beautiful and great; and if the people submit to the strength and force of *tsar'* Batu, then it will not be destroyed" (*Voistinu divno est' mesto se, i krasota sego i velichestvo; i ashche by vedali liudie sii silu i dr'znovenie tsaria Batyia, pokorilisia emu, i ne by razoren byl grade sei i mesti sii*). The verb "to submit" (*pokoriti*) is employed in the *vita* of Aleksandr Nevskii to convey a change in political sovereignty, and the word for "destroyed" (*razoren*) echoes the "Tale of the Destruction (*razorenie*) of Riazan' by Batu." Mikhail of Chernigov's scene with the Tatar envoys is further adulterated from his *vita*; Mikhail now refuses, on religious grounds, a request to bow (*pokloniti*) to *tsar'* Batu. (The Tatar genealogy is further mangled to read that the *kan* who died was not of the clan of Batu, though beloved of him. This excludes Batu from the Chingisids and further confuses the matter.) Upon leaving Kiev, Batu installs an official in the city (*Batu zhe posadi v grad Kiev voevodu svoego*).

Mengu kan's dialogue in this version at least raises the question of Kiev's submission and subordination, though the narrative does not conclude by saying that this occurred. However, the Nikon account does interpolate the installation of a governor, albeit one with a Russian title, *voevoda*, and no name. This sign of Mongol administration may be another echo of the *vita* of Mikhail of Chernigov, which mentions the delegation of *namestniki* (governors) to all of the Russian cities. Still, even at this late date, in the sixteenth century, there is no explicit connection between the seizure of the city and Batu's appointment of a governor.

For all its vivid presentation of Batu's sack of Kiev, this tale throughout its history, with the late and incomplete exception of the Nikon redaction, maintains a discreet silence about the consequences of the Mongol invasion for Russia's political independence.

The "Lay on the Ruin of the Russian Land" (*Slovo o pogibeli russkoi zemli*) is extant only in what is presumed to be a fragment. Its authorship is unknown,[70] and though it is thought to be about the Mongol conquest, even this is uncertain for it does not mention the Tatars by name. Its most thorough student believes that a southerner composed it about the Tatar invasion of Vladimir-Suzdalia, some time between 1238 and 1246.[71] The "Tale of the Sack of Kiev" in the chronicle of Galicia-Volhynia concludes with the line, "behold the Russian Land perishing from the unclean." Words with the same roots (*gibnushchuiu* and *pogibel'*) appear in the "Lay." This may indicate a relationship between the two works or may merely be coincidence.

If we accept the assumption that the "Lay" is about the Mongol conquest, whether of 1237-1238 or of 1240 and whether written in Vladimir-Suzdalia or in the Kievan region, it still tells us little. The most that can be said of its interpretation of the Mongols' arrival is that Russia was devastated, her past glory and fortune destroyed, and the good old days gave way to an abhorrent present. The "Lay's" poetic and literary qualities notwithstanding, this text does not appreciably alter our understanding of the Russian reaction to the Tatar conquest.[72]

Since the Mongols feared and respected the clergy of all religions, Chingis Khan decreed that in his empire all religions would be tolerated, indeed, tax-exempt. The khans of the Golden Horde largely adhered to this policy, even after their conversion to Islam.[73] Yet the *vita* of Mikhail of Chernigov records that Batu

ordered Mikhail's execution in 1245 or 1246 for failure to perform a
pagan ritual.   Mikhail's refusal and martyrdom won him
canonization in the Russian Orthodox Church.   The contradiction
between the Mongols' well-known religious toleration and the
alleged cause of Mikhail's execution is indicative of the distorted
view of Russo-Tatar relations as seen through the prism of
medieval Russian religious ideology.

Mikhail's martyrdom appears in the Laurentian and Hypatian
Chronicles and in the older recension of the Novgorod First
Chronicle.   His full *vita*, however, occurs for the first time in the
younger recension of the Novgorod First Chronicle and thus cannot
be attested before the fourteenth century.   It was probably written
several decades after the event by an eye-witness, not in
Chernigov or even in the Ukraine, but in Vladimir-Suzdalian
Rus'.[74]   The author was probably working for either Mikhail's
daughter, Maria, the widow of Vasil'ko Konstantinovich, or for
Mikhail's grandson, Boris.   These aspects of its provenance cannot
be disregarded in its interpretation.

According to the younger recension of the Novgorod First
Chronicle,[75] Tatar envoys had approached Mikhail in Kiev and
deceitfully sought the surrender of the city.   After ordering their
execution, Mikhail flees to Hungary and remains absent during the
Tatar "campaign" (*nakhozhdenie*), i.e., the sack of Kiev in 1240.
"For a certain time" (*po koletsekh vremena*) the Tatars "sat"
(*osadisha*) in the cities of *Rus'*; they took a census (*chislo*) and
began to collect tribute (*imati dan'*).   The taxation of his people
leads Mikhail to return to Russia, where the Tatars inform him
that it is improper for him to live on the land "of the khan"
(*zemli kanove*) without having made obeisance (literally, bowed:
pokoniv'shesia) to Batu.   Accordingly, Mikhail travels to the Horde
(*orda*).   He balks, however, at the ritual of walking between two
fires to show that he comes without evil intent.   Though told it is
asked of everyone, he remains obstinate.   Batu sends his courtier
(*stolnik*) Eldega to persuade Mikhail to perform the rite; otherwise
he cannot be received.   Mikhail states: "I bow to you, oh *Tsar'*,
for God has given you the tsardom and the glory of this world
. . .," but he will not violate his religion.   Batu orders Mikhail
beheaded;   the pagan Doman, a criminal (*zakonoprestupnik*),
performs the deed.

A number of details in this narrative require comment.   It is
not clear why the Tatar envoys who request the surrender of Kiev

are "deceitful." Perhaps their offer to spare the city if it surrendered was considered a trick, but this is only speculation. Mikhail's execution of the envoys is reminiscent of the fate of the first Tatar envoys who came to *Rus'* in 1223. It is odd that Mikhail does not have to pay for this violation of diplomatic immunity and affront to Tatar honor when he is summoned to the Horde.[76] There is no evidence outside of the *vita* that the Tatars remained in Kiev and other southern cities following the campaign of 1240; the Mongol army, after all, had moved on to Central and Eastern Europe. Nor is there confirmation elsewhere in the chronicles that the Mongols immediately took a census and began collecting tribute. This would surely have interfered with their military agenda, and we know that the censuses in Vladimir-Suzdalia and Novgorod came only in 1257, at the command of the Grand Khan in Karakorum. Given that the *vita* was written after the census of the northeast, it seems possible that the census it mentions is an invention, an anachronism devised to motivate Mikhail's return from exile.[77] The fire ritual is a standard Inner Asian purification rite, the same one that Zamarchus, the Byzantine ambassador to the sixth-century Türk Empire, was asked to perform.[78] There can be no question but that all Russian princes who came to the Horde, like the Catholic missionaries and representatives, were required to walk between the two fires. It is peculiar that of all these only Mikhail is too religiously fastidious to do so and prefers death. The courtier who tries to persuade him to obey Batu's request is given a Russian rank, *stolnik*, but Eldega is certainly not a Russian name.[79] The executioner's identity is even more confusing. In later chronicles the pagan Doman becomes the apostate Doman or a Severianin, a citizen of the Russian city of Severa. His name has no recognizable ethnicity, and his various identities in different texts suggest that the scribes too were puzzled. If Doman is described as an apostate it lends drama to the story, though it detracts from its plausibility.

Mikhail is also asked to bow to an idol (*idol'*, *bolvan*) or in some cases the sun and the moon, the sky, or a sacred bush. All are genuine elements of Mongol shamanism; the idol would be the embodiment of Chingis Khan himself. However, it is simply not credible that the Mongols would ask a Christian outsider to perform such rites.[80] They would have required mutual religious respect of Mikhail and nothing more. One suspects that the

hagiographer embellished his account with Tatar shamanist rituals
he had himself observed at the Horde. This possibility is
consistent with the general assumption that the author of the *vita*
was a cleric or *boyar* who had accompanied Mikhail to the Horde,
or at least someone who had spoken to a member of Mikhail's
retinue.

Mikhail, as Cherniavsky recognized, seemed to concede the
political authority of Batu. St. Paul preached that "The powers
that be, are of God," and Mikhail echoes this statement as he
acknowledges Batu's power and proclaims his willingness to defer to
it. He refuses, however, to compromise his religion. Yet to the
Mongols his refusal was a political act, one of treason rather than
of personal religious conscience.[81] In fact it is hard not to think
that both Batu and Mikhail were fully aware that politics underlay
their confrontation. Mikhail had been party to a loose coalition of
anti-Tatar Russian princes that also included Daniil Romanovich of
Galicia-Volhynia and Andrei Iaroslavovich of Vladimir-Suzdalia,
the brother of Aleksandr Nevskii. None of the princes acted at the
same time, and the coalition fizzled. Nonetheless, Mikhail had
attempted rebellion, and the intransigence of both sides in this
incident probably reflects this tension. Mikhail's refusal to walk
between the two fires may well have been a political gesture
cloaked as a religious expression—a truer reflection of his political
loyalties than his allusion to St. Paul. Batu's harsh response
(especially compared to his relatively mild treatment of the other
two rebels, who were more diplomatic) tends to support this view.
Centainly it is hard to imagine why, if even the Franciscans, let
alone the other Russian princes, performed the rite, Mikhail alone
could not be persuaded it was harmless.[82]

The *vita* of Mikhail of Chernigov skirts the issue of Tatar
suzerainty in a curious manner. The Tatar invasion is a campaign,
as a result of which the Tatars begin to govern (what could be
more governmental than collecting taxes?). Even Mikhail
recognizes Batu's legitimate authority. Still, the text never states
that a conquest preceded the collection of taxes, nor does it specify
that Russia had become part of the Mongol Empire (though one of
the Tatar officials does describe Chernigov as the "land of the
kan"). Since the text is not really political, it is hard to ascertain
whether the *vita* is politically anti-Tatar. The Tatars martyr a
Christian saint, which hardly makes them look good, but at the
same time the text does not celebrate or even bring up the issue

of political opposition. After all, within the conceptual framework of the story Mikhail is martyred for religious reasons alone.[83]

This picture does not alter significantly in the *vita*'s subsequent appearances in the Russian chronicles. In the mid-fifteenth-century Tverian Chronicle[84] a new introduction blames Russian sins for the Tatar "campaign" (*nakhozhdenie*). It asserts that many cities were "plundered" (*popleneny bysha*) and remain empty "to the present day" (*i donyne*). This last seems literary license rather than journalistic update. In the "*Batyevo i tsarevo zemlia*" (Batu's and the tsar's land—an interesting combined form which translates *kan* into the standard form, *tsar'*) many Russian princes did bow down, but not Mikhail. This heightens his devotion but also emphasizes the oddity of his behavior. The Sofia I Chronicle[85] curiously retains the use of *kan/kanovi*, but intensifies the *vita*'s dramatic tension. In this version the bishop of Chernigov warns Mikhail before his departure not to sacrifice his religion as the other Russian princes had done. Mikhail also bears the anachronistic title, "Russian Grand Prince" (*velikii kniaz' russkii*). In the Voskresensk Chronicle of the sixteenth century, the Tatars offer the throne of the just-executed Mikhail to his *boyar*, Fedor, on condition that he performs the rite. In all earlier redactions Fedor had followed the example of his prince, refused the rite, and died. The offer of the throne of Chernigov, or perhaps even of Kiev, is an innovation, however, and a patently fictitious one. The Mongol sense of royal legitimacy was very strong. They never imposed a non-Riurikid on any Russian throne and would not have dreamed of doing so. The sixteenth-century chronicler probably intended this embellishment of the narrative to impugn Tatar morality and to enhance the devotion to church and prince apparent in Fedor's sacrifice. In another minor sixteenth-century alteration, in the *Vologodsko-Permskaia letopis'*, Mikhail hears that "scribes of the tsar'" (*tsarevye pistsy*) were writing down the people in order to collect tribute (*dan'*); *pistsy* is a sixteenth-century Muscovite administrative term and clearly an anachronism.[86]

The Nikon Chronicle shares some of its innovations with other sixteenth-century texts like the Chronograph (*Khronograf*) of 1512 and the Book of Degrees (*Stepennaia Kniga*). In its version, Batu has "enslaved" (*porabotati*) the Kievan area, a phrase used in a number of Nikon annals dealing with the Tatars. He also installs "officials" (*namestniki i vlasteli*) in all the Russian cities. These

are Russian administrative terms, and such generalizations are
typical of the Nikon chronicler. In this version Mikhail's eloquence
impresses Eldega, just as his bravery impresses Batu. Their
reaction perhaps mitigates their villainy. The Nikon account also
asserts that Batu wanted to institute the false faith of Persia in
Rus'. It is not clear whether this extravagant exaggeration refers
to Zoroastrianism (perhaps extrapolated from the symbolism of thc
fire rite) or to Islam, also anachronistic since Batu was a pagan.
Prince Boris of Rostov appears in a new role as a loyal servant of
the Horde who tries to persuade Mikhail to perform the rite rather
than to be martyred like Boris's own father, Vasil'ko
Konstantinovich. In the end Eldega reports to Batu that Mikhail
cursed all who did not properly follow his own religion and spoke
many words not fit to be repeated in Batu's "realm" (*dr'zhava*).
This reworked and massively edited version of the *vita* well
illustrates the literary and political proclivities of the Nikon
Chronicle but resolves none of the contradictions of Mikhail's
martyrdom.[87]
     It is not surprising that these endured. There was no way
for the hagiographer or later redactors to present a coherent
explanation of Mikhail's execution—that is, a political
one—without addressing Mikhail's status as a rebel and the
attendant implications of Tatar suzerainty. Morover, the
hagiographer had no need to confront these issues. Mikhail died
because he was a prince of Russia. As Cherniavsky has elucidated,
this made his sainthood automatic, since to die *pro patria*, for the
Holy Land of Christian *Rus'*, was by definition to die *pro fide*.
Much as western kings supposedly had the "royal touch," i.e., the
miraculous healing ability of saints, so too all medieval Russian
princes participated in a princely cult. By dying as a prince
Mikhail imitated the passion of Christ and earned canonization.[88]
Given this conception of the religious nature and function of
Mikhail's sacrifice, any examination of his political motives would
have been superfluous and even sacrilegious. Hagiography has no
room for such matters, and only the details reinforcing the religious
nature of the story were relevant to the author and to the later
scribes, copyists, and redactors who perpetuated the text. There
was no way for the Russian intellectual elite to make sense of the
death of Mikhail of Chernigov except through the distorting lens of
religious ideology. A simple act of political reprisal became one of
divine providence in which a devout Christian proved the strength

of his faith. However well informed the hagiographer may have been of the unattractive political realities of Mikhail's career and execution, the *vita* itself refuses to analyze Russo-Tatar relations outside of the confines of the Christian world-view.

Another who fled before the oncoming Tatar hosts was Grand Prince Daniil Romanovich of Galicia-Volhynia. Like Mikhail he returned when the Tatar armies were gone, only to be summoned to the Horde. Here the similarity ends, for where Mikhail was martyred, Daniil was honored. The story appears in an entry in the Galician-Volhynian Chronicle often cited as illustrative of the greater hostility toward Tatar rule among the people of Galicia-Volhynia (read: Ukrainians) than among the people of Vladimir-Suzdalia (read: Russians). However, this conclusion is far from obvious.

According to the chronicle, in 1245-1246 (1250)[89] the envoy (*posol*) Moguchei summoned Daniil to Batu; Daniil could refuse only at the expense of his patrimony (*otchina*). Travelling through Kiev, Daniil meets Dmitri Eikovich, *boyar* of Grand Prince Yaroslav of Vladimir-Suzdalia. After passing through Pereiaslavl', Daniil encounters Kuremsa and his Tatars who send him on to Batu's camp on the Volga. At this point in the narrative the chronicler pauses to present a litany of the abominable sins Daniil witnessed among the Tatars, including the usual drinking, fornication, and sorcery. Then Daniil meets Yaroslav's "man" (*chelovek*), S"ngar, who advises him to obey the Tatar rituals and to bow to Batu. Though the chronicler has just finished equating these Tatar practices with the machinations of the Devil, Daniil agrees. He bows to Batu and drinks "black milk" (kumiss), though later Batu sends him wine instead as a courtesy. Daniil also bows to the "grand princess" (*velikaia kniaginia*) Barakchin. Daniil sinks to his knees; he is called the "slave" (*kholop*) of the Tatars, promises to pay the tribute (*dan'*), and swears fealty. Here the voice of the chronicler intrudes again, exclaiming, "Oh the greatest disgrace is to be honored by the Tatars (*kakaia zlaia chest' v Tatare*)." He goes on to recall how Daniil's father, Roman, ruled the Russian Land (*russkaia zemlia*), was its *tsar'*, had "plundered" (*pleni*) the Polovtsy and "made war on" (*voevati*) neighboring lands. And now his son is called slave and receives false and evil honor!

This emotional and rather effective literary effort raises a number of questions. Is the *boyar* Dmitri Eikovich in Kiev the same Dmitro who defended the city as Daniil's *boyar* in 1240? We will recall that Batu spared the wounded Dmitro's life. However, if this is the same *boyar*, he has switched overlords and now serves Yaroslav of Vladimir-Suzdalia. Though the chronicle mentions neither the religion nor the ethnicity of Yaroslav's man, S"ngar, he is identifiable as the same Christian Polovtsian *boyar* whom Carpini had met.[90] It is unusual for a converted Polovtsian to have retained his Turkic name. Barakchin's title, "grand princess," is incorrect; surely she is the *tsaritsa*, though in this annal Batu is not termed *tsar'*, this honor being reserved for Daniil's father! Though certain aspects of this account should be taken at less than face value, it is on the whole a credible relation of the events, probably the report of an eyewitness.

The extravagant jeremiad comparing Daniil's fortune and character with those of his father appears to derive from a speech in the "Alexandriad" in which Alexander relates the fall from glory of King Darius.[91] Given this original context, the use of *tsar'* to describe Daniil's father may simply be apolitical rhetorical imitation. The chronicler's contempt for honors the Tatars awarded is not typical. No comparable revulsion is apparent elsewhere in the chronicles, for example, in their description of Batu's reception of Alexandr Nevskii, and northeastern chronicles never sneer at honor (*chest'*) from the Tatars.[92] The Galician-Volhynian chronicler invidiously compares Daniil with Mikhail of Chernigov and his *boyar*, Fedor, both of whom chose martyrdom rather than violate the Christian faith. The implication is that Daniil's behavior cost him eternal salvation. The chronicle entry does not employ the lexicon of political suzerainty to explain why Daniil performed a vassal's act of obeisance. It is apparent that he is acting under duress, yet he does obey, and the chronicler damns him for it.

Though Daniil submitted personally to Batu, political relations between the Horde and Galicia-Volhynia, as subsequent annals attest, were by no means settled. Daniil pursued an anti-Tatar policy and sought an alliance with Catholic Europe. In exchange for homage to the pope, he received a royal crown and a promise of military support. In keeping with his opposition to the Tatars, he took reprisals against the "Bolokhov princes" (*Bolokhovskie kniazi*), who are supposed to have agreed to sow wheat for the Tatars.[93] He also severely punished his man Milei, who in 1255 surrendered to the Tatars and became their *baskak* (administrator).[94] Aid from the pope never materialized, however, and Burundai, Kuremsa's successor as Tatar factotum in Galicia-Volhynia, proved a less lenient overseer. Burundai rode into Galicia-Volhynia in 1261, but Daniil refused to meet him. Burundai sent him a message with this choice: Daniil could either become one of the *mirnitsi* (peaceful subjects?) of the khan or be in disgrace (*opala*) before him. Daniil fled to Poland and Hungary again. A Tatar attempt to storm the city of Kholm is foiled, since the city has been secretly warned not to obey the Galician-Volhynian princes (minus Daniil) when they order it to surrender. Galician-Volkynian contingents join the Tatar campaign against Poland and Lithuania,[95] a practice which became common after Daniil's death.

One assumes that Daniil's submission to Batu was merely intended to gain time while Daniil strengthened his position with links to Rome and to Nevskii's brother, Andrei Yaroslavovich, and that his actions after returning from the Horde reflect his real leanings. Thus the anti-Tatar sentiments apparent in the account in the Galician-Volhynian Chronicle actually represent Daniil's own feelings, or at any rate those of the elite of Galicia-Volhynia. Be that as it may, Daniil's anti-Tatar activities after 1250 were not effective, and Tatar influence in Galicia-Volhynia increased even further following his death.

The chronicler distorts the record of Roman, Daniil's father, to tendentious purpose. Roman never bore the title *tsar'*, which would have to echo Byzantine imperial aspirations here, nor was the ideology of the Russian Land much in vogue in thirteenth-century Galicia-Volhynia. Roman was a powerful prince, but the chronicler exaggerates his ideological pretension by according him an exalted and otherwise unattested title. The chronicler accuses Daniil of failing to live up to a fictitious past.

Interpretation of the account of Daniil's career in the Galician-Volhynian Chronicle must begin with an appreciation of the nature of the chronicle itself.[96] It is entirely a product of the thirteenth century, though where lies the seam between the Galician and the Volhynian portions is a matter of dispute. Also open to question is the social position of its authors; some have seen ecclesiastical, others, secular (chivalric: *rytsarvstvo*) values in the prose. Regardless of whether the chronicle was composed in Daniil's chancellery or in the episcopal court of the bishop of

Kholm, as a whole it is favorable to Daniil with the exception of the entry on his visit to Batu, which is infused with religious hostility to the Tatars and Daniil alike. Daniil's union with the Roman Catholic Church, though part of his machinations against the Mongols, would necessarily have aroused intense suspicion among the Orthodox hierarchy. Further, it is safe to assume that any well-informed chronicler would know that the Mongols exempted the Orthodox Church from taxation. Any cleric trying to deal with Daniil's submission to Batu would have experienced mixed emotions.

Daniil's Tatar policy might better be described as one of reluctance than as one of resistance. Not above taking advantage of his Tatar connection, he once dressed his troops in Tatar clothing to intimidate the Hungarians, and the ruse worked.[97] The diatribe against him in the submission episode may reflect a response to his failed policy of mixed bluster and blunder, flight and reconciliation, and his failure to put up any genuine resistance.

The attitude toward the Tatars in the Galician-Volhynian Chronicle is generally similar to that in the chronicles of Vladimir-Suzdalia. The narratives of 1223, 1237-1238, and 1240 graphically describe Mongol destruction but do not treat the question of political suzerainty. Therefore the account in the Galician-Volhynian Chronicle of Daniil's submission is something of an anomaly, in that its attack on Daniil, though couched in religious terms, is a political one. It exhibits a clear consciousness of the political implications of Daniil's submission: Daniil is Batu's "slave" and will pay tribute. Nonetheless, though the author does discuss the political relationship between the Mongols and Galicia-Volhynia, it is fundamentally irrelevant to his concerns. It is the religious dimension of the relationship that occupies the author, and it is the infidel rites themselves rather than the political significance of the act that upset him. It is difficult to assign the uncompromising religious fanaticism of this entry to any serious segment of the Galician-Volhynian establishment. Clearly Daniil's was the ox being gored; perhaps further study of the chronicle will reveal the identity of the bull.[98]

Of all Batu's Russian visitors, the most famous today is probably Aleksandr Nevskii, whose renown rests upon his victories over the Swedes and the Teutonic Knights in 1240 and 1242. Nevskii, however, was also a Tatar collaborator, and this aspect of his career has long been a source of embarrassment to patriotic Russian historiographers. The debate revolves around Nevskii's *vita*, written, it is currently thought, at the behest of his son Dmitrii and metropolitan Kiril in the Rozhdestvenskii monastery in Vladimir in the 1280s.[99] At the time of composition, Nevskii and Batu had both been dead for several score years.

In the reconstructed primary text of the work,[100] which also recounts Nevskii's rescue of Novgorod and Pskov from Catholic knights and his rejection of the pope's attempt at ecclesiastical union, Nevskii receives a summons from Batu. The text describes the Mongol leader as "a powerful *tsar'* of the eastern land, to whom God had subordinated (*pokoril*) many lands, from the east to the west." Batu's message is as follows: "You know that God has submitted (*pokoril*) many nations (*iazytsy*) to me. Why have only you not wished to submit (*pokoritesia*) to my strength? But if you wish to protect your land, then quickly come to me and look upon my imperial honor (*chest' tsarstva*)." Nevskii accordingly does journey to the tsar's horde (*k tsareve k orde*), where Batu greets him with great honor and remarks that reports of Nevskii's awe-inspiring qualities have proved true. Nevskii departs.

Subsequently Nevskii's younger brother, Andrei, angers Batu, who sends his commander (*voevoda*) Nevrui to make war on (*voevati*) the Suzdalian Land. In the wake of Nevrui's plundering (*po plenenii*), Nevskii restores the land, rebuilding cities and churches, and regathers the people. Next Nevskii travels to the Horde bearing gifts, for there is great distress (*nuzhna*) in the land because of foreigners (*inoplemenniki*) who want to make war on the Christians. His embassy is successful, but he sickens and dies on the return journey. Altogether the three episodes involving the Tatars comprise only a fraction of the *vita*.

The text is nonetheless an important one for our purposes, and its presentation of Russo-Tatar relations requires explanation. The *vita* describes Batu as a *tsar'*, a legitimate emperor, who has conquered many lands from the east to the west (the repeated verb *pokoriti* unambiguously connoting political submission). The lands in question are not named, nor is there any indication that Russia is among them. Batu's message to Nevskii, like his message to Daniil of Galicia-Volhynia, indicates that the prince will lose his land unless he swears obedience. The *vita*, however, fails to make the connection between Batu's right to make this demand and the oath of fealty sworn by Nevskii's father, Grand Prince Yaroslav, following the Tatar campaign of 1237-1238. (It was at Yaroslav's nomination that Nevskii served as prince of Novgorod, and the son was surely bound by the oath of the father.) The *vita* leaves this political context of Batu's request unexplained and never refers to Yaroslav's trip to Karakorum. Nevskii goes simply to avoid being the cause of harm to his land. Though Batu insists that Nevskii alone has yet to submit to him, none of the other Russian princes who have responded to summonses are specified; presumably they include Mikhail of Chernigov and Daniil of Galicia-Volhynia, as well as numerous princes of the northeast. Nor is there mention of any such rites as walking between fires, drinking kumiss, and so forth such as were required of Mikhail of Chernigov and Daniil of Galicia-Volhynia, or of political obligations like the tribute Daniil agreed to pay. Nevskii is simply honored and dismissed. The narrative merely focuses on Nevskii's gracious treatment at the hands of a powerful eastern tsar.

Batu's anger with Nevskii's brother, Andrei Yaroslavovich, also is left unexplained (when in fact Andrei was part of the anti-Tatar coalition that got Daniil of Galicia-Volhynia into trouble). Batu dispatches Nevrui to "plunder" the Suzdalian Land; again it is clear that the verb *pleniti* does not refer to conquest.[101] Nevskii is not implicated in the breakdown of peace, simply appearing afterward as the restorer of the Suzdalian Land. His role here parallels that of Ingvar Ingvarevich in the "Tale of the Destruction of Riazan' by Batu."

The final Tatar episode in Nevskii's *vita*, in which Nevskii travels to the Horde because foreigners are causing "great distress" among the people, presumably refers to the 1262 *veche* uprisings against Muslim tax-farmers in numerous cities of northeastern Russia.[102] Nevskii's purpose, apparently, was to dissuade the Tatars from launching raids to punish the revolts; in any case no punitive expeditions were sent. Nevskii's embassy seems to indicate that he himself was not involved in the uprisings, but the language of the *vita* so obscures the political reality behind the events that more detailed analysis is difficult.[103] As in the case of Andrei's provocation, Nevskii stands apart from the source of trouble. His role in Russo-Tatar relations is that of a mediator and arbitrator rather than of an activist.

No interpetation of Nevskii's Tatar policy based on his *vita* can be taken seriously unless it takes into account the ideology and tendentiousness of the work itself. The Eurasianists, for example, believed that Nevskii was trying to use the Tatars and their religious tolerance to protect Russian Orthodoxy from Catholic conversion efforts. This argument is founded on a belief in Nevskii's profound piety substantiated only by the *vita*,[104] an ecclesiastically sponsored work[105] deliberately designed to enhance Nevskii's chances of canonization. Surely such a work cannot be taken at face value in assessing Nevskii's religious commitment. On the other hand, Nevskii was certainly more than an unprincipled opportunist of minor importance.[106] His military and political skills saved Novgorod and Pskov from hostile Latin neighbors, and he appears to have been an effective prince, fully capable of exercising his authority when necessary. He saw that he could either suffer martyrdom and the destruction of his land and people or collaborate with the Tatars, and he chose the latter. Not enjoying Daniil's advantage of distance from the Horde, Nevskii simply did not have the same options.

By the 1280s, when Nevskii's *vita* was written, Mongol authority was firmly established in Russia. The *baskak* system had been implemented, the census taken, and tribute collection regularized. Yet in this text none of this is mentioned. It is either taken for granted or swept under the rug. Indeed the entire political context of Russo-Tatar relations, let alone their theoretical implications, is omitted from the text, which virtually presents Nevskii's encounters with the Tatars in a political vacuum. Was this merely "camouflaging" (to use Fennell's term) of the embarrassing fact of Nevskii's collaboration?

Even literary analysis of the *vita* has sometimes foundered on the seeming disparity between Nevskii the patriotic hero who fends off the Catholics, and Nevskii the collaborationist who serves the Tatars.[107] Such problems arise from trying to make his policies conform to modern secular political conceptions of how he should properly have acted.[108] The solution lies in understanding the ethos of our ideological text. Cherniavsky discovered the key to the *vita*'s picture of Nevskii.[109] To use his epigrammatic formulation, Nevskii is both the saintly prince and the princely saint. As the former, he battles Catholics to save the Russian Land;[110] as the latter, he sacrifices himself for the same purpose in his tireless and ultimately fatal attempts to secure Tatar mercy. Much of the sacrifice lies in the necessity of showing humility before the Tatars. This portrait of Nevskii's dual yet distinct heroisms is of course not real psycho-history. Instead it is the *vita*'s sophisticated and carefully orchestrated ideological image of its hero, a compounding of abstract political myths. Nevskii vigorously defends his land against one set of enemies and also imitates Christ in his humility before another set of enemies, though they are his inferiors. Since both actions qualify as heroic, there is no conflict. Of course the heterogeneity of Nevskii's *vita* leaves many loose ends, even in the Tatar episodes alone. After all, Nevskii's reception by Batu seems to glorify the Russian rather than humiliate him. The fact remains that the *vita*'s political theology must be our first consideration as we seek to answer questions about the historical Nevskii's politics and character.

The *vita* probably was not written to be included in the chronicles, and when it was, it was usually cannibalized, different parts of it appearing in different annals, rather than reproduced in its entirety. While the dissemination of Nevskii's cult was perhaps slower than has been thought, this was not because his Tatar policies lessened his popularity. Despite the sponsorship of the metropolitan, Nevskii was merely a local saint, and it was not until the middle of the fifteenth century that a redaction of the *vita* associated him with the Russian Land, the "national" myth of the medieval Russian elite. It is not clear which northeastern chronicles between the thirteenth and the early fifteenth centuries contained the full *vita* or its Tatar segments.[111] A fifteenth-century redaction from Novgorod musters the historical perspective to compare Nevskii's restoration of the Suzdalian Land with that of his father Yaroslav, "after the first great Tatar seizure (literally: taking)" of the Suzdalian Land (*po pervom velikom vziatii tatarstem*). This has not been mentioned previously in the text's literary tradition, but the construction is awkward and strained, and even at this great remove finesses the Tatar conquest. Other embellishments in this version expound on Nevskii's use of wealth to ransom Nevrui's prisoners.[112]

Sixteenth-century Muscovite chronicles show interesting revision of the Tatar passages. Typically, the Nikon chronicler gives Andrei a speech to explain his flight from Nevrui. Here Andrei insists that the Russian princes must not allow the Tatars to turn them against one another and that it is better to flee than to serve the Tatars. This certainly casts a less favorable light on Nevskii's later behavior. The true inhibitions and prejudices of the Nikon chronicler, however, come through in another passage. The writer rationalizes Batu's honorable treatment of Nevskii as divine intervention, for otherwise the minds of the unclean could think only of insulting and shaming Christians.[113] This clearly reflects the more expansive anti-Tatar rhetoric of the sixteenth-century Muscovite bookmen.

Aleksandr Nevskii will remain a controversial figure in Russian history, for there is no question but that he profited from the Mongol conquest and built his career on Mongol support. Perhaps it was statesmanship rather than opportunism which enabled him to realize that military and political opposition to the Mongols could lead only to defeat and death, or perhaps he had no genuine conception of what he was doing. We can only infer his motives from his actions, of which we know little, or from the point of view of his *vita*, which we know to be tendentious.

The accounts of the visits to Batu of Daniil of Galicia-Volhynia and of Aleksandr Nevskii could hardly differ more in their interpretation of these events. The narration of Daniil's submission speaks of the protagonist's enslavement and relentlessly castigates the Tatars, while Nevskii's *vita* is apolitical and largely neutral in its treatment of the Mongols. Yet these differences may arise less from differing attitudes toward the Tatars than from different attitudes toward the princes themselves. The discreet tone in Nevskii's *vita*, which avoids the usual opprobrious remarks about the Tatars, is inevitable, given that the work is intended to glorify a collaborator. Nonetheless, both works stress that the humiliation involved is religious rather than political and do not concern themselves with the real central issue—that of suzerainty. Nevskii's *vita* differs in degree but not in kind from the standard thirteenth-century Russian intellectual stance with regard to the Tatars.[114]

The traditional perception of the Mongol conquest in Russian historiography is quite a simple one. The Mongols, almost an elemental destructive force animated only by greed and blood-lust, overwhelmed the Russian principalities, leaving only ruins in their wake. They instituted an arbitrary and cruel administration, executing innocent patriots like Mikhail of Chernigov and subverting Quislings like Nevskii. In a minor variation, Nevskii too is a true patriot who sacrifices his own honor for the survival of his land. The accepted vision of the Tatars and their motives is a selective extrapolation from their portrayal in the medieval Russian sources, one which is tendentious, ideologically inspired, and distorted.   The medieval bookmen explained Tatar actions as motivated by a hatred of Christians (more recent, secular historians have done little more than translate this into the antipathy to be expected from pastoral nomads and "Asiatics").   There was no need to explain Tatar behavior beyond this, since infidel evil was self-explanatory.   In the Russian texts of the time, Mongol strategy, politics, and culture were irrelevant; after all, the Tatars were no more than God's instrument for punishing Russian sins. The modern prejudiced perception of the Tatars is a secularized recension of this religious mentality.

But the medieval Russian bookmen who articulated the perceptions of the elite went even further in their distortion of Russo-Tatar relations.   In theory God's punishment of the Christian Russians could have included infidel conquest, and the bookmen had ready access to a lexicon that would have clearly conveyed this political reality.   Instead they presented Russo-Tatar relations as a series of violent incursions by marauding bands of nomads from the steppe.   The bookmen simply did not discuss what had really happened.   This is less surprising in such works as the *vita* of Mikhail of Chernigov and Aleksandr Nevskii; hagiography had no place for political theory.   Yet the same is true in all other records of the day as well.   A good example is the "Tale of the Destruction of Riazan' by Batu," the ending of which is pure fiction.   The ideology of silence, by means of which improper fraternization with religious enemies was ignored, was characteristic of the entire medieval ethno-religious frontier. Intellectual rejection of the very fact of conquest was a uniquely Russian variation.

It would be a mistake to assume that the Russian sources went about this in a simplistic fashion.   Both writers and readers, of course, were aware of the true situation, so manifestations of Tatar rule can be found in the texts—princes travelling to the Horde, tax collection.   Even the existence of Mongol authority was acknowledged in the echo of St. Paul's dictum concerning the powers that be.   Moreover, the political establishment understood Mongol imperial politics very well, and by the time most texts concerning the events of the thirteenth century were written, Batu was being referred to as *tsar'* (i.e., khan, a title Batu never used). In fact, the Russians were intimately familiar with many Tatars and Tatar ways.   Though it served Russian ideological purposes to write as though the Tatars were an alien and entirely unknown people, the bookmen continually betray their expertise in Tatar affairs, thus confounding their literary pose. In short, the medieval Russian texts dealing with thirteenth-century Russo-Tatar relations reveal the contradictions implicit in the position of the Russian elite, who were well acquainted with their overlords but knew they were not supposed to be.

Thus these texts must be read critically and cautiously. For example, it is easy to assert, after reading the medieval sources, that the conquest was a religiously traumatic experience for the Russian people, but we must keep in mind that much of the Russian population in the countryside was still pagan. The religious interpretation of the conquest in the texts reflects the ideology of the elite and would have been meaningless for the greater part of the population. Furthermore, the texts record Russian shock in a traditional, highly rhetorical language with inevitably distorting effects. And lest some argue that because the sources present Tatar victories as the will of God, the texts are therefore "pro-Tatar," we must recall that within the Christian providential world-view no other interpretation was possible. Though Russian defeats were punishment for Rusian sins, the Tatars were still instruments of the Devil, and Russian redemption would result in their demise. This is hardly a pro-Tatar vision of the future. The full complexities of the presentation of the Tatars in the Russian narrative sources can only be identified and analyzed by penetrating the ingrained ideological motives of the medieval bookmen, studying what they literally say, and remaining sensitive to what they reveal in spite of themselves.

The thirteenth-century Russian sources refuse to deal with the Mongols in terms of conquest or to draw conclusions about Tatar politics outside of a religious framework. They attempt to conceal Russian familiarity with the Golden Horde, and will not modulate their religious animosity to accomodate such incidents of social understanding as Batu's occasional honorable treatment of Russian princes or warriors. These patterns in the Russian perception of Tatars in the sources shaped the style and content of Russian accounts of Russo-Tatar relations both for the duration of Mongol rule and in the years following its collapse.

Chapter III:

Tatar Oppression

Between the death of Batu, c. 1255, and the Battle of Kulikovo Field, 1380, Russian bookmen often referred to the Mongols' mistreatment of Russia as "Tatar oppression." We find the first hint of the expression in the Laurentian Chronicle, which explains that the *veche* uprisings in northeastern Russian cities in 1262 occurred because the Christians could not endure "the oppression of the infidels" (*ne terpiashe nasil'ia poganskykh*).[1] Though the "pagans" in this case were actually Central Asian Muslims, the entry *sub anno* 1266 in the *Troitskaia letopis'* changes the modifier, observing that, "In that same year Khan Berkai died, and *Rus'* suffered less from Muslim oppression" (*Togo zhe leta umre tsar' Tatarskii Berkai i byst' oslaba Rusi ot nasil'ia besermen*). Muslim here refers to the Tatars,[2] though in fact the Golden Horde had not yet converted to Islam. The fifth sermon of Serapion, Bishop of Vladimir, probably composed in the 1270s,[3] alludes to the "many sorrows and pains, expeditions, hunger [which Russia has endured] from pagan oppression" (*ot poganskikh nasil'ia*). Then, looking again in the Laurentian Chronicle, we find that in 1300 Metropolitan Maksim left Kiev for the Suzdalian Land "because he was unable to endure Tatar oppression" (*ne terpia Tatarskogo nasil'ia*). This actually marks the first appearance in the sources of the adjective "Tatar" joined with the noun "oppression."[4] Later, the *Troitskaia letopis'* declares that after Ivan Kalita of Moscow became grand prince of Vladimir in 1328, the Russian Land enjoyed forty years of peace "from Tatar oppression" (*ot nasilia Tatarskogo*).[5] Finally, the Novgorod Fourth Chronicle records that in 1357 Metropolitan Alexei was trapped in the Horde amidst violent civil war and just barely managed to escape alive "from pagan oppression" (*ot nasilia poganskikh*).[6] These examples illustrate the permutations of a phrase linguistically and semantically akin to "the Tatar Yoke." However, since contemporary Russians never used the latter expression, "Tatar oppression" seems a more apt and legitimate heading for our discussion of texts written between Batu's death and Donskoi's victory.[7]

In the winter of 1237-1238, the Mongol armies, having swept through northeastern *Rus'*, bore down on Novgorod. After coming within a hundred *versts* of the city, however, the Tatars turned back. The Novgorodian Chronicle hailed divine intervention. Historians, on the other hand, have been less inclined to credit the Virgin for the Mongols' departure, and have assumed that it was the spring thaw that discouraged them. Another proposal is that the Tatars were merely chasing refugees from the border city of Torzhok (which they had just stormed), and never intended to attack Novgorod at that point. This theory is supported by the fact that Novgorod would have required a full concentration of Mongol forces, and by the time these could have been mobilized, the spring thaw would have made transport of heavy siege equipment impossible. This is a cogently reasoned military analysis of the Mongol "feint" toward Novgorod,[8] and is the probable explanation for Novgorod's escape from destruction in 1237-1238.

What remains unexplained is Novgorod's continued good fortune, for it is not clear why the Tatars did not reduce the city during any of the subsequent winters. Had Novgorod actively opposed Mongol authority (in accordance with its carefully maintained image as a democratic, freedom-loving, and anti-Tatar city), the Mongols would have had no choice but to bring the city to its knees. That they did not suggests to me that the Novgorodian Chronicle has omitted to record secret negotiations whereby the city surrendered peacefully and a *modus vivendi* for the future was arranged. We know that some cities of northeastern Russia made such arrangements with the Mongols, and it is impossible to imagine that the Mongols would have shrunk from the challenge of besieging Novgorod had they needed to.

Novgorod's reputation for uninhibited antagonism toward the Tatars arises from the account in the Novgorod First Chronicle of Nevskii's visit to the city accompanied by Tatar census-takers.[9] These latter (*chislenitsy*) had conducted, in the winter of 1257, a census of the Suzdalian, Riazanian, and Murom Lands, setting up decurions, centurions, chiliarchs, and ten-thousand men (*desiatniki i sotniki i tysiachniki i temniki*).[10] Only persons connected with the Russian Orthodox Church were exempted. While the Laurentian Chronicle records no resistance to the census in Vladimir-Suzdalia, Novgorod was to be a different matter.

According to the Novgorod First Chronicle, "evil news" came

to Novgorod in 1257: the Tatars wanted to collect the *tamga*, a customs tax, and the *desiatina*, a tithe. (The latter term is suspicious, previously used only in a dubious episode concerning the attack on Riazan' in 1237–1238.) The city is in such uproar that several mayors (*posadniki*) lose their lives. Then Aleksandr Nevskii arrives with Tatar envoys (*posly*). This Nevskii is grand prince of Vladimir and hence overlord of Novgorod, but he has already, nay, long since, become a faithful Tatar vassal. Nevskii's son Vasilii, who held the throne of the city at Novgorod's pleasure and his father's, has fled to Pskov upon hearing the news of his father's impending visit. Though gifts for the Tatars divert them from their intention of extracting taxes and tribute, Nevkii's vengeance on his son's *boyare* is horrible. For leading Vasilii astray, he has various of them mutilated. Vasilii himself is later driven from Pskov.[11]

Interpreters of this account and the event it describes have paid too much attention to Novgorod's apparent ability in 1257 to bribe its way out of a census, and too little to the peculiarities of the story. First of all, it is implicitly clear that Novgorod was *not* in a state of active opposition to the Tatars; the Mongols' first demand to an unfriendly city was for capitulation, not taxes. Nevskii, who was both a Tatar friend and the rightful overlord of Novgorod, had no doubt already made the arrangements committing the city to subservience. Second, the author of the entry does not in fact call the envoys census-takers. He believes that they have come for the *tamga* and the *desiatina*, but he may have misunderstood their real purpose, which might well have been simply to lay the groundwork for the census the Mongols did conduct in Novgorod two years later. If the events of 1257 were a Tatar trial balloon, then the chronicle has remained silent on some aspects of the situation. The relationship between Nevskii and his son is also confusing. The chronicle allows us to infer that Vasilii Aleksandrovich and his *boyare* opposed Nevskii's cooperation with the Tatars,[12] but this is never made explicit. The political maneuverings of the next two years are not recorded, and the denouement is confusing.

The chronicle says that in 1259[13] Mikhail Pineshchinin, a Novgorodian in the service of Grand Prince Aleksandr Nevskii, came from the "Low Country" (*Niz*, a typical Novgorodian appellation for Vladimir-Suzdalia) "with a lying message" (*so lzhyvim posolstvom*): either Novgorod would carry out a census or there were Tatar troops. The message is incomplete and cryptic, since it doesn't say what the Tatar troops would do; nonetheless the nature of the threat is obvious. As a consequence, the Novgorodians "carried out a census on themselves" (*iashasia po chislo*). This is extraordinary, since the East Slavs had never had the administrative expertise to conduct a census before. The chronicle does not comment on its principles, procedures, or its equity (the last is of particular interest in light of subsequent events). Certainly the Mongols did not regard any census not carried out by their own officials as adequate. Perhaps Mikhail Pineshchinin's was a "lying message" because he knew this, but the chronicle does not make this clear.

In that winter census-takers arrived in Novgorod, "the accursed Tatars, eaters of unclean flesh (*syroiadtsy*) Berkai and Kasachik and their wives and many others." Accompanying them were the three most powerful princes of northeastern *Rus'*, Aleksandr Nevskii, his brother, Andrei Yaroslavovich of Suzdal',[14] and Boris Vasil'kovich of Rostov.[15] A riot (*miatezh*) erupts in the city. The Tatars try to collect the *tuska* (tuft, a tax?) throughout the province, but the disorder is too great. The Tatar envoys seek Nevskii's protection, and inform him that unless they receive adequate security, they will leave. Though the chronicle does not say so, the implied threat is that they will return with a punitive force.

Here we must interrupt the chronicle's narrative of these swiftly moving events to note a few curiosities. First it is rare for Tatar officials in the Russian forest zone to be accompanied by their spouses. This is especially unusual if the Berkai referred to is the same Bitsik whom the *Yüan shih* (the annals of the Mongol Yüan Dynasty in China) says was named "to count the people in Russia" since his spouse would have had to accompany him from China or at least Mongolia. Second the narrative does not mention translators. Third the chronicle presents the Tatars' demand for Nevskii's protection as an unforeseen contingency, a situation unexpectedly forced upon him. In fact it is evident that Nevskii was present for this very purpose, to ensure the orderly completion of the Novgorod census.

The chronicle goes on to say that Nevskii's response to the Tatars' demand is to order the *posadnik* (mayor) and *deti boyarskie* (minor servitors) to guarantee their safety. In the morning the common people (*chern'*) express their willingness "to die honorably

for St. Sophia and the churches" (*angelskie domy*). The people
were divided into two groups, the "good folk" (*dobrie*), who stood
for St. Sophia and the true faith, and the "richer" (*viatshii*), who
conspired to count the poorer in the census. The Tatars, under
Nevskii's protection, survey Novgorod, writing down the Christians'
houses. The *boyare* have arranged it so that they were counted
"lightly" (*lcgko*) "and the lesser folk harm" (*i men'shie zlo*, i.e., the
lesser folk were taxed more harshly than the nobles). Nevskii and
the Tatars leave the city, but Nevskii installs his son Dmitrii
Aleksandrovich on Novgorod's throne.

While the Novgorod First Chronicle's account is dramatic and
describes some anti-Tatar agitation, there is not much basis for
contrasting it, as an anti-Tatar document, with the laconic
narration of the census in the northeast that appears in the
Laurentian Chronicle. If we examine the text itself, rather than
the events it describes, we find that its omissions and ambiguities
are as great in their own way as those in the Laurentian Chronicle.
For example, the Novgorod chronicler variously describes those who
oppose the census as the "common folk" (*chern'*), not usually a
complimentary term, the "good folk" (*dobrie*), a moral description,
and the "lesser folk" (*men'shie*), an equally uninformative term.
Are these all the same people? Similarly, the *boyare* and the
"richer" (*viatshii*) appear to be synonymous, but we must not
overlook the looseness of the lexicon.

It is also not clear whether the regressive taxation (i.e.,
heaviest taxes on those least able to pay) was part of the Mongol
policy[16] or the result of manipulation by the *boyare*. Mongol
taxation, and that of steppe nomads in general, was usually
proportional, and a fairly applied tithe would certainly have been.
One theory is that the Novgorodian elite were awarded special
privileges in return for the military support necessary for
completing the census.[17]

In interpreting the ambiguous data in the Novgorod First
Chronicle's account of the Mongol census of 1259, we must first
examine the provenance and prejudices of the sourse itself. To
take everything at face value is not enlightening[18] and an
appreciation of the tendentiousness of the text makes it much
easier to discriminate betwen fact and fiction in the narrative.
Remarkably, considering the significance accorded to the events it
describes, no one has previously attempted to dissect the 1259
annal with attention to its sponsorship and biases.

The Novgorod chronicles emerged from a complex political *milieu*. Chronicle-writing was carried out in the archbishop's chancellery, which was probably manned by lesser clergy and monks of the cathedral of St. Sophia. The archbishop himself was selected from among the abbots of the main monasteries within the city. The ecclesiastical establishment was thus highly integrated with the social, economic, and political oligarchy that dominated every aspect of the city's life. Though the *boyare* ran Novgorod, they were highly prone to factionalism, feuding, and strife. Usually they controlled the *veche*, but sometimes one faction would turn the *veche* against another, and at other times the lower classes actually acted on their own (though this was just as likely to result in a riot, or *miatezh*, as in a *veche* meeting). Because of these variables, the Novgorod Chronicle was sometimes sympathetic to the *veche* and the lesser folk and sometimes not.[19] This is especially true since contested archepiscopal elections might be the result either of rifts within the oligarchy or of heightened antagonism between the elite and the masses.

Given that the chronicle was the instrument of ecclesiastics with vested interests in the city's social and political turmoil, it seems reasonable to assume that its presentation of the events of 1259 is not disinterested. The chronicler vents his disapproval on the rich and powerful of Novgorod, though he presents the story in a demonstrably religious and moralistic light. The census is attacked as sacrilege, since it means paying taxes to infidels, and the alleged scheming of the Novgorodian *boyare* adds insult to injury. The *boyare* Nevskii punished for misleading his son may well have been one of the factions within the oligarchy. One of the most interesting aspects of the chronicle's stance is that it almost entirely dissociates Nevskii from blame. Perhaps this is because the author feared retribution, or perhaps Nevskii had a hand in producing the chronicle. Be that as it may, it treats his collaboration in a neutral, matter-of-fact way, so much so that one wonders why his peace-keeping role in the Novgorod census could not have been worked into his *vita*. The villains in the chronicle account are the Novgorodian *boyare*, and they are castigated for conspiring against the common people. Thus the Novgorod Chronicle casts more doubt on the assumption that Nevskii's policy of collaboration was a source of extreme discomfort in medieval *Rus'*, and buttresses our suspicion that the 1259 narrative is less an anti-Tatar tract than an "internal" Novgorodian argument. As so often happens in oligarchic societies, the welfare of the common people was an idea used for its political leverage, rather than a genuine philanthropic goal.

There is another peculiarity in the narrative which has hitherto passed unnoticed. The chronicler, probably himself an ecclesiastic, insists that the "good men" of Novgorod stood for St. Sophia and the faith and opposed the census. (Given the context, "St. Sophia" probably refers to the cathedral and its properties.) Yet the Church itself was undoubtedly exempt from both the census and all taxation. We know that this was the case in the northeast, and it was the Tatars' invariable policy with regard to religious institutions among their subjects. Though the chronicler manages to imply that the Church both suffered and resisted, he actually says nothing one way or the other about the Church's status in the census or any role in the resistance. Ecclesiastics were certainly among those "counted lightly" (indeed they were not counted at all), but to acknowledge this significant fact in an ecclesiastic tract would have woefully impaired its self-righteous attack. Here too the chronicler has been disingenuous.

Almost all we can say with certainty concerning the events in Novgorod in 1259 as revealed in the chronicle is that the Tatars conducted a census and Nevskii assisted them. The extent of the opposition should not be exaggerated, and it should be remembered that it was miserably ineffective. A show of force quashed the riot and the census was carried out without further incident. The Novgorodian nobles' betrayal of the city, if taken at face value, should lay to rest Novgorod's reputation for heroic resistance, and Novgorod's subsequent history suggests a long and peaceful accommodation. There is no justification for reading the 1259 entry as proof of Novgorod's patriotic opposition to the Tatars and its forthright defense of national independence. The chronicle's cries for social justice seem special pleading, and its objections to paying taxes are rooted in religious bigotry rather than in some mythic democratic values allegedly acquired from the Hanseatic League. Indeed, the story of Novgorod's 1259 census is, on the contrary, prophetic of the submission of the Novgorod establishment to Mongol rule on negotiated terms.[20] The denouement was essentially the same as in the rest of thirteenth-century *Rus'*.

Nowhere was the "oppression of the infidels" more graphically painted than in the sermons (the only thirteenth-century ones extant) of Serapion, bishop of Vladimir. The first task of the Russian Orthodox Church in the aftermath of the catastrophic Mongol conquest was to provide "solace and spiritual comfort" to the survivors,[21] and the sermon was the natural vehicle for this undertaking. Serapion's writings merit our close attention.[22]

Serapion came from the Kievan Monastery of the Caves, and only five of his sermons have survived. Of these, four are found in a fourteenth-century manuscript of the *Zlataia tsep'* (Golden Chain), an anthology of ecclesiastic literature. The first three also occur in numerous manuscripts of two anthologies, the *Izmaragd* and *Zlatoust* (the latter title means Chrysotom, indicating that its contents are attributed to St. John Chrysotom, the Golden-Tongue). Serapion's fifth sermon first appears in another miscellany, the *Paisevskii sbornik* (miscellany of Paisii) from the end of the fourteenth or the beginning of the fifteenth century. Though all five are sometimes attributed to Efrem the Syrian or to Byzantine authors such as Chrysotom, and though other sermons are occasionally and probably spuriously attributed to Serapion, the five sermons assembled by Petukhov are reliably considered the bishop's work.

Serapion began his career in Kiev and ended it in Vladimir, where he died not long after participating in the Church Council in that city in 1274. His first sermon, which mentions the earthquake that shook Kiev in 1230 (the allusion to Tatars must be an interpolation), was clearly written there, and his last sermon was surely written in Vladimir. Whether Serapion delivered his second, third, and fourth sermons in the north or the south is a matter of contention. Whether the answer to this question affects our interpretation of the sermons' allusions to the Tatars remains to be seen.

In his first sermon, Serapion asks rhetorically, "Have not a merciless people been sent against us by God, who devastated our land, plundered (*plenisha*) our cities, destroyed (*razorisha*) our holy churches, killed our fathers and brothers, and desecrated our mothers and sisters?"[23] In his second sermon, Serapion continues: "Has not our land been plundered (*plenena*)? were not our cities taken (*vziati*)? did not our fathers and brothers fall swiftly like twigs to the earth? were not our women and children taken into captivity (*v plen*)? were not the survivors enslaved with bitter slavery by these foreigners (*ne poraboshcheni bykhom ostavshem gor'kuiu si rabotoiu ot inoplemenniki*)?"[24]

The most extensive discussion comes in the third sermon. "Thus He (God) released upon us merciless heathen, a violent people having mercy neither for the young, for the weak and aged, nor for infants. The wrath of the Lord descended on us . . . The sacred churches were destroyed; the sacred vessels were defiled, the saints were trodden upon, the prelates were victims of the sword, the bodies of the blessed monks were laid out as food for birds. The blood of our fathers and brothers, like water, soaked the earth. The strength of our princes and commanders (*voevody*) disappeared. Our brave (warriors) were filled with fear and fled. Many of our brothers and children were led into captivity (*v plen*). Our villages are overgrown with weeds, our greatness (*velichestvo*) has vanished, our beauty has perished (*krasota nash pogobe*). Our wealth has been stolen from us; the pagans have inherited our work, the foreigners (*inoplemennikom*) have received our land as their property. We are jokes to our enemies."[25]

The fourth sermon lists Russia's ills in brief: "War (*rati*), hunger, frost, and plague; we have been given finally to the foreigners not only for death and captivity but to bitter slavery (*ne tokmo na smert' i na plenenen'e no i na gor'kuiu rabotu*)."[26] And in the fifth and last sermon: "And what evils have we not seen in our years? Many burdens and suffering (*bedy i skorby*), campaigns (*rati*), hunger, from infidel oppression (*ot poganskikh nasil'ia*)." The pagans, who do not follow God's law, treat their own kind better than we Christians do, neither robbing nor stealing from each other, not slandering each other, not selling each other into slavery, but helping each other.[27]

Serapion was clearly well versed in Byzantine and scriptural literature, for his sermons describing the Mongol conquest echo those of Patriarch Photius which describe the Russian attack on Constantinople in 860, and also Byzantine accounts of the sack of that city in 1204 during the Fourth Crusade. He was also familiar with the more theological sermons of the twelfth-century master, Kirill of Turov. Thus Serapion's sermons derive their literary quality and great emotional force from a lengthy tradition of sermon literature. While his language is stylized and appropriately rhetorical, his genuine sympathy for the victims of the Mongol invasion is self-evident.[28] It is also apparent that what we have is a single description of the Mongol devastation of Russia, unequally distributed throughout the five sermons.[29] The Byzantino-Christian world-view mandated the basic framework of Serapion's analysis of Russia's fate, which was, essentially, that the coming of the Mongols was God's punishment for Russia's sins. The same interpretation, of course, had been advanced in the Russian accounts of the Battle on the River Kalka and in Tatar-related literature since. What remains to be said concerning Serapion's intellectual response to the Tatars?

Serapion's sermons employ the same vocabulary of Russo-Tatar political relations as all Russian sources of the thirteenth century. Russian cities and villages are taken (*vziati*) and plundered (*pleniti*), but there is no intimation of a change in political status. Though the survivors of the Mongol holocaust find themselves in slavery (*rabota*), this is a didactic and moral conception rather than a political one. None of the *realia* of Tatar rule—the census, the payment of tribute, princes' trips to the Horde or to Karakorum—appear in Serapion's pathetic list of Russia's misfortunes. Interestingly, though scholars have not previously noted it, Serapion never refers to the Tatars explicitly. His allusions are to "pagans" (*poganye*) and "foreigners" (*inoplemenniki*). Though Russia in the thirteenth century suffered at the hands of pagans such as the Lithuanians and of Catholics such as the Swedes and Germans, there is no question, from the magnitude of the oppression Serapion describes, that he is referring to the Tatars. Is this just an example of the tendency of Byzantine Christian literature toward the general and the abstract?

The voice of Serapion also appears unmistakably in the rules of Metropolitan Kirill adopted at the Vladimir Church Council of 1274.[30] Whether the 1274 text is by Serapion or taken from his writings, the language is clearly his: "Has not God turned his face from us? Are not our cities taken? Have not our strong princes fallen on sharp swords? Have not God's holy churches been destroyed? Do we not suffer daily from godless and unclean infidels (*ot bezbozhnykh i nechestikh pogan*)?"[31] Again, as if the identity of the pagans was a mystery, the Tatars remain nameless. And in an admonition to priests attributed to Serapion, nothing more specific than "pagan oppression" (*nasilie poganskoe*) appears.[32] Clearly Serapion's fastidious aversion to referring to the Tatars by name found sanction in the Russian Orthodox Church's formal ecclesiastical canons. (Only Feognost', bishop of Sarai, could not avoid designating the Tatars by name. He inquired about the procedures for baptizing Tatars who wished to convert, and he wondered if priests who had nomadized with the Horde or

committed murder could perform the liturgy.)[33]   Furthermore,
Serapion's stance almost certainly met with the approval of Kirill,
who was Metropolitan of Kiev and of all *Rus'*.   The two men
must have known each other well, and even if they had not met
before Serapion's move to Vladimir-Suzdalian *Rus'*, they shared the
same residence in Vladimir.   Kirill would only have delegated the
task of writing the rules of the council of 1274 to someone who
fully shared his own views.   Thus it is surely safe to assume that
Serapion and Kirill were in agreement concerning the proper
position of the Church vis-a-vis the Tatars.[34]

How then can the pervasive hostility toward the Tatars
evident in Serapion's writings, which clearly earned the approbation
of Kirill and the Church hierarchy, be reconciled with Kirill's own
pro-Tatar behavior, patterned on that of Alexandr Nevskii?[35]   The
answer lies in the curious nature of the *modus vivendi* which the
Church, having no choice but to protect its institutional base, had
established with the Tatars.   The Mongols respected all religions
and granted the Russian Orthodox Church fiscal and judicial
immunities, requiring in return only that the Russian clergy pray
for the health of the khan and his clan.   Though it was impossible
to inscribe the name of an infidel khan in the dyptychs, the
Russian ecclesiastics carried out their part of the bargain, and
indeed any priest who did so with mental reservations was guilty
of mortal sin.[36]   Kirill's pro-Tatar sections reflect this reluctant
but pragmatic approach of the Church to its new circumstances.
However, the concordat between the Church and the Horde did not
prevent ecclesiastics from venting their hostility towards Russia's
oppressors.   Serapion's sermons may not have mentioned the Tatars
by name, but they were flagrantly anti-Tatar, and the sermon is a
highly public means of expression.

It may be peculiar that the Mongols would tolerate such
inflammatory rhetoric.   Of course the Church dealt with the
Mongol presence in moral rather than political terms, and
Serapion's sermons were intended to inspire moral rather than
political change.   Not having recognized the Mongols' conquest of
Russia, he could hardly call for their overthrow.[37]   Nonetheless, his
diatribes, like any anti-Tatar statement, must have had some
political relevance, and the Mongols, who were well informed of
developments in Russia, would have been aware of it if the
sermons came into their hands.   However, the Mongols were simply
indifferent to anything other than direct political and military

action against their authority which threatened revenues. The opinions of intellectuals, even if disseminated among the masses, were of no concern as long as they were not associated with tangible resistance. The Mongols, who were always pragmatists, indulged intellectual dissent because their political and military might was so great that they could afford to. In short, the Mongols respected free speech.[38]

Even since Tacitus' *Germania* it had been a commonplace in moralizing rhetoric to shame one's own civilization by comparing it unfavorably with "barbarian" peoples. Just as Byzantine authors bewailed the fact that the hated Ottomans had higher ethical standards than decadent Constantinople, Serapion in his fifth sermon deviates from his customary execration of the infidel to make the point that Russia's erring Christians are even more debased. Thus Serapion's praise for Tatar morality in the final sermon is no more than an ideological ploy. The question is not that his ethnology may be faulty (Carpini painted a different picture of Tatar ethics, and when poverty struck the Horde in the fourteenth and fifteenth centuries, Tatars did indeed sell each other into slavery). Nor should Serapion's brief idealization of Mongol morality be cited as proof of a "rehabilitated" attitude resulting from his move to the more pro-Tatar environment of Vladimir-Suzdalia—the earlier part of the sermon is as strident as ever about infidel misdeeds. Even if the Mongols had learned of Serapion's laudatory remarks in the fifth sermon, the contempt of the pastoral nomad for the sedentarist was so great that they would have been as meaningless as his attacks.

Serapion's sermons show that the attitudes toward the Tatars of a spokesman for the Church were as ambivalent as those of other thirteenth-century writers. Like the authors of the other texts we have examined, Serapion does not face the Mongol conquest in political terms, but in religious and moral ones. Like them he falls back upon the standard interpretation of the Tatars' ascendancy, blaming it on the sins of the Russian people. Whether or not the chronicle and narrative accounts of the events of the thirteenth century were written by laymen, the religious *Weltanschauung* apparent in them is the same as that of the ecclesiastic texts.

Of the texts in the medieval Russian chronicles, none better illustrates the horrors Serapion lamented than the story of *Baskak*

Akhmat of Kursk. However, both the text's provenance and its internal contradictions pose major obstacles to its interpretation. In addition, it is doubtful that Akhmat's activities, as described, can be taken as typical of *baskaks*, the Mongol officials stationed within the Russian forest zone and charged with collecting tribute, supervising conscription, and maintaining law and order.[39]

This complex narrative will require an extended summary.[40] Akhmat, an evil Muslim, held the *baskach'stvo* in Kursk and farmed out the Mongol taxes (*otkupasha dani u Tatar*). He established two settlements (*svobody*) in the patrimony of Oleg, prince of Rylsk and Vorgol, into which many people flocked. In the Kursk district Akhmat's men committed great oppression on the Christians (*nasilie tovriakhu khristianom*). To complain about Akhmat, Oleg, with the assent of Prince Sviatoslav of Lipetsk, his relative, goes to *Tsar'* Nogai. Akhmat slanders Oleg as being not a prince but a bandit (*razboinik*), and suggests that the *tsar'* test Oleg's loyalty by inviting him on a hunting expedition. Though the real culprit was Sviatoslav, who had, without Oleg's permission, attacked a settlement at night like a bandit, Nogai is infuriated when Oleg fails to respond to the invitation to the hunt, and he sends his Tatar troops against the blameless prince. Nogai's troops take (*vziati*) Oleg's principality, but Oleg flees to Telebuga and Sviatoslav escapes to the forests of Voronezh. Akhmat compensates for the escape of the two princes by ordering the execution and mutilation of the captured *boyare*. Their clothing he gives to some merchant-pilgrims (*gosti polomniki*) whom his punitive expedition has also seized. Akhmat releases them with the admonition: "You are merchant-pilgrims, travelling through many lands; let it be known that this is the fate of anyone who has a dispute with his *baskak*." Though Akhmat himself cannot remain in *Rus'* with the two Russian princes still at large, he leaves his two brothers in charge of the settlements. His forces impose tribute (*iasak*) upon the district, but few people are left to pay it.

In the following year Prince Sviatoslav comes out of the forests and attacks a party of two Muslims and thirty Russians travelling from one of the settlements to the other. Twenty-five Russians and the two Muslims are killed. Hearing the news, Akhmat's brothers flee and entirely evacuate the two settlements. Sviatoslav had attacked without consulting Oleg, who now returns from the Horde and holds a mass for his executed *boyare*. Oleg accuses Sviatoslav of acting like a bandit, and his envoys (*posly*) tell Sviatoslav that he has violated Tatar custom (*obychai*) and will have to answer to the Horde. Rather than living like a bandit when a Tatar army (*rat'*) rode against them, he should have accompanied Oleg to the Horde. Sviatoslav has also violated Russian custom, for he knew it was evil to oppose a Muslim by force. Oleg concludes, "And if you do not go to your *Tsar'* Nogai, God will be the judge between us." Later, with the permission of the *tsar'*, Oleg comes from the Horde with Tatars and kills Sviatoslav. In revenge, Sviatoslav's brother, Prince Aleksandr, later killed Oleg and Oleg's son, David, giving joy to the Devil and Akhmat, his assistant.

This unedifying tale of political conflict concerns actions in the south of Russia. Kursk is in Chernigov province, and Rylsk, Lipetsk, and Vorgol are petty districts of that area. However, the story does not appear in the thirteenth-century Galician-Volhynian Chronicle, which paid little attention to the Dnepr' river valley. Yet the chronicles of the northeast, which generally show even less interest in the area, scarcely noting the sack of Kiev in 1240, do include the curious story of Akhmat. It occurs in the compilation (*svod*) of 1305, a Tverian grand-princely chronicle which served as the basis of the Laurentian Chronicle, copied by Lavrentii in 1377. Likewise, the tale was repeated in the *Troitskaia letopis'*, which concluded with 1408. However, the narrative is strangely absent from the two chronicles which derive from the hypothetical compilation of 1448, the Novgorod Fourth and Sofia First Chronicles. Despite this lacuna in its transmission, the text reappears in a variety of late fifteenth-century and sixteenth-century chronicles.[41] Thus the pattern of the tale's preservation does not conform to the norm for texts in the medieval Russian chronicles. Since Oleg's and Sviatoslav's domain were probably too petty to sponsor chronicles, the tale must first have been written down elsewhere, perhaps from the stories spread by the merchant-pilgrims. Vladimir, Tver', Rostov-Suzdal', and even Novgorod have been proposed as sites for the tale's literary composition.[42] That the tale was written at a distance from its origins and probably from oral sources may account for some of its narrative peculiarities. Other obvious but overlooked confusions arise from the fact that the events recorded *sub anno* 1283-1284 seem actually to have occurred over a longer period, probably 1287-1293.[43] One example of the contradictions is that Oleg is presented as blameless before Nogai, when in fact it was at his petition that Telebuga ordered the destruction of the settlements. Sviatoslav is ostensibly the guilty party because of his bandit attack on the settlement, yet we are also told that Sviatoslav only became a bandit after Nogai's punitive expedition under Akhmat had ravaged the Russian principalities. Indeed, no bandit attack on a settlement is described, merely Sviatoslav's attack on the travelling party. It is also strange that this incident compromises Sviatoslav before Telebuga, given that Telebuga had ordered the destruction of the settlements and that the party in question was presumably loyal to Telebuga's rival, Nogai. Oleg's taunting suggestion that Sviatoslav betake himself to his *tsar'*, Nogai, may even be facetious, since it was Nogai's troops that originally drove Sviatoslav from his principality, and the tale specifies that it was Sviatoslav rather than Oleg who was guilty before Nogai.

Telebuga and Nogai were the two rival powers within the Golden Horde at the end of the thirteenth century[44] and the tale of Akhmat clearly recounts the adventures of two Russian princes caught in the crossfire. (The princes of Vladimir-Suzdalia took sides in the dispute in accordance with their own rivalries. Thus Grand Prince Andrei Iaroslavovich, Prince Fedor of Iaroslavl', and Prince Konstantin of Rostov back Telebuga, while Princes Daniil of Moscow, Mikhail of Tver' [later his great enemy], and Dmitrii Aleksandrovich of Pereiaslavl' supported Nogai.)[45] Precisely how the feud between Oleg of Rylsk and Vorgol and Sviatoslav of Lipetsk became involved with the rivalry between Telebuga and Nogai is not clear.

The tale of Akhmat is intriguing partly because it contains elements not found elsewhere, but for the same reason it is not clear which can be accepted as true or typical. Since it is the only extended narrative in the medieval Russian chronicles about a *baskak*, there is no way of knowing if Akhmat's activities were the usual ones. It appears from the tale that Akhmat, in addition to being the *baskak*, held the tax farm as well. Normally in the Golden Horde these functions were distinct; the *baskak*'s responsibility to supervise the collection of the tribute implied that someone else did the actual work, usually other Mongol tax-collectors or Muslim tax-farmers from Central Asia. It is perhaps note-worthy that the tale refers to Akhmat as a Muslim but never as a Tatar.[46]

Another curiosity is the settlements (*svobody*, in later Russian language, *slobody*) Akhmat is alleged to have founded. No other *baskak* is known to have done such a thing. Their purpose, presumably, was economic exploitation, but it is not clear how this worked, and it is not apparent whether the inhabitants were local or immigrant Russians or even Russians at all.[47] The travelling party ambushed by Sviatoslav presents a final obscurity. Was it a military unit with Tatar officers and Russian enlisted men, as Roublev assumes, or an economic caravan? If the settlements were in fact commercial, and if Sviatoslav was able to annihilate the contingent with only his own retinue, the latter supposition is the more likely.

Since no northern prince had any vested interest in the fate of such petty southern princelings as Oleg and Sviatoslav, the tale's appearance in northeastern chronicles seems to have been accidental. Doubtless its appeal lay in its curious subject matter and complex plot. Certainly the tale would not have been selected for its merits as an anti-Tatar tract.[48] Admittedly it paints Akhmat in the darkest possible colors, especially in his barbaric mutilation of the executed *boyare*. Further, the Tatars under Akhmat's command and Tatars in general are the servants of the Devil. Yet the Tatar khans Nogai and Telebuga are spared such epithets, and indeed, Telebuga is the source of justice in the story. He sends his force to destroy the settlements galling the Russian princes, shelters Oleg from Akhmat's fury, and finally provides the means for Oleg's defeat of Sviatoslav, who was a bandit in Russian as well as Tatar eyes. Nogai, though Telebuga's enemy, also behaves rationally. He dispatches his troops only after Oleg has failed a legitimate invitation, and in any case, the khan has been manipulated by his *baskak*.

Interestingly, the fact that the two Russian princes are still at large keeps Akhmat from returning to *Rus'*.[49] This suggests that even a *baskak*—or at any rate this *baskak*—did not necessarily have enough military might at his immediate command to protect himself from rebellious Russians. Nonetheless, the moral of the story, which Oleg more or less explicitly states, is that unilateral armed resistance to the Tatars is self-defeating. Banditry might result in small victories, but when the power of the Horde is mobilized the Tatars could easily crush recalcitrant southern principalities. The pragmatic political logic of Oleg's dictum is obvious. Its astonishing theoretical implications are left unexplored.

The tale's resolution is inconclusive. Akhmat and Nogai, who have major roles in the first half, disappear from the second segment. Obviously Nogai did not provide Sviatoslav sanctuary from Telebuga's death writ, but whether by that time he was still in a position to do so is not clear, and the tale does not supply the denouement of the struggle between the rival khans. The passing reference at the end of the narrative to the vengeance of Aleksandr surely obscures some lapse of time, and after that the history of Kursk, Rylsk, Vorgol, and Lipetsk cannot be traced, for it escaped the attention of the chroniclers of the northeast. The narrative's incompleteness, like its contradictions, may reflect its confused origin. On the other hand it must be said that other passages in the chronicles, such as the story of the census in Novgorod, did not suffer such literary handicaps but perpetrated similar intellectual errors.

Whatever its failings and despite the questions it raises and leaves unanswered, the tale of Akhmat, *baskak* of Kursk, is an interesting work for the study of both the *baskak* system and of Russo-Tatar relations. Once unity had been restored in the Horde, the *baskak* system in the Russian forest zone was dismantled. Whether deportment like Akhmat's had anything to do with this development is impossible to say, for his actions only make sense within the framework of the feuding of the rival khans. In the tale Akhmat is evil because he is a Muslim, though his sadism is also a blunt political warning. While Muslims and the Devil definitely have evil designs on Russian Christians in this story, the khans themselves (in keeping with Russian respect for Chingisid legitimacy) appear blameless. The tale of Akhmat is hardly a call for liberation from the Tatar Yoke.

Though the *baskak* system seems to have been liquidated in northeastern *Rus'* during the early fourteenth century, the Mongols replaced it with another. The new representatives of Tatar authority were non-resident "envoys" (*posoly*), several of whom enjoyed reputations as black as Akhmat's. Through these envoys, who could always call upon supporting armies from the nearby steppe, the Golden Horde maintained its influence—or interference—in Russian affairs.

These affairs were dominated during the fourteenth century in Vladimir-Suzdalian Russia by the struggle for supremacy between the princes of Moscow and Tver'. Possession of the throne of Vladimir and the title "Grand Prince of Vladimir and all *Rus'*" ratified this supremacy, and the privilege of awarding the patent (*iarlyk*) to this throne belonged to the khan.   The Tverian-Muscovite rivalry consequently was played out in consort with the Horde.   Though Tver''s bid for "national" power eventually failed, the city did enjoy a period of apparent ascendency in the Volga-Oka mesopotamia, marked by two episodes, the martyrdom of Mikhail Aleksandrovich and the Tverian uprising of 1327.   The texts recounting these incidents warrant close attention.

Mikhail's martyrdom occurred in 1317-1318, and he was subsequently canonized.   The tale (*povest'*) about the events surrounding his execution was written by a contemporary, presumably a cleric in his suite.   However, although the earliest chronicles, such as the Novgorod First and the Trinity, do mention Mikhail's death, they do not contain the full tale.   Later manuscript miscellanies (*sborniki*) contain texts of the tale that may actually reflect earlier redactions,[50] but there are no major discrepancies between the standard text from these non-chronicle manuscripts and the oldest extant chronicle redaction, that of the Sofia First Chronicle of the mid-fifteenth century.   Analysis of the text may begin with the latter version.[51]

The tale begins with a flashback to eight years before its primary action, explaining how Mikhail of Tver' had secured the throne of the grand prince by travelling to the Horde "as the princes before him then had the custom to do" (*akozhe i prezhe ego kniaz obychai tamo vzimati velikoe kniazhenie*)[52]   Though Mikhail's rival, Prince Yurii of Moscow, had promised Metropolitan Maksim not to contest the throne, the Devil inspired him to go to the Horde anyway and offer the Tatars more tribute (*vykhod*—the first appearance of this term in the chronicle) in exchange for the *iarlyk*.   As the chronicle observes, it was the custom (*obychai*) of the Tatars to encourage feuding (*vrazhda*) among the princes so as to receive more gifts (*dary*—a euphemism) and the result was a great burden (*tiagota velika*) on the Russian Land.[53]   Nonetheless, Yurii's attempt failed.

This explained, the real action of the tale begins, concerning a renewed challenge to Mikhail from Yurii, who now has the support of the Saracen *tsar'*, Uzbek, and the latter's general, Kavgadii.   Yurii and Kavgadii ride on Tver', where Mikhail, who has tried to avoid a battle, defeats them (though Kavgadii seems to have avoided committing his full strength).   In this battle, Mikhail's body suffered no wounds.[54] Kavgadii, who was captured and later released, returns to the Horde, where, though Mikhail had treated him honorably, he lies to *Tsar'* Uzbek and accuses Mikhail of "making war on the authority of the khan without his word and permission" (*voevali esmi vlast' tvoiu bez tsareva slova i poveleniia*, i.e., unlawfully using force on the khan's representative, Kavgadii).   To answer these accusations, the envoy Akhmyl summons Mikhail to the Horde.   Mikhail joins the Horde on the Don river where it flows into the Sea of Surozh, and for a month and a half he is tried and tortured as the Horde nomadizes. Kavgadii is the prosecutor and the charges are that Mikhail "did not give the imperial tribute, battled against an imperial envoy, and poisoned the princess of Grand Prince Yurii"[55] (*tsareva dani ne daval esi, protivu posla bilsia esi, a kniaginiu velikogo kniazia Yurii umoril esi*).   Though this is the first mention in the Sofia First Chronicle of Yurii's wife, Agafiia, her role in these events is critical, for her original name was Konchaka, and she was the sister of Khan Uzbek.   Captured along with Kavgadii, she had somehow died while in Tverian custody, and Kavgadii and Yurii apparently accused Mikhail of murder.   Mikhail protests his innocence, but is forced to wear a wooden yoke or collar around his neck and is eventually executed by the otherwise unidentified Romanets.   His martyrdom occurs when the Horde is on the Terek river at the *Yas'* and Cherkess (Alan and Circassian) hills at the city of Tetiakov on the river Sevench beyond the Iron Gates (toward Derbend on the eastern Caucasus).   Tatars and Russians alike loot the martyr's tent and abuse his corpse, until Kavgadii reproaches Yurii for tolerating such treatment of a fellow Christian. The tale notes the aptness of the Turkic name for the nearby river Adysh, for it means sorrow (*gorest'*).   Mikhail's body is removed to Mozhd'zhchara, and from there merchants (*gosty*) transport it to Bezdezh.   Eventually it is taken to Moscow, where the Tverians must ransom their prince's relics from the hated Muscovites.

The story of Mikhail's martyrdom was obviously written by an eyewitness to the main events, indeed, one exceptionally well informed concerning the geography and topography of the steppe. The account contains the most extensive description of the Horde's nomadic cycle that has survived.   It is also apparent that the author modelled his narrative on the *vita* of Mikhail of Tver'''s namesake, Mikhail of Chernigov, with Kavgadii taking Eldega's role of accuser, and Romanets replacing Doman as the executioner.[56]

In its later evolution, the story of Mikhail was altered in

accordance with the biases of its redactors, in particular becoming
more hostile to Kavgadii. The Tverian Chronicle thus excoriates
the Tatar general as evil and thrice-accursed, besides calling Uzbek
a lawless *tsar'*. Though the capture of Konchaka is mentioned in
one of the earlier annals of the Tverian Chronicle, her death is not
among the charges brought against Mikhail, who is accused instead
of withholding tribute with the intention of absconding with it to
Germany! This version also adds the detail that Romanets cut out
Mikhail's heart.[57] In the Moscow compilation of 1479, Kavgadii
acts without the khan's permission, which diminishes to some
extent Uzbek's responsibility for later events. More significantly,
this account relegates to the past tense the "custom" of receiving
from the khan the patent for the throne of Vladimir. This surely
reflects the changing relationship between *Rus'* and the Golden
Horde on the eve of the "liberation" of 1480.[58]

In the sixteenth century, Moscow had a monopoly on
chronicle-writing, with the predictable result that the villainous
role of Yurii of Moscow was diminished. This was simply
accomplished by making Kavgadii and Uzbek even more obviously
evil. (Tver' by this time had no political significance, hence
Metropolitan Makarii was able to include Mikhail's *vita* in the
Great Menology, and Mikhail's icon could be painted on the walls
of the Kremlin Cathedral of Archangel Michael, without concern for
the anti-Muscovite animus of his cult.) The "Expanded
Redaction" of the non-chronicle variants of the tale vilifies Uzbek
as a Muslim fanatic and criminal, directly responsible for Mikhail's
execution.[59] The khan is likened to unjust rulers in history such
as the Byzantine emperor Phocas, and the author castigates the
Tatars for their greed in selling the *iarlyk* to the highest bidder.
While this redaction indulges in rhetorical amplification, however, it
does not distort the narrative core of the original tale.

The same does not hold true for the later chronicles, in which
ignorance and fantasy resulted in considerable deviation. According
to the Ustiug Chronicle, Mikhail expelled (*prognal*) Yurii, poisoned
the khan's daughter, and killed Kavgadii.[60] The Nikon Chronicle
heightens the drama without improving the tale's historical
accuracy; here the Tatars accuse Mikhail of planning to flee with
his treasury to the Pope in Rome (the Pope, in fact, was in
Avignon at that time). The Nikon Chronicle account does not,
however, present Uzbek as the major villain as in the "Expanded
Redaction" of the non-chronicle variants. Still, this is only a

preserved characteristic of earlier redactions.[61]

However, much later redactors and copyists altered the text of the tale of Mikhail, freely rearranging the roles of Yurii, Kavgadii, and Uzbek, eliminating and interpolating passages. The crux of Mikhail's martyrdom—that he was executed for crimes of which he was innocent—remains unchanged. (The only exception is the late and distant Ustiug Chronicle.) Mikhail opposed Kavgadii only when he had no choice and then treated the captive general with full honor. Mikhail always disclaims any wrongdoing in the death of Konchaka (and in fact the historical Mikhail would never have made the fatal blunder of harming a Tatar princess of the imperial clan). Indeed, he denies deliberate rebellious activity of any kind. Within the context of the tale, Mikhail must be innocent of crimes against the Tatars, or the story loses its religious significance as the account of a martyrdom, i.e., the death of an innocent. Consequently the tale of Mikhail cannot be a celebration of anti-Tatar activities.

At the same time, this story of the Mongols' savage murder of a blameless Russian prince can hardly be taken as pro-Tatar.[62] Of course the original Tverian account was extremely hostile to Yurii, for the excellent reason that the Tverians hoped to serve the interests of their city by undermining the reputation of the Muscovite princes among the political and ecclesiastic establishment of northeastern *Rus'*. Nonetheless, the Tatars are clearly ultimately responsible for Mikhail's torture and death, and their rule is presented as cruel and arbitrary. (The tendency in later redactions to make Kavgadii more culpable and Uzbek less so reflects the continued respect in medieval Russia for the Chingisid khans.)[63]

In any case, the tale's concerns are religious rather than political, and Mikhail's martyrdom must be explicated within a theological framework. Cherniavsky[64] showed how the tale presents Mikhail of Tver' as if he were a martyr for the faith like Mikhail of Chernigov, when in fact he was not. The author creates and exploits parallels with the deaths of other great martyrs. Summoned to the Horde to face almost certain death, Mikhail submits voluntarily, like the classic medieval Russian passion-sufferers, Boris and Gleb. By doing so he protects other Christians, i.e., his subjects, from suffering. The parallels between the stories of the Mikhails of Tver' and Chernigov have already been noted. Before Mikhail of Tver' is finally executed, Kavgadii taunts him that no one will help him bear his wooden yoke, yet one man steps forward to do so, like Simon of Cyrene who helped Christ to bear the cross. Mikhail dies both in Christ and like Christ, a voluntary sacrifice to save others. As Cherniavsky observes, since Mikhail did die at the hands of the Tatars, other Tatar-related themes could be worked into the narrative, but in a manner thoroughly consistent with the medieval Russian perception of the Tatars and their authority over *Rus'*. But without the political theology of the princely saint and the saintly prince, there could have been no *vita* of Mikhail of Tver'. The author's point of view can only be appreciated within the circumscribed limits of multiple intellectual and political restraints.[65]

The tale of Mikhail's martyrdom cannot be taken as either a pro-Tatar or an anti-Tatar tract without distorting its religious import and theological framework. There are evil Tatars in the tale, but evil Russians as well, and though the depiction of Tatar rule is hostile, the author does not advocate its overthrow. (Nor, of course, does he explicitly address the real nature of Russia's relationship with the Horde.) Mikhail's *vita* was in no way intended as ideological preparation for the Tverian uprising of 1327.

The prince of Tver' a decade after Mikhail's martyrdom was his son, Aleksandr Mikhailovich. Aleksandr's brother Dmitrii had avenged their father by murdering Yurii of Moscow at the Horde, but was executed by the Tatars for having done so without the khan's permission. Then, in 1327, the Tatar envoy Chol Khan (in Russian, variously Shevkan, Shevkal, Shchelkan, Shchevkan) arrived at Tver' with his retinue, only to be met by an uprising in which Chol Khan and nearly all of his men lost their lives. The inevitable result was a punitive expedition from the Horde against Tver', commanded by Fedorchiuk, who was assisted by Ivan Kalita of Moscow. Aleksandr found refuge in Pskov, but Metropolitan Feognost', who was of Greek origin but acted in the interests of Moscow, placed an interdict upon the city until Aleksandr should abandon its shelter. To save the souls of his protectors, Aleksandr left Pskov. Strangely, the Tatars allowed him to reclaim his throne, though two years later he was summoned to the Horde and executed for unknown reasons. Such in outline form were the events of the Tverian uprising of 1327. Since the chronicles that record them vary considerably in their accounts, we must analyze them individually.

According to the Tverian Chronicle,[66] the Devil inspired the godless Tatars to poison the mind of the lawless *tsar'*, Uzbek, persuading him that his authority (*vlast'*) in *Rus'* remained vulnerable as long as Aleksandr and the other Russian princes were alive. Uzbek responds by sending the thrice-cursed servant of the Devil, Chol Khan, oppressor of Christianity, to attack the Christians and kill the princes. Arriving in Tver', Chol Khan expels Prince Aleksandr from his palace (*dvor*) and begins to oppress (perpetrate "great distress" [*velikoe gonenie*] on) the people. One day as the deacon Dud'ko leads his donkey to the square to water it, a Tatar seizes the animal. Dud'ko cries out for assistance, and the eventual result is a *veche* uprising in which all of the Tatars within the city walls are killed. Only the Tatars tending the horses outside the city escape, fleeing first to Moscow, then back to the Horde. The Tatars retaliate by sending an army (*rat'*) under the command of *voevoda* Fedorchiuk, accompanied by Turalyk, Siuga, and five unnamed *temniki*. Aleksandr flees their "slander" (*kramola*) that he was responsible for the uprising, and in his absence his principality is subjected to massive reprisals.

The Trinity Chronicle describes Fedorchiuk's expedition but not the Tverian uprising that motivated it.[67] Fedorchiuk and Ivan Kalita, "at the order of the khan" (*po poveleniiu tsareva*), plunder (*plenisha*) Tver' and Kashin and other cities and villages. They "take the entire Tverian principality" (*vse kniazhenie Tverskoe vziasha*), lay waste the land, cause much harm, kill many and take many prisoners (*polon*). This suffering, adds the chronicler automatically, was because of our sins.

The responsibility, according to the Novgorod Fourth Chronicle, was Aleksandr's.[68] Although he does not start the confrontation, he is eager to avenge the blood of his father and brother. Chol Khan wants to "sit" (*sidet'*, i.e., rule) in Tver' and to convert the Russians to the Muslim faith, prompting Aleksandr to lead a revolt. Aleksandr's fellow Russian princes, inspired by the Devil to follow the order (*povelenie*) of the cursed *tsar'* Uzbek, participate in Aleksandr's punishment. Ivan Kalita of Moscow deplores Aleksandr's incautious attempt at vengeance which has produced such disastrous countermeasures, and he berates Aleksandr for causing Christians to suffer so at the hands of Tatars. Denying improper conduct, Aleksandr asserts that the Tatars had already taken (*vziasha*) and plundered (*plenisha*) Tver' and that he had had no choice but to defend the life and property of Christians. To spare his people further suffering, he will flee. The Novgorod

Fourth Chronicle goes on to say that he sought refuge in Novgorod before being taken in by Pskov. Novgorod denied him sanctuary, yet even still only the power of the Virgin (Hagia Sophia), augmented by two thousand silver rubles, saved the city from Tatar retribution.[69]

The Pskovian chronicler by and large follows the narrative as it appears in the Novgorod Fourth Chronicle, with certain alterations.[70] Chol Khan wants to sit in the Tverian principality (*kniazhenie*). The "strength of the Russian Land" (*sila russkoi zemli*) is brought to bear on Aleksandr, but cannot avail against the steadfast support of Pskov.[71] Nonetheless, Aleksandr voluntarily leaves the city so as not to imperil Christian souls. Kalita and Pskov subsequently reach an amicable accord, establishing an eternal peace (*vechnii mir*) based upon patrimonial tradition (*po otchine i dedine*). Only then is the interdict lifted.[72] A final variation appears in the Nikon Chronicle of the sixteenth century, which gives Chol Khan the patronymic Diudenovich and calls him *tsarevich*. That Chol Khan was the son of Diuden' (Tydan) and therefore a Chingisid and cousin of Uzbek is faintly possible; however, the Nikon chronicler's notorious inaccuracies in other areas cast doubt on this genealogical interpolation.[73] There is no reason to follow some scholars in calling Chol Khan a *baskak*; no Russian chronicler ever does so, and the designation *posol* (envoy) is undoubtedly accurate.[74]

What is important, of course, is neither Chol Khan's ancestry nor his bureaucratic title, but his mission in coming to Tver'. Scholars have universally admitted the implausibility of the claim that he intended to exterminate the Russian princes and impose Islam on the populace. (Some have seen this fantasy as a demagogic concession to popular credulity and prejudice,[75] while others regard it as no more than a slight exaggeration of the effects of Tatar oppression.)[76] It is inconsistent with everything we know about the Golden Horde in the first half of the fourteenth century to believe that Chol khan, a Muslim, desired to establish his own appanage (*udel*) in Tver' as part of a policy of replacing Russian princes with Tatar begs.[77] In addition, the further explanation in the chronicles that Uzbek felt insecure with Aleksandr on the throne is difficult to accept, especially considering that the prince was allowed to continue his reign following the suppression of the rebellion.[78]

It is at least apparent that Chol Khan and his men did not

comport themselves with circumspection in Tver', and this observation has led to the theory that their mission was to act as *agents provacateurs*. In this view, the Tatars considered Aleksandr Mikhailovich politically unreliable because of the actions of his father and brother and hoped to provoke popular resistance to Tatar representatives, resulting in the forfeiture of Aleksandr's throne.[79] While the Tatars were fully capable of devising such a strategem, the cost and complexity of this one seem to far exceed the demands of the situation. The Horde was always able to dispose of a troublesome prince through fabricated charges of embezzlement or dealings with hostile powers. It is hard to believe that the Mongols, who were committed to expending the minimum in resources and manpower to extract from Russia the maximum in profits and manpower, would have needlessly sacrificed a number of men, only to leave Aleksandr on the throne again.[80] It is far more likely, in my opinion, that the Golden Horde was at this time preparing another expedition against the Ilkhanids of Persia, in hopes of seizing the rich pastures and profitable caravan routes of Azerbaidjan. The Horde commonly used Russian soldiers in such undertakings, and Chol Khan's mission to Tver' may well have been to muster recruits and revenue. He apparently misplayed his hand, provoking an uprising that cost lives and required still more troops to put down.

The Tver' *veche* uprising, like almost any riot, was a spontaneous outburst rooted in long-term discontent. On a market day the town would have been especially crowded, and tensions between Tatars and Russians were no doubt running high. The incident of Dud'ko's donkey merely provided the spark in an already explosive situation, and the result was mass violence.[81] It is unlikely that Tver''s Prince Aleksandr was oblivious to the trouble brewing, but equally unlikely that he had any hand in planning a revolt.

The Tverian Chronicle took shape in the mid-fifteenth century, more than a hundred years after the events of 1327. While we may accept as accurate such mundane narrative details as the donkey incident, the reasons given for Chol Khan's visit to the city are, as we have seen, highly distorted. The question arises whether the fantastic charges concerning the Tatars' motives reflect contemporary claims or whether they result from the changed circumstances of Russo-Tatar relations in the fifteenth century. True, it is easier to invent details about past events as they recede in time, but our study thus far of the Russian sources shows that remarkable distortion even of contemporary events was always justifiable when it served ideological purposes. It is difficult to accept the assertion that this account's explanation of Chol Khan's intent is attributable to fifteenth-century Russian sensibilities.[82] The kinds of anti-Tatar charges considered credible in the fifteenth century are not a mystery. During the Muscovite civil war, Vasilii II was accused of paying the Tatars excessive ransom and of allowing them to insinuate themselves into the Russian cities.[83] There is no mention anywhere of any scheme to impose Islam on Russia or to exterminate the Russian princes.[84] The verisimilitude of these claims would have been no greater in the fifteenth century than in the fourteenth. Consequently, they may just as easily have originated at the time of the uprising as on the desk of the later chronicler.

The Tverian chronicles preserve what was doubtless the official Tverian interpretation of the 1327 uprising, and naturally in this account Prince Aleksandr Mikhailovich is held to be blameless. The "compilation" of 1448 must have utilized a Muscovite redaction; in this version Aleksandr is censured (though Ivan Kalita does not entirely escape blame for his role in the campaign with Fedorchiuk). The attitudes expressed in these accounts are contrary to all expectations in that the Tverian political establishment disclaims any part in anti-Tatar activities, and Muscovite bookmen opposed to Tver' castigate Prince Aleksandr for successfully annihilating a Tatar bureaucratic delegation. This anomaly severely tarnishes Tver''s reputation among scholars for having been in the fourteenth century a center of heroic liberationist ideologies and programs.

Certainly the Tverian version does not deprecate anti-Tatar activity out of fear of what the Tatars might think. The Mongols did not follow the Russian chronicles,[85] and even if they had, they would hardly have placed more credence in them than in the first-hand reports of those Tatars who had survived in the uprising. If Aleksandr had a hand in stirring up the rebellion, the Tatars would have learned about it.[86] The audience for which the chronicles were intended was the Russian elite, and it is to this audience that we must look if we are to explain the fact that the Tverian Chronicle, while it makes no attempt to minimize Tatar oppression,[87] also seeks to exonerate Aleksandr from charges of having resisted it. To the articulate Russian elite of the fourteenth century, it had become apparent that while the Tatars were evil, it was also true that open opposition had evil results. Resistance was noble but brought consistently disastrous consequences for Russia. Almost certainly this attitude, which violated the very ideological foundations of Russian society, was never stated bluntly. Nonetheless, Kalita's reproach to Aleksandr in the Novgorod Fourth Chronicle adumbrates the logic of just such an argument.

There is another reason why the Tverian account strives to distance Aleksandr from the anti-Tatar rebellion among his people. For a Riurikid prince to be associated with the uncontrolled lower-class mob violence of a *veche* was simply unseemly. It was proper for a Russian aristocrat to slay Tatars, indeed in theory it was his duty. But it should be in a struggle among warriors in open battle, not fighting side-by-side with the rabble in the streets. It is of course impossible to judge to what extent this social context influenced Tverian and Muscovite reactions to the 1327 uprisings, but it was surely a factor.

The conceptual framework of Russo-Tatar relations and the vocabulary used to describe them in the tales of 1327 largely conform to the patterns we have observed elsewhere. The chroniclers describe events in which the power of Uzbek in *Rus'* is obvious, but make no attempt to explore the significance of this premise. It is especially interesting, given the fact that the events of 1327 constituted a rebellion of sorts, that there is no hint of the theme of "liberation from the Tatar Yoke." (And of course while it is difficult from a modern perspective not to ascribe socio-political aims to the Tverian masses, we can never know to what extent they simply wanted to get even with a particularly obnoxious group of Tatars.)[88] The usual religious animosity infuses the narrative. Uzbek, Chol khan, and Fedorchiuk, because they are Muslims in the service of the Devil, all have the same goal: to oppress and kill Christians. The Tatars in fact had no interest in *jihad*, and this fixation on the religious aspect of Russo-Tatar relations largely obscures real Tatar policies. To a certain extent, the accusation in these narratives that the Tatars wanted to impose Islam on Russia reflects the increasing Islamization of the Horde under Uzbek. Still, the fantasy that the Mongols intended to convert the Russians distorts the real picture of Russo-Tatar relations even further.

According to the tales of 1327, Chol Khan and Fedorchiuk either intend to take and plunder Tver' and its territories or else they succeed in doing so.[89] (The use of the verb *pleniti* proves that it has not acquired the sense, "to conquer.") More unusual is the assertion made in the Novgorod Fourth Chronicle that Chol Khan intended "to sit" in Tver'. This verb, *sideti*, describes the assumption of his throne by a legitimate Russian prince; the prince "sits" in the capital city. This usage is noteworthy in that it alludes explicitly to the concept of suzerainty. The implication is that the Tatars wish to impose a direct Mongol rule which will constitute a political revolution involving a change of dominion. However, the unusual use of such a concept in chronicle accounts of Russo-Tatar relations is greatly mitigated by two factors. First, Chol Khan's plan is conceived as only a higher form of religious oppression, part and parcel of his program of killing the Russian princes and destroying Russian Christianity. Thus any meaningful political context is omitted. Second and more obvious is the fact that the Tatars' desire to rule in *Rus'* is presented as failing. Thus the use of the verb *sideti*, apparently a fifteenth-century innovation, does touch upon the delicate subject of suzerainty, but in a misleading way entirely divorced from the reality of the situation.

Non-Tverian accounts downplay the role of Ivan Kalita of Moscow in assisting the Tatars. His participation in Fedorchuk's punitive expedition would not impress the elite of northeastern Russia, so it is excused with an allusion to the khan's "permission" (*povelenie*). It is possible that the term has connotations of coercion; as Uzbek's vassal, Kalita was at his beck and call. Kalita and his patrimony benefited by being spared from Tatar raids. This was not a bad bargain.

The Nikon Chronicle further exonerates Kalita as a divine favorite[90] in its interestingly different redaction of the tale of the Tverian uprising. Dud'ko and his donkey are absent, and it is Aleksandr Mikhailovich who arms the Tverians and stirs them to action. Uzbek, furious, summons Kalita to the Horde and then sends him back with Fedorchuk "to plunder the Russian Land." Novgorod is spared for a price of five thousand silver rubles. But now God also saves Kalita and his principality from Mongol bloodletting and destruction (which sounds gratuitous). Aleksandr had abandoned Tver' because he could not endure "evil devilish Tatar slander and oppression" (*lukavye besovskie kramoly i Tatarskago nasilie*). Upon his return to the plundered city, he holds services for the dead and restores cities and villages. The extra verbiage in the Nikon Chronicle adds little of substance, but it hardly minimizes Uzbek's role or the horror of Tatar cruelty.[91] What the aristocrat who wrote this chronicle does eliminate is the *veche*, thus allowing a proper Russian prince to lead the fight.

Nasonov observed that it is hard to appreciate the difficulties of writing chronicles during the Mongol period.[92] If by this he meant that the Tatars kept a strict eye on chronicle-writing, he clearly is wrong. If, on the other hand, he had in mind the religious and ideological complexities of dealing with Russo-Tatar relations, then he was decidedly right. In their zeal to uncover princely partisanship in the chronicles, scholars have neglected the more diffuse and intangible intellectual dilemmas the Russian bookmen faced. Ivan Kalita's participation in Fedorchuk's punitive expedition against Tver' provides a good example. No Russian could applaud Kalita's collaboration with the Tatars in committing acts of violence against Russian Christians. At the same time, Kalita's was a wise policy which spared Moscow from Tatar raids during his reign. Moscow's chronicler thus had to both deplore the actions of the Mongols, Russia's bitterest enemies, and celebrate the deeds of Ivan Kalita—no easy task. Yet while the chroniclers whitewashed the actions of their own princes and often found it useful to distance the khan from the actions of "the Tatars" in general, no chronicler ever wrote favorably of the Mongols. If some accounts are less vehement than others, this hardly qualifies them as "pro-Tatar." No Tatar in the chronicles, apart from the khan, ever acts other than badly toward Russian Christians.

Chronicle accounts of events between the death of Batu and the Kulikovo era perpetuate the overwhelming emphasis on the religious aspect of Russo-Tatar conflicts, and this is just as true in the accounts of the 1327 uprising as elsewhere. The two Tverian texts from the early fourteenth century—the *vita* of Mikhail of Tver' and the story of Aleksandr and the Tverian uprising—adhere to the tradition of religious hostility toward the Tatars, unaccompanied by any articulation of the real political relationship between Russia and the Golden Horde. This, combined with the fact that the Tverian uprising of 1327 did not in the least loosen the Mongols' grip on Russia, makes untenable the position that the events of 1327 represent a step, deliberate or otherwise, in a war of "national liberation." The Horde was then at the height of its power, and military opposition still guaranteed disaster. Later in the fourteenth century internal strife weakened the Horde and this situation changed; the result was Kulikovo.[93]

Chapter IV:

The Kulikovo Epoch

According to the great Imperial Russian historian Sergei M. Soloviev, the Russian defeat of the Tatars at the battle of Kulikovo Field in 1380 was an event of global significance. He ranked it with such other great victories of "Europe" over "Asia" (i.e., Christianity and civilization over barbarism) as the Battle of Catalon, at which Rome stopped the Huns, and the Battle of Tours, at which the Franks stopped the Arab advance into Europe.[1] That two years later Khan Tokhtamysh rode unopposed to Moscow and sacked the city, initiating another century of Mongol domination, considerably undermines Soloviev's judgement. Nonetheless Dmitrii Donskoi's victory at Kulikovo over Emir Mamai was significant as Russia's first major military triumph against the Mongols. It has received such attention in both medieval texts and modern scholarship that the years between 1378, when a preliminary battle occurred on the river Vozha, and 1408, when Emir Edigei besieged Moscow, for our purposes may legitimately be called the Kulikovo epoch.

Even patriotic Russian scholars who have acknowledged that the Mongols did not subsequently vanish from Russian history have hailed the Battle of Kulikovo as a moment of great importance for Russian liberation.[2] More germane to our interests here, in interpreting those monuments of Old Russian literature devoted to Kulikovo and related events, they have not freed themselves from the nationalist ideology of liberation from the Tatar Yoke. The result has been a body of scholarship which reads into the medieval texts concepts of national liberation. The texts themselves suggest other perspectives on the meaning of the medieval narratives.[3] That the Muscovite bookmen at the end of the fourteenth and the beginning of the fifteenth century would incorporate into their writings the concept of liberation from the Tatar Yoke is inherently implausible. During the preceding century Russian bookmen had never addressed the issue of Russo-Tatar relations in terms of a conquest involving a change of suzerainty. It was, as a consequence, ideologically impossible for them to anticipate or celebrate the casting off of a yoke they had never acknowledged. In addition, Russian writers had consistently cast Russo-Tatar relations in the light of a religious struggle. While, as Joan of Arc demonstrated, religion and nationalism can go hand-in-hand, the predominance of religious matters in the Russian stance toward Russo-Tatar relations may have impeded the emergence of a politically-oriented ideology of national liberation.

Before beginning a close textual reading of writings from the Kulikovo period, it will be helpful to review briefly some of the salient characteristics of the age. Russia during the second half of the fourteenth century was experiencing a major cultural flowering, part of what Likhachev had called the East European Pre-Renaissance. A new mystical movement of monastic contemplation called Hesychasm, which originated in Byzantium and spread throughout the Orthodox Slavic world, was a powerful force in the cultural activities of the time.[4] Strong elements of Hesychasm are apparent in the work of two of the great artists of the day, Andrei Rublev, painter of frescoes and icons, and Epifanii Premudrii, a hagiographer. However, as important as Hesychasm was in the cultural life of fourteenth-century Russia, it is a mistake to draw too direct a connection between such cultural phenomena and political history. There are, for example, many optimistic elements in Rublev's paintings which seem to mirror the political optimism of an ascendent Moscow, but his iconography also included many apocalyptic themes, such as Tatar depredations, famine, plague, and flood.[5] The aim of Hesychasm was not the liberation of Russia from the Tatar yoke,[6] and to ascribe to Byzantine and Russian Hesychasts a homogeneous foreign policy of opposing Muslims does not do justice to the theological foundations of the movement.

Nonetheless, elements of the Russian Pre-Renaissance do figure in our study of the treatment of Russo-Tatar relations in the medieval sources. The most visible of these in the writings from the Kulikovo era is Historicism, the search for political, literary, legal, ideological, and artistic antecedents in the Golden Age of Kievan *Rus'*.[7] Likhachev has identified the seeming historical distortion this produced in Russian literature from the end of the fourteenth century. In the sources from this period, the Tatars are sometimes called the Pechenegs or Polovtsy. These were Turkic pastoral nomads with whom *Rus'* had had lengthy and intimate relations in Kievan times. It follows that the "Tatar Land" or "Tatar steppe" (*tatarskaia zemlia/step'*) became the "Polovtsian Land" (*polovetskaia zemlia/step'*) in many texts. Thus Russo-Tatar relations were seen as part of a continuum with relations between Kievan *Rus'* and the steppe.[8] Russian intellectuals had in fact been applying to the Mongol period the conceptual framework of the earlier period ever since 1223, so this development was more the continuation of an earlier trend than an innovation. Still, the fusion/confusion of the Tatars with the Pechenegs and the Polovtsy occurs for the first time in the sources from the Kulikovo era.

The Battle of Kulikovo was the subject of three textologically related works, the so-called "Kulikovo cycle," comprising the epic, *Zadonshchina*, the extended narrative, *Skazanie o Mamaevom poboishche*, and a tale found only within the corpus of the Russian chronicles. Each survives in more than one redaction. The other events of Russo-Tatar relations following 1380 were also immortalized in tales, usually within the chronicles and often with more than one redaction. The result of this situation is that we often have strikingly different accouts of the same episodes. These differences do not reflect random, aribtrary, or merely literary embellishments of the same narrative, and more is involved than the conflicting accounts of eyewitnesses. These literary works, in effect, are engaged in a hidden dialogue, a polemic about political programs and political identity conducted by anonymous authors and the social and political factions they represented. In addition, new events and changing circumstances necessitated adjustments in orientation and induced re-editing of the texts to keep them in line with new ideological developments. The stages of this evolution might be identified, and the various literary works of the period be correlated with the different phases of Russian intellectual thought concerning Russo-Tatar relations.[9] Although this approach is highly fruitful, it must be applied with respect for the rules of textological analysis which determine the dating and literary history of a work, and with respect for the literal lexicon of the texts themselves. Failing this, a scholar's conclusions attest more to his own imagination than to the intellectual inventiveness of the medieval Russian bookmen. With these general observations in mind, it is possible to proceed to an analysis of those works from the Kulikovo era which reflect Russian attitudes toward the Tatars at a time when the Horde's power was at low ebb.

The Battle of Kulikovo was preceded in 1378 by the clash of the river Vozha, in which forces sent by Grand Prince Dmitrii Ivanovich of Moscow defeated a Tatar raiding party dispatched by Emir Mamai, the power behind the throne in the Golden Horde. Perhaps because neither Dmitrii nor Mamai participated personally, the incident received little attention in medieval Russian literature.[10] The short chronicle narration devoted to it lists the Tatar generals who were killed: the commander-in-chief and Mamai's favorite, Begich, as well as Khazibei, Koverga, Karataluk, and Kostrok. (As usual, Russian familiarity with individual Tatar personnel is extensive.) The surviving Tatars fled to Mamai at the Horde, "because Mamai had a *tsar'* with him in the Horde, but the *tsar'* ruled no one; Mamai stood in front of him. Mamai held all seniority (*stareishinstvo*) in the Horde and ruled everyone in the Horde." (This passage is of special interest as an accusation of *lèse-majesté*. Mamai was not a Chingisid. Barred from the throne, he ruled through puppet-khans. While all infidel oppressors ought to have been equally abhorrent to Russian Christians, the author of the narrative attacks Mamai by emphasizing his illegitimacy. The text was designed for domestic consumption, and the Russian elite may well have found it easier to bring themselves to oppose a mere emir than a member of Chingis' imperial clan.)[11] Insulted and enraged by the ignominious defeat of his troops, Mamai began gathering his forces for a critical assault on Dmitrii. The Muscovites forced the issue by marching into the steppe in 1380, meeting Mamai's army at Kulikovo Field.

Of the works in the Kulikovo cycle, the so-called "chronicle tale" (*Letopisnaia povest'*) about 1380 will be discussed first because of its continuity with the tale of the Battle on the river Vozha. The shorter redaction is found in the *Troitskaia letopis'*, completed in 1408. The longer redaction was included in the hypothetical "compilation" of 1448, and is preserved in the two chronicles which derive from it, the Novgorod Fourth and the Sofia First.[12] It is difficult to exaggerate the amount of controversy surrounding the relationship and dating of these two redactions among Soviet specialists.

Salmina has made the case that it is the Short Redaction of the chronicle tale that is primary, having been written for inclusion in the *Troitskaia letopis'*. In her view the Long Redaction was written in the 1440s for inclusion in the "compilation" of 1448 and based directly upon the Short Redaction without intermediaries.[13] This conclusion is consistent with the general schema of chronicle-writing of the period advanced by Lur'e. That the *Troitskaia letopis'* was prepared in the chancellery of Metropolitan Kiprian is generally recognized.[14] Rejecting the idea of intermediate texts, he asserts that the "Great Russian Chronicle" referred to in the Trinity Chronicle was not a Muscovite work. He also denies the existence of the Vladimir Polichron of c. 1418-1423, another hypothetical compilation thought by some to have been the intermediate between the chronicles of 1408 and 1448, and associated with Metropolitan Photius. Lur'e doubts that Moscow composed any chronicle compilation between the *Troitskaia letopis'* and the *svod* of 1448.[15]

The conclusions of Salmina and Lur'e have aroused considerable dissent. Azbelev has criticized Salmina's analysis of the chronicle tale of 1380, in particular her reliance upon the anachronistic inclusion of Prince Fedor Torusski among the casualties of Kulikovo in the Long Redaction. Since Torusski in fact died in 1437, Salmina contends that the Long Redaction must have been written later than this. Azbelev, however, argues that the Torusski alluded to in the tale was actually an eponymous ancestor. He returns to the more traditional scholarly position that the Long Redaction was primary, and that the Short Redaction is a contraction.[16] Another who has taken issue with Salmina's conclusions is I. B. Grekov, who also dismisses the Torusski anachronism and faults Salmina's conception that in dating medieval Russian sources, textological analysis supercedes historical investigation.[17] Salmina has replied to these objections at length and seems, on textological grounds, to have had the upper hand.[18]

Lur'e's schema has met with objections from Prokhorov, Plugin, and Kuchkin, all of whom defend the existence of Muscovite chronicle-writing in the second half of the fourteenth century and of the Vladimir Polichron. They are inclined to believe that the Great Russian Chronicle was in fact a Muscovite work and that it included the Long Redaction of the chronicle tale of 1380, which they believe to be primary. In their view the Trinity Chronicle omitted this full tale because it was not of Muscovite provenance, but the full tale was included in either the Vladimir Polichron or the *svod* of 1448.[9] In spite of the furor Lur'e's schema has stirred up among Soviet scholars, his conclusions have met with general acceptance in the West.[20]

That the relationship between the Long and Short Redactions of the chronicle tale of Kulikovo has proven so controversial is not difficult to understand, for the entire issue of chronicle-writing in the fourteenth and the first half of the fifteenth century hangs in the balance. Furthermore, it makes a great difference in interpreting the tale whether it was written in the 1380s by Muscovite bookmen or in the 1440s by members of the metropolitan's chancellery. My assumption is that the Short Redaction came first, since it is unlikely that the Trinity Chronicle would have omitted a longer version already in existence.[21] In all the maze of textological polemic about the chronicle tale, not enough attention has been paid to its actual contents and in particular to the language in which the tale deals with Russo-Tatar relations. A fresh look at the tale itself provides a different perspective on its dating and interpretation.

According to the Trinity Chronicle, in 1380 the godless and evil-honored (*zlochestivyi*) pagan Mamai gathered many troops from the Polovtsian and Tatar Lands, *Friazi* (Genoese),[22] *Cherkasy* (Circassians), and *Yasy* (Alans), to march against the Christians. The evil Ishmaelite wished to avenge the defeat on the river Vozha and to plunder (*pleniti*) the Russian Land. Dmitrii Donskoi learns that Grand Prince Jagailo of Lithuania is allied with Mamai, but when the armies meet at the confluence of the Don and Nepriadva rivers, Donskoi's men slaughter the infidel Polovtsy without mercy. The Hagarenes are smitten by an unseen force, and Mamai flees with his pretty retinue (*malaia druzhina*) to the Tatar Land. After pausing to bury on the field of battle the many fallen Russian nobles, Donskoi marches home, his men laden with the booty abandoned by the fleeing Tatars. When Donskoi learns that Oleg of Riazan' had intended to aid Mamai, he sends a punitive expedition against that city. However, since Oleg himself has fled the city, the expedition is recalled, and a delegation of Riazan' *boyare* petitions for mercy. Muscovite governors (*namesniki*) are installed in Riazan'.[23] After a time Mamai raises another army, but he is compelled to use it against Tokhtamysh, an eastern *tsar'* who challenges his control of the Horde. On the river Kalka (the chronicler ignores the irony) Mamai's regiments desert him, and he is caught and executed by Tokhtamysh's men. As a result of this victory, Tokhtamysh "took the Mamai Horde and *tsaritsa* and his treasury, and possessed his *ulus* entirely, and took Mamai's riches, dividing them among his retinue." He then sends envoys to Oleg of Riazan' and the Russian princes, informing them of his arrival and installation (*kak v'tsarisia*) "and how he had defeated his enemy and their's, Mamai" and sat on the Volga *tsarstvo* (the Golden Horde khanate). The Russian princes, including Donskoi, send gifts to the new khan.

This narrative is anything but pro-Tatar. The chronicler uses all the usual religious epithets,[24] and when divine intervention (the "unseen force") turns the tide of battle in favor of the Russians and they show no mercy to the infidels, it is obvious that the Tatars are getting what they deserve. Mamai, too receives his just desserts. Just as in the tale of the Battle on the river Vozha, he is never referred to as *tsar'*, and when the true Chingisid *tsar'* Tokhtamysh defeats him, the political ramifications are spelled out in Tatar terms. The chronicler explains that Tokhtamysh has seized the throne of the Volga khanate and *ulus*. Although he manages discreetly not to explain why the Russians had to submit to the new Volga khan, it is evident that the victory over Mamai had not altered Russia's relationship with the Horde. Tokhtamysh's message that he had defeated their common enemy was not a sign of political respect, but merely a ploy to gain Russian support. The Russian princes recognized this of course, but were too canny not to perform the necessary political courtesy.[25]

It is hard to believe that it took a score of years for this precise and sensitive narrative of the Battle of Kulikovo to be written. If it was written in 1408, it is even harder to understand its respectful treatment of Tokhtamysh, who in the 1390s lost a titanic struggle with Timur (Tamerlane, Temir-Aksak in the Russian sources) and fled the Horde. He became a puppet of Grand Prince Vitovt of Lithuania, but after Emir Edigei, Timur's client, smashed the Lithuanian-Tatar army in 1399, Tokhtamysh fled again. The Russian chronicles record his death in the Siberian khanate in 1406.[26] In 1408 it was rather late to be worried about his reputation.

In any event the Short Redaction of the chronicle tale of 1380 gives no indication that its author saw in Donskoi's victory anything beyond a glorious triumph over a particular Tatar. He not only makes no allusion to any Russian libertion, but describes the symbolic submission of the Russian princes to the new khan.

The concept of Russian liberation is nowhere to be found in the Long Redaction either, though the expanded version does add a number of details. *Besermeny* (Central Asian Muslims), Armenians, and Burtas are now included among Mamai's recruits, all understandable interpolations. The chronicler refers to Mamai only as a "prince" (*kniaz'* = emir), and in a new sentence adds disdainfully that "the accursed Mamai puffed himself up in pride and considered himself a *tsar*" (*mnev sebe aki tsaria*). Mamai's motive for mounting a war now includes Donskoi's refusal to pay tribute (*vykhod*) beyond the amount stipulated in an earlier (otherwise unknown) agreement between the prince and the emir. In the engagement itself, Donskoi and Mamai's puppet-khan (*Mamaevo tsar'*) Teliak fight hand-to-hand.[27] Mamai loses successive battles with Donskoi, then Tokhtamysh (said to be from the Blue Horde, *Siniaia orda*), but this time, rather than dying at the hands of Tokhtamysh's Tatars, Mamai seeks asylum with the Genoese of Kaffa. The latter, greedy for his treasure, slay him. Besides these new narrative details, the expanded redaction contains a considerable amount of added material of religious and miraculous nature on Prince Oleg, on the Orthodox Lithuanian princes who join Donskoi's forces, and on the role of St. Sergius. The conclusion, however, is the same, as the new khan, Tokhtamysh, exhanges envoys with the obedient Russian princes.

The addition in the Long Redaction with the most significance for the study of Russo-Tatar relations is the accusation that Mamai styled himself a khan. It provides a key to the ideological orientation of the text, and this in turn is of use in trying to date the work. Thus while we need not accept the accusation of *lèse-majesté* at face value,[28] we cannot dismiss it as some have done.[29]

The author of the Long Redaction knew that in reality Mamai had not tried to make himself khan; after all, the same text records the presence at Kulikovo of the puppet-khan, Teliak. Yet this false claim served a distinct ideological purpose. If Mamai, a non-Chingisid, tried to become a khan, he was a renegade and a usurper in the eyes of both Rusians and Tatars. Thus opposition to him was justified from both perspectives and did not constitute rebellion. The chronicler is taking pains not to call into question the legitimate relationship between Russia and the Horde, even stressing that Donskoi objected not to paying tribute, but to paying it in excess and to a usurper. And at the end of the tale, when a Chingisid *tsar'* restores the "constitutional" relationship with Russia, the Russians, who have just won a great battle against Tatar power, meekly send him gifts.

The accusation of *lèse-majesté* conflicts with the theory that the work dates from the 1440s; more than half a century after the battle, such an invention would have served no purpose. Furthermore, the Long Redaction, as we have just seen, is extremely conservative, adhering closely to the conceptual framework of Russo-Tatar relations found in the Short Redaction of the tale. In the lengthier text the amount of anti-Tatar rhetoric is naturally greater, but the ideology remains the same, and the Long Redaction in no way reflects the changed political situation vis-a-vis the Horde in the mid-fifteenth century. One would also expect a text written during the Muscovite civil war of the 1440s to serve the interests of one or the other of Donskoi's competing grandsons, but there are no obvious signs of this in the longer text.[30] On the whole, the Long Redaction of the chronicle tale seems to make the most sense as a reflection of the Russian point of view after Tokhtamysh's defeat of Mamai but before his attack on Moscow in 1382. Whether both of the redactions were actually written during that period appears to be an unanswerable question.

That most subsequent chronicles retain the *lèse-majesté* motif seems to coroborate the idea of its importance to the text.[31] In certain of the later sources, the chronicle tale is partially or entirely eclipsed. The Vologodsko-Perm' Chronicle replaces the tale with the *Skazanie o Mamaevom poboishche*, and the Nikon Chronicle combines the two texts. The results of this fusion were not always felicitous, especially when the redactor also used his imagination. For example, the chronicler asserts that Mamai, out of jealousy, had the khan murdered, but the sentence about Teliak's hand-to-hand battle with Donskoi remains in the text, creating a certain contradiction.[32]

The chronicle tale of 1380 is obviously both pro-Muscovite and anti-Tatar. Yet no matter when the two redactions were written, it simply will not serve as evidence of Russian liberationist attitudes. It shares with earlier texts that conceptual framework for Russo-Tatar relations in which the fact of Tatar rule is left unspoken. Like earlier texts, the narrative includes some of the *realia* of Mongol rule, such as the payment of tribute, without explaining them or addressing their ideological implications. An ideology which rejects the fact of conquest cannot accommodate the concept of liberation, and in any case the Long Redaction more or less explicitly rejects the idea of rebellion by emphasizing the illegitimacy of Mamai's power. In the political vision of the redactor, Donskoi fought Mamai at least partly in the name of Chingisid legitimacy, making Moscow "plus royaliste que le roi" with regard to Mongol dynastic succession.[30] The tale does not reflect a Russia that sensed freedom within its grasp.

Of all the works in the Kulikovo cycle, that with the greatest current aesthetic appeal is the epic, *Zadonshchina*.[34] Like the chronicle tale of 1380 it has aroused enormous controversy, in this case because of the peculiarities of the manuscript tradition and the incestuous relationship between the questions of its literary history and of the authenticity of the *Slovo o polku Igoreve*. However, canonical wisdom holds that the Igor' tale is authentic, and that it was the basis for a complete text of the *Zadonshchina*. It follows, in this view, that the earliest manuscript of the epic, the Kirillo-Beloozerskii from the end of the fifteenth century, is not a short primary redaction but an abbreviation of the full original. Soviet textologists and literary specialists answer any objections to this schema with alacrity and determination.[35] One textological analysis within this dominant schema attempts to demonstrate that Sofronii of Riazan' was not the epic's author.[36] The argument is cogent enough to raise grave doubts about Sofronii's authorship, and further comment from specialists will certainly be forthcoming.

Likhachev, in his numerous publications, has continued to propound and restate his interpretation of the text's ideological significance,[37] and I know of virtually nothing recently published that contests his view. Likhachev holds that the author of the *Zadonshchina* has reversed the imagery of the tale of Igor' so as to present the Russian victory in 1380 as revenge for the Russian defeat of 1186 (in which the Polovtsy triumphed over an expedition which Prince Igor Sviatoslavovich had unadvisedly led into the steppe). According to Likhachev, the author's goal was to encourage in Russia a war of national liberation under Muscovite leadership.

Likhachev's suggestion that the struggle with the Tatars was viewed as a continuation of the Kievan struggle with the Polovtsy is both literally and literarily true. The author of the *Zadonshchina*[38] refers to the Tatars as Polovtsy, and the Tatar Land is also called the Polovtsian Land.[39] Like the Polovtsy in the tale of Igor', the Tatars in the *Zadonshchina* are associated

(inaccurately) with the Don and Dnepr' rivers. The text alludes to
the long-past Russian defeat on the Kalka river, conflated with the
Kaiala river of the Igor' tale, to suggest how long *Rus'* has suffered
at the hands of infidels. Poetic license permitted a certain degree
of historical and geographical astigmatism in fusing the pastoral
nomads of the Kievan and Mongol periods into a single, constant
enemy.

　　This enemy's intent in 1380, according to the *Zadonshchina*,
was to take (*vziati*) the Russian Land. Grand Princess Evdokiia
prays for a Russian victory on the Don, and that the disaster that
took place on the Kalka will not be repeated. The monk-warrior
Peresvet declares that he prefers death in battle to capture, and
his wish is granted, though the Tatars are defeated. They "fled
each for himself along unprepared roads to the sea coast, gnashing
their teeth and rending their faces, saying, 'no longer, brethren,
shall we live in our land, nor see our children, nor fondle our
women. We must fondle the moist earth,[40] we must kiss the green
grass, and no longer shall we go in battle against the *Rus'*, nor
shall we take tribute (*vykhod*) from the Russian princes.'" Mamai,
also in flight, seeks refuge in Kaffa, but the Genoese deride him:
"Why did you, infidel Mamai, encroach on the Russian Land?
That was the *Zaleskaia orda*[41] from olden times. And you are not
like *tsar'* Batu. *Tsar'* Batu had 400,000 warriors and he made war
on (*voeval*) the entire Russian Land. He plundered (*plenil*) from
East to West.[42] And God punished the Russian Land for its sins.
And you, Prince Mamai, come to the Russian Land with many
forces, with eight hordes, with seventy princes. And now you run
away to the sea coast. There is no one to winter with you in the
steppe" (*zimovati v pole*). After thus shaming the luckless
commander, the Genoese send him away in dishonor.

　　Although the *Zadonshchina* thus ends with Mamai's utter
undoing, the narrative makes no allusion to his loss to
Tokhtamysh, nor does it mention the roles of Oleg of Riazan' or
Jagailo of Lithuania. This paring down of the narrative is typical
of many epics, and allows the military clash between the Russians
and the Tatars to take center stage. Also in accordance with the
demands of the epic form, the Tatars are formidable and noble
adversaries, for otherwise there is no glory in besting them. Their
numbers are of course greatly exaggerated; Batu did not have
400,000 men, and Mamai had one horde rather than eight. The
seventy princes are also hard to credit.

The epic's author was obviously familiar with the fauna and flora, sights and sounds of the steppe, not to mention its geography. In addition, he shows a keen awareness of the exigencies of nomadic life. When the Genoese send Mamai off to winter alone in the steppe, the author is clearly aware that this for a nomad was the ultimate dishonor, and for a nomad without people and herds, tantamount to a death sentence. Thus the derision in this passage is balanced by an undertanding of the hardships of nomadic life and a real sense of the pathos of Mamai's position.[43]

Also striking is the author's empathy for the fleeing Tatars, whose speech he has copied, if not textologically then in substance and literary function, from that of the Kolomna widows in the tale of Igor'.[44] (The shift in the ethnic identity of the mourners is interesting.[45]) The passage, in its own way, illustrates the expressive-emotional style that emerged in Old Russian Literature at the end of the fourteenth and the beginning of the fifteenth centuries.[46] In any case, the defeated infidels are portrayed in very human terms, and express themselves in a manner immediately understandable to contemporary Russians. That the *Zadonshchina* could depict the Tatar warriors both as Russia's archenemies and as noble adversaries with human characteristics is typical of the kind of mutual martial respect found all along the medieval ethno-religious frontier. Such attitudes are of course well suited to the epic genre, and can be traced in such works as "El Cid," "La Chanson de Roland," "Digenis Akritas," and of course the "Tale of the Host of Igor'."

There is nothing in either the lament of the fleeing Tatars or Mamai's pathetic end to indicate that Tatar domination of Russia was over. The defeated warriors bewail the fact that they will never again battle Russians or collect tribute from them, but this is because they, the followers of the usurper Mamai, are doomed, not because the Tatar Yoke is shattered.[47] The Genoese speech emphasizes Mamai's illegitimacy, according him for the first time in the narrative a title, "prince" (*kniaz'*, equivalent to emir), only to compare him with a true *tsar'*, Batu. Clearly the humiliation of a false pretender to the throne does not constitute the overthrow of the Goden Horde. The lexicon and conceptual framework of the *Zadonshchina* warrant no other interpretation. In the traditional vocabulary of Russo-Tatar relations, the Tatars want to "take" the Russian Land, a task apparently left undone by Batu, who merely "plundered" from east to west (perhaps a stock phrase from the Alexandriad). Donskoi's victory does not spell the end of the Tatar Yoke for it has never existed.

The closest approach to genuine historical perspective occurs in the lament of Grand Princess Evdokiia, creating some conflict with the more pervasive historicist reliance on the imaginary continuum with Kievan circumstances. Evdokiia prays that God will not allow what happened on the river Kalka to be repeated on the Don.[48] Although the princess conflates the Kalka with the Kaiala river (of the Igor' tale), and the defeat of 1223 with the campaigns of 1237-1240, there is implicit in her lament an awareness of a distinct Tatar era that began with Batu. However, she says only that since the time of Batu the Russian Land has suffered, and that when Donskoi wins the Russian Land will be happy. In recognizing a Tatar period, Evdokiia violates the historicist pose that struggles with the Polovtsy and the Tatars are all one. On the other hand, Evdokiia's lament remains firmly within the framework of established Russian ideology in making no allusion to the concepts of conquest or liberation.

The *Zadonshchina* is concerned only with a Russian prince's spectacular defeat of an over-ambitious Tatar emir. Assuming an offensive defensive strategy, the Russians march into the steppe to intercept the line of Mamai's advance, triumph despite enormous losses, and march home again. The author of the *Zadonshchina* claims that the news of the battle will spread from one end of the Golden Horde to the other, from Urgench (the Iron Gates) in the Caucasus or Khwarizm in the East to Bulgaria in the West, and to Rome, Constantinople, and Bulgaria.[49] But the victory is celebrated for its own sake, not for its political ramifications. Some modern researchers claim that Kulikovo was an event of world significance, since its spreading fame served as a prophecy of the liberation of the Balkan Slavs from the Ottomans.[50] Yet the idea that the *Zadonshchina* hails the liberation of Russia would have astounded its author.

The ideological position of the *Zadonshchina* may provide one of the few clues to its dating. On textological grounds little can be said with assurance except that it was written after 1380, and in time to have become known to the scribe Efrosin, who abbreviated it in the 1470s.[51] How long it took for the epic to take shape depends on how much of it derived from oral traditions; folkloric composition is usually regarded as a slower process than written composition. I see no indication that the *Zadonshchina* prefigures the imminent "liberation" of 1480. Indeed, from its content and ethos, it seems entirely possible that the epic comes from the same time as the chronicle tale, i.e., the brief interlude between Donskoi's victory and Tokhtamysh's sack of Moscow. Different in genre, in treatment of Donskoi, and even in cast of characters, the epic and the chronicle tale are compatible in their presentation of Russo-Tatar relations. The differences probably reflect varying perspectives on relations with Lithuania or among Russian princes, but the similarities bespeak the common perception of the Tatars among Russians of the Kulikovo era.

The contest of Russian and Tatar in the *Zadonshchina* takes shape as a timeless epic confrontation. The agony of defeat on the Kaiala/Kalka river had turned into the thrill of victory on the Don. But within the political ideology of medieval Russia, the recent victory was as devoid of consequences for Russia's political status as was the ancient defeat. Regardless of who wrote the epic, and when, the *Zadonshchina* does not violate that intellectual framework of medieval Russian thought which precluded discussing Russo-Tatar relations in terms of suzereignty. No adulteration in later manuscripts of the epic could penetrate that obstacle[52] and no interpretation of the text should overlook it.

The last of the three works that constitute the Kulikovo cycle, the *Skazanie o Mamaevom poboishche*, is by far the most religious. It presents Donskoi's campaign against Mamai as a full-fledged religious crusade, in which fallen Russians achieve martyrdom, and miracles and visions abound.[53] Although manuscripts of the work are numerous, dating has proved a complex task. Of the more than one hundred manuscripts surviving, the vast majority were written in the seventeenth century. Only a few, in chronicles and autonomously, are extant from the sixteenth century, and none from the fifteenth century appear to have survived, though new manuscripts continue to turn up.[54] Given this situation, without a definitive list of manuscripts, or a comprehensive analysis of the redactions and the text's literary history, or a critical text, the dating of the *Skazanie* must remain open, and any proposal problematical.[55] The least accepted theory dates the text to the 1390s,[56] while the majority of scholars is inclined toward the mid-fifteenth century.[57] Another minority holds out for the late fifteenth or even the early sixteenth

century.[58]   The text is particularly receptive to glosses and
interpolations of all kinds, and this must be taken into account in
analyzing the *Skazanie*.[59] However, it must be conceded that the
text is fairly homogeneous, far more so than, for example, the
"Tale of the Destruction of Riazan' by Batu."

The *Skazanie*'s cohesiveness depends upon its heavy emphasis
on religion and the crusading ethos that pervades the narrative.
Indeed, the Church's role in the narrative is greater than in any
other text.   The text's hallmark is the role (entirely fictitious) of
Metropolitan Kiprian in the events of 1380, and both St. Sergius of
the Trinity Monastery and Bishop Gerasim of Kolomna have parts
to play.[60] (Texts of this sort are the least likely to have arisen
from oral or folkloric sources. However, certain motifs appearing in
later redactions may reflect such influences.)[61] It will come as no
surprise that the *Skazanie* is not a clarion call for the Russian
people, under the leadership of Moscow, to overthrow the Tatar
Yoke;[62] and in fact the crusading vision of the text makes the
realia of Russo-Tatar relations almost irrelevant.   Yet the text
does contain a number of interesting and novel readings, in
addition to the usual lexicon.   The conception contained in the
Skazanie of Russia's relationship with the Horde merits close
attention, but on its own terms.

Of the surviving redactions of the *Skazanie*, the oldest is the
Basic Redaction (*Osnovnaia redaktsiia*).[63] In this narrative[64] the
Devil instigates Mamai, a prince from the Eastern country (*strana*),
to try to destroy Christianity. Mamai asks old Tatars (Tatars are
indiscrimately referred to as Polovtsy, Pechenegs, Hagarenes, and
Ishmaelites) to tell how *Tsar'* Batu had plundered (*plenil*) the
Russian Land, taken (*vzial*) Kiev, Vladimir, and all of *Rus'*.   He
then informs his officials (*alpauty, yasauly*), princes, and
commanders of his intention to kill the Russian princes and to sit
(*sideti*) in the Russian cities, to rule (*vladeti*) quietly and without
trouble (*vladeem tikho i bezmiatezhno*).   Mamai gathers many
hordes (*ordy*) to ride against *Rus'*.

In its opening passages, the *Skazanie* correctly alludes to
Mamai as a "prince" (*kniaz'*), and the distinction between the emir
and *Tsar'* Batu is clear.   Further along in the narrative, as we
shall see, the distinction disappears, in this manuscript and all
others. It is impossible to know whether the error appeared in the
original text—it may not have.   The *Skazanie* describes Batu's
accomplishments with the standard verbs (take and plunder), but is

somewhat more unorthodox in its assertion that Mamai planned "to sit" and even "to rule" in the Russian cities. Of course mid-fifteenth-century redactions of the tale of the Tverian uprising of 1327 mention that Chol Khan meant "to sit" in the Rusian cities, but the use of the verb "to rule" is most atypical even for the mid-fifteenth century. Be that as it may, the *Skazanie* naturally draws no connection between Mamai's ambition and Batu's "plundering." One Tatar simply wishes to match the exploits of another, and Mamai seems to be planning not the continuation of Mongol rule, but the initiation of it. And as the readers of the *Skazanie* knew, Mamai failed.

The *Skazanie* continues with Mamai receiving an obsequious letter from Oleg of Riazan', who identifies himself as Mamai's client or vassal (*posazhenik i prisiazhnik*; literally, he who was installed and is sworn). Oleg states that he has learned that *Tsar'* Mamai (the title is retained throughout the remainder of the text) is riding against Mamai's servitor (*sluzhebnik*) Dmitrii Donskoi. Oleg announces that he and Olgerd of Lithuania are Mamai's slaves (*raby*) and will lend him their support. Olgerd (Jagailo misidentified) also writes to say that he too is Mamai's vassal and that he is aware that Mamai wishes to punish/execute (*kazniti*) his servitor Donskoi and his *ulus*, because Donskoi has insulted Mamai's *ulusnik*, Oleg of Riazan'. As a reward for their services, Oleg and Olgerd expect to receive *yarliki* from Mamai to sit (*sideti*) in the cities of Kolomna (which Moscow had seized from Riazan') and Moscow, respectively.

This is a striking passage which has not been fully explored. True, the letters are meant to be fawning and manipulative, and the reader is not expected to take all of their statements at face value. Nonetheless, the lexicon of vassalage and clientage is explicit. It is also a severe distortion of reality. Mamai was not a khan and could not have, would not have, and did not issue *yarliki* in his name. In any case, as the author has just explained, Mamai intended to keep the Russian cities for himself. It is equally impossible that a Lithuanian Grand Prince would ever declare himself the vassal, much less the slave of a Tatar. Finally, the use of the terms *ulus* and *ulusnik* is most curious. The *ulus*, or inheritance, was the key concept of Inner Asian socio-political structure, and the Golden Horde was the *ulus* of Chingis Khan's son and grandson, Juchi and Batu. Since Russia lay outside of the steppe, it is not clear whether it could have been part of a

nomad's *ulus*, though Russians in the fourteenth and fifteenth
centuries occasionally alluded to Russia as the *tsarev ulus* when it
served their purposes to do so.[65] The Russification of the term to
produce the nominative *ulusnik* in the *Skazanie* betrays both
Russian expertise in steppe affairs and considerable assimilation of
Tatar concepts. The pro-Muscovite bookman who wrote this text
clearly intended the historical inaccuracies in the epistles to blacken
the reputations of Oleg and Olgerd. Yet in the process he
inadvertently revealed information about concepts and relationships
that he had never meant to convey.

Mamai's response is arrogant: "I am worthy of being and
defeating a *tsar'*, one equal to myself, and to receive the honor of
a *tsar'*" (*Mne ubo tsariu dostoit' pobediti tsaria, podobna sebe, to
mne podobaet i dovleet tsarskaa chest' poluchiti*). In the mistaken
belief that he can handle Donskoi by himself, he disdains the
proferred assistance of his allies. With many hordes (a common
misuse of the term) he approaches Russia, imitating the mindless
(*bezglavomu* = headless?) Batu. Donskoi meanwhile prays that
God will not allow to happen to him what happened to his
ancestors when God sent the evil Batu against the Russian
cities—"Fear and worry are still great among us because of that."

Donskoi's prayer deftly skirts the issue of political suzereignty.
His fear is that Russia will once again be plundered, and he hopes
that this time Russia's sins are not so great that God will cause
this to happen. The prayer is free of any political context and
offers no explanation of why Oleg, Olgerd, and Mamai all consider
him a vassal of the Horde. The lacuna widens during Donskoi's
conversation with Metropolitan Kiprian, in which the prince asserts
that since he has actually paid four times the regular amount of
tribute (*vykhod*), Mamai has no cause to plunder the Russian Land.
Yet Donskoi will take the field against him as a loyal and obedient
servitor wronged by his overlord. (This last image is taken from
the chronicle tale of 1380 and echoes the rather passive and
self-righteous poses of Mikhail of Chernigov and Mikhail of Tver'.
Perhaps such responses to outrageous demands from infidels are
meant to show Christian humility.) Donskoi does send Tiutchev
and two interpreters (*tolmachi*) versed in the Polovtsian language
to Mamai in an attempt to negotiate. Though the idea that the
Tatars spoke the Polovtsian tongue is to be expected in a text
from this period, the reference to the use of interpreters between
Russians and Tatars is a rarity. In the Basic Redaction, Tiutchev

learns of Oleg and Olgerd's duplicity and does not actually negotiate with Mamai.

The *Skazanie* finds time before the battle for another of Evdokiia's laments. This time the Grand Princess prays that should Mamai not be stopped, the Russian Land will not be destroyed (*razorenie*, a term best-known from the title of the "Tale of the Destruction of Riazan' by Batu"). She asks God to prevent a recurrence on the Don of what the Russians suffered on the Kalka river at the hands of the Polovtsy and Hagarenes. The Russian Land still weeps from that sorrow, from that "great Tatar battle" (*velikogo poboishcha tatarskago*). As in the *Zadonshchina*, the battle on the Kalka is conflated with the campaigns of 1237-1240. The similarity between the two great battles, the one past, the other imminent, is brought out by the use of the noun *poboishche* (battle), an echo of the full title of the *Skazanie*. As always in Evdokiia's laments, she speaks only in terms of victory and defeat, not of conquest and liberation. There is no hint of any political continuity between Batu and Mamai, and although the princess allows that Russia still suffers from the effects of the earlier battle, her point is simply that Russia's wounds still have not fully healed.

On the eve of the battle Dmitrii Bobrok Volynskii puts his ear to the ground of the battlefield and hears women mourning both the Russian and the Tatar dead. A Tatar woman bewails the number of fallen Tatars in the Hellenic tongue (Hellenic meaning pagan or infidel). Especially in a text of such crusading ardor, we need not look for too much sympathy for the widows of dead infidels,[66] still, the "sign" (*primet*) which Bobrok hears does indicate a certain empathy for all those bereaved by battles. Once the conflict has begun, the monk-warrior Peresvet engages in personal combat with a Pecheneg. The Tatars cry out in the Hellenic tongue as they are slaughtered, and Mamai watches the ruin (*pogibeli*) of his army. He flees in utter defeat.[67]

In the potency of its crusading religiosity, the *Skazanie o Mamaevom poboishche* stands alone within the Kulikovo cycle. A number of features from the chronicle tale and the *Zadonshchina* are adjusted accordingly, and certain novelties of terminology and language may indicate a later date of composition. Nonetheless, the *Skazanie* does not transcend the reluctance of medieval Russian bookmen to discuss Russia's relationship with the Horde in terms of political suzerainty. Indeed, the heightened religious mood of the work may well have made it especially resistant to violations of the ideology of silence as it was practiced in medieval Russia.

Many of the later redactions of the *Skazanie* do little to alter the ambivalent treatment of Russo-Tatar relations. While the Chronicle Redaction, found in the *Vologdsko-Permskaia letopis'*, corrects the name of the Lithuanian grand prince from Olgerd to Jagailo, the only relevant revision occurs in a prayer by Dmitrii Donskoi. He prays that Russia will not be given over to slavery (*porabotati*) to her enemies, but that God will show mercy.[68] The concept of slavery (*rabota*) with regard to Russo-Tatar relations started to appear after the 1480 "Stand on the Ugra River," especially in sixteenth-century Muscovite works associated with Metropolitan Makarii. It is, however, a religious rather than a political term. Taken from Exodus, it implies that the Russians are the new Israelites and reflects the increasingly ambitious ideology of the Muscovite tsardom in the sixteenth century.

The "Kiprian Redaction" of the *Skazanie* appears in the Nikon Chronicle and is a fusion of the *Skazanie* with the Long Redaction of the chronicle tale of 1380. In the midst of effusive moralizing and endless prayers, there are no substantive alterations with regard to Russo-Tatar relations. Peresvet's opponent is now named Temir-Murza; Donskoi claims to have paid the tribute as set by *Tsar'* Uzbek (who perhaps carries more weight than Chanibek); and Tiutchev's interpreters speak Tatar rather than Polovtsian. Otherwise the added prose of this version is just stylistic adornment.[69]

The Expanded Redaction (*Rasprostranennaia redaktsiia*)[70] is probably from the late fifteenth century, judging from its tale of Novgorodian participation at Kulikovo, which may reflect recent Muscovite annexation of that city. The attitude toward the Golden Horde in this version is unlike that found in any previous redaction. In this version Mamai tells his *ulus* not to grow grain since his men will be feasting on Russian grain (pastoral nomads, of course, do not eat grain). In another addition, Olgerd's envoy to Mamai returns to his master with a description of the Tatar leader. The envoy, Bartiash from the Czech Land, describes Mamai as a man of middling size and not much intellect, not memorable in speech but great in pride. Olgerd nearly executes Bartiash for his candor. Later in the text Vladimir Andreevich of Serpukhov tells Dmitrii Donskoi, his cousin and lord, that he would rather die than be in slavery (*rabota*) to the evil Mamai. The sentiment echoes other passages in the literary history of the text.

By far the most significant addition in this version of the *Skazanie*, however, concerns Donskoi's envoy to Mamai, Tiutchev. Tiutchev arrives at the Horde bearing gold Donskoi has sent in hopes of dissuading Mamai from attacking Russia. The Tatar leader haughtily distributes it among his Cossacks (*kozaki*, a peculiar usage), with the observation that soon he will have all of Donskoi's gold. Tiutchev dares to contradict his boast, thereby enraging the "princes of the tumens" (*temnye kniazi*) who are prepared to take his head. Mamai, however, is impressed with both the envoy's bravery and his loyalty to his lord. He restrains his men and invites Tiutchev into his service. A wrong answer would have meant certain death, but Tiutchev brilliantly talks his way out of this tight spot. He flatters Mamai by saying that "it is better to serve a *tsar'* badly than a prince well," implying that he is both eager and unworthy, but goes on to say that before he can switch allegiance, he must complete this final mission for Donskoi. Mamai cannot but respect the envoy's sense of duty, not to mention his eloquence, and sends Tiutchev back to Russia alive and well. He is accompanied by fifty Tatars and four envoys, all of them princes and high officials at Mamai's court: Kozebaem, gentleman of the khan's bedchamber (*postelnik tsarev*); Urai, the khan's best clerk (*lutchei tsarev d'iak*); Agish, equerry (*koniushii*); and Siuidiuk, master of the house/key (*kliuchnik?*). Tiutchev bears a letter to Donskoi "from the eastern terrible (*graznago*) *tsar'*, from the Great Horde (*Bol'shaia orda*, an anachronism), from the strong Tatar *tsar'* of tsars, Mamai, who rules many *tsarstva* and hordes and *ulusy*." The letter gives Donskoi the choice of bowing down before Mamai or being executed (*kazniti*, as in Mamai's plans for Donskoi according to Olgerd in the Basic Redactions). Tiutchev cleverly manages to alert his countrymen of his approach in the company of Tatars, and the Russians ambush the embassy. The triumphant Tiutchev tears Mamai's letter in half and tells one of the surviving Tatars to return it to Mamai, since Tiutchev does not deliver stupid (*bezumie*) epistles. Upon his return to Moscow, he receives many honors for the masterful completion of his mission.

Other alterations found in the Expanded Redaction of the *Skazanie* include a full narrative of the return from the steppe of the victorious Muscovite army. However, since this is nothing but

the first portion of the *Skazanie* told in reverse, it contains little of
interest.

These new episodes of the envoys Bartiash and Tiutchev are
integral to the Expanded Redaction, and clearly reflect a new stage
in the written "history" of Kulikovo. The facts have become
almost irrelevant, and invention and distortion have become the
rule. The Tiutchev episode appears to be the work of an informed
writer, but a writer of fiction. Such details as the names and
offices of the Tatar envoys, he either borrowed or invented.
Mamai was harldy a figure of fun during the Kulikovo period, but
the attitude of the author of the Tiutchev episode is almost
playful, and the obvious purpose of both this and the Bartiash
episode is to make Mamai look stupid.[71] Bartiash describes Mamai
as a fool, and Tiutchev plays him for one.

Only a considerable lapse of time and the waning power of
the Golden Horde could have permitted such liberties. The new
treatment of Mamai in the Expanded Redaction of the *Skazanie*
reflects a later stage in Russian perception of the Tatars, which,
while it did not permanently influence mainstream attitudes, at
least produced a number of attractive literary works. The revision
of Mamai's image is less surprising when one considers that the
vita of Mercurius of Smolensk and the "Tale of the Death of
Batu," also products of the later fifteenth century, went so far as
to report that Russia had defeated Batu in battle.

Yet for all the liberties with the text taken in the Expanded
Redaction of the *Skazanie*, we still find no retrospective attempt to
impose upon the events of the Kulikovo period a political
framework of conquest and liberation.[72] Despite the enormous
flexibility of the work and the obvious ease with which it has been
subjected to variation and adulteration, interpolation and
extrapolation, the medieval perception of the Tatars at its core was
never altered. The durability of that perceptual framework
becomes apparent only after close analysis of the changes in the
text.

With the passage of time, the *Skazanie* retained its popularity
while losing its relevance to Russian political concerns. By the
seventeenth century the Golden Horde had long since ceased to
exist; Moscow had annexed the khanates of Kazan' and Astrakhan',
and the Kasimov khanate was nothing but a vestigial remnant of
former Tatar power. While the Tatars of the Crimea continued to
pose a threat, popular cultural interest centered instead on the

Ottoman Turks, and war with the "west" began to supercede war with the steppe as Russia's dominant preoccupation. Yet the *Skazanie o Mamaevom poboishche* continued to appear in new redactions and subredactions, and the text found new life within the *Synopsis'* of Innokentii Guizel', which became the textbook on East Slavic history for much of the eighteenth century. After the Time of Troubles, however, the *Skazanie's* evolution had become a function of purely literary concerns, for the Tatars of the Golden Horde were both historically and politically irrelevant. Increasingly literary and historical works influenced by Polish and Latin books shaped Russia's perceptions of her own past. The *Skazanie* became less religious and more belleslettristic, less serious and more entertaining. With these developments, the *Skazanie* passes out of our realm of interest.

Future research, however, will continue to enrich our understanding of the original structure and purpose of the *Skazanie*. Scholars have only begun to discover, for example, how the author of the Basic Redaction employed an entirely different lexicon and vocabulary in describing identical actions of Donskoi and Mamai, thus heightening the distinction and antagonism between the text's hero and its villain.[73] Other research, textological analysis of the illustrations that accompany many of the manuscripts, and in some cases, unaccompanied illustrations, has begun, but much remains to be done. Only those conversant with the ritual and etiquette of the visual symbolism can draw the real meaning from the miniatures; sometimes even the use of colors conveys information.[74] Linguists and art historians will make greater and greater contributions to the study of the *Skazanie o Mamaevom poboishche.*

The texts of the Kulikovo cycle vary greatly in their approach to the events surrounding Russia's first and most celebrated victory over the Tatars. The epic *Zadonshchina* takes a chivalric stance that brings out the mutual understanding that linked the military elites of enemy peoples; the chronicle tale of 1380 emphasizes Mamai's illegitimacy from a Chingisid perspective; and the *Skazanie* envelopes the entire affair within a crusading religiosity. Nonetheless, despite the variety among the works, they all share the same conceptual framework of Russo-Tatar relations, and not one of them suggests that when Donskoi defeated Mamai, Russia threw off a Tatar Yoke.

The truce between Dmitrii Donskoi and Khan Tokhtamysh

broke down in 1382. Tokhtamysh led a punitive expedition which
laid waste the land on its way to Moscow, then sacked the city.
The "Tale of the Sack of Moscow by Tokhtamysh" describes this
event with graphic horror.[75]

The *Troitskaia letopis'* contains the Short Redaction of this
tale, which is the earliest. Chronicles which derive from the
"compilation" of 1448 include an Expanded Redaction, and still
later chronicles feature a "compilative" redaction which mixes
several variants together.[76] Textologically, then, the history of this
tale is analogous to that of the chronicle tale of 1380.[77] To be
convincing, any interpretation of the tale's ideological importance
must be based upon its textological schema,[78] and must begin with
the Trinity Chronicle annal for 1382.[79]

According to this account, Tokhtamysh began by seizing and
robbing the Russian merchants (*gosty*) in the land of the Volga
Bolgars, so that they could not warn their compatriots of his
intentions. This accomplished, he rides against the Russian Land.
"Hearing that the *tsar'* himself was coming against him with all his
strength, [Grand Prince Dmitrii] did not stand in battle, did not
raise his hand against him, against *Tsar'* Tokhtamysh."[80] Instead,
Donskoi leaves Moscow for Kostroma, and a recently arrived
Lithuanian prince, Ostei, assumes command of the city.
Tokhtamysh arranges with "deceptive speeches" (*lzhivymi rech*), a
"false truce" (*lzhivym mirom*), and then has Ostei murdered. The
khan's forces sack the city, though a contingent of his men
encounter a Russian force at Volok led by Vladimir Andreevich of
Serpukhov. Rather than allow the Muscovite princes time to
regroup, Tokhtamysh elects to make off with the booty and
captives, pausing on the way to loot the principality of Riazan',
whose prince, Oleg, fled. The Muscovites follow suit, as the Short
Redaction ends, by ravaging Riazan' territory.

The Short Redaction gives a fairly clear picture of the real
events: Tokhtamysh rode to Moscow without encountering any
serious opposition, failed to take the city by storm but gained
entry through a ruse and reduced the city to smoldering ruins,
deporting many of the survivors as slaves. This blow to Moscow's
prestige, not to mention its economy, was enormous and surely
constituted a grave setback for Muscovite political aspirations.
(Fortunately for the Muscovite bookmen, they had not proclaimed
Russia'a liberation after the Battle of Kulikovo two years earlier,
and were not faced with the ideological problem of reconciling such

a claim with the ashes around them.) Moscow's vulnerability in 1382 was due in part to its political isolation; Tokhtamysh had blackmailed the princes of Suzdal', Donskoi's own in-laws,[81] into collaborating with the Tatars, and Oleg of Riazan' practically volunteered to do so. Oleg, as the Short Redaction shows, paid a high price for his perfidy, since the Tatars treated Riazan' as enemy territory on their way back to the steppe, and angry Muscovites wreaked havoc in Riazan' not long after.[82] Despite the magnitude of the disaster, Moscow remained too powerful for Tokhtamysh to revoke the *yarlik* for the throne of Vladimir. Still, the payment of tribute no doubt resumed (probably in larger amounts than before), and Donskoi's son and heir-apparent, Vasilii Dmitrievich, remained for several years a hostage at the Horde.[83] Tokhtamysh had succeeded in restoring a *quid pro quo* favorable to the Horde.[84]

Even this Short Redaction of the tale contains a strong appreciation of the Chingisid principle and its importance in Russo-Tatar relations. Later chronicles make it clear that in the aftermath of the Pyrrhic victory at Kulikovo, Donskoi was simply unable to raise the troops necessary to mount a defense. The narrative, however, is at pains to point out that Donskoi is reluctant to do battle because this time it is the "khan himself" who rides against Moscow. The significance of this is apparent only in light of the Muscovite accounts of Kulikovo, which go to great lengths to make it clear that Mamai is not a khan, whether they accuse him of *lèse-majesté* or not. This combination of contempt for Tatars and respect for Chingisid khans characterizes the Short Redaction of the tale of Tokhtamysh, and indeed almost all of the texts we have thus far examined. It is amplified in the Expanded Redaction.

The Expanded Redaction contains many "facts" not found elsewhere. Since they are unattestable before the 1440s, they may have been invented.[85] According to this redaction,[86] 1382 was the year that saw the "campaign" (*nakhozhdenie*) of Tokhtamysh and the "taking" (*vziatie*) and "plundering" (*plenenie*) of Moscow, other cities, and the Russian Land. Donskoi learns of the impending attack from some "advocates of the Russian Land" (*pobornitsi russkoi zemli*). Though he wants to stay and fight, he cannot because of divisions among his servitors and the difficulty of raising troops. The Tatars' arrival is followed by three days of saber-rattling and curses traded between the Russians on the city

walls and the Tatars outside them. There is some inconclusive
fighting, during which a merchant from Surozh (*sukonnik*) named
Adam manages to kill a Tatar prince, making Tokhtamysh very
sad. The khan, frustrated in his attempts to storm the city,
resorts to a strategem. A delegation of Tatar princes approaches
the walls and makes the following speech:

> The *tsar'* wishes to pardon you, his people; you are
> innocent and not deserving of death. The *tsar'*
> gathered his forces against the grand prince [Donskoi],
> not against you. The *tsar'* demands nothing from you
> other than that you come out to meet him with your
> prince [Ostei], with moderate (*legkimi*) gifts. The *tsar'*
> wishes to see his city and to give all of you his peace
> and love.

The sons of Dmitrii Konstantinovich of Suzdal', Donskoi's
brothers-in-law, now approach the walls, reminding the Muscovites
that they are of the same religion and guaranteeing the sincerity of
the Tatar offer. This is good enough for the Muscovites, who
accept the terms and surrender, though the chronicler points out
that Muslim deceit was great. When the delegation with Ostei
emerges from the city, the Tatars first separate Ostei from the
delegation and murder him, then slay the entire delegation and
sack the city. Many are taken into "infidel slavery" (*v rabotu
poganskuiu*) in the Tatar country (*strana*), and other cities are
plundered as well. Tokhtamysh sends his envoy Shikhmat with a
communique to the docile Dmitrii Konstantinovich of Suzdal',
explaining his activities, and in the spring the khan sends his
envoy Karach to Dmitrii Donskoi. So ends the Expanded
Redaction.

The obvious approach to interpreting the Expanded Redaction
is to examine those elements that set it apart from the Short
Redaction. The first of these is the "advocates of the Russian
Land" who warn Donskoi of the khan's plans. The identity of
these mysterious Russian sympathizers has become the subject of
much controversy, in part because the question is sometimes
connected with that of the literary milieu in which this redaction
was made. For example, some have taken the "advocates" to be
merchants like those that figured so prominently in the defense of
Moscow, such as Adam the *sukonnik*, and have concluded that this
redaction was written in a commercial environment.[87] Others have
seen the "advocates" as Mordva or Mari. These were non-Slavic

tribes who dwelt along the Volga under Tatar domination; since they were favorably disposed toward the Russians, they might have served them as scouts or border guards.[88] Yet another theory holds that the "advocates" were pro-Russian Tatars.[89] Intriguing as these possibilities are, there is still another which is more likely, especially if we accept the later dates proposed for this redaction, or credit its author with a degree of imagination and literary flair. The Russian merchants on the Volga were incarcerated, yet Donskoi has to learn of Tokhtamysh's approach in time to leave the city. The vaguely described "advocates of the Russian Land" may simply have been the invention of a redactor faced with a small problem of narrative logic. One more problem of identity is worth noting, that of Ostei. Though some have accepted the claim in some manuscripts that he is Olgerd's grandson, this only compounds the mystery.[90]

The greatest deviation in the Expanded Redaction from the narrative line of the Short Redaction lies in a description of a *veche* uprising in Moscow. In this account Donskoi and his wife, much of the aristocracy, and Metropolitan Kiprian all abandon the city. A riot breaks out, and while the "evil" people break into the winecellars of the nobles and get drunk, the "good" people pray to God and organize a disciplined defense of the city. Obviously the redactor was using this episode (whether he invented it or not) to make a point of some kind. Probably it was designed to embarrass those who did not contribute to the defense of the city, though he uses no names.[91] Whatever the polemic purpose of this episode, it seems to have outlived its usefulness after the composition of the "compilation" of 1448. Later chronicles, such as the Ermolin, castigate all the participants in the *veche* and credit the *boyare* with organizing the city's defense.[92]

The vocabulary of Russo-Tatar relations in the Expanded Redaction of the tale of Tokhtamysh is standard—the Tatars launch campaigns, take and plunder cities. Once again it is apparent that none of these words implies conquest, since the Tatars have now been taking and plundering *Rus'* more or less continually since the time of Batu. The captured inhabitants of Moscow are taken into literal slavery (*rabota*) to be sold to the Ottomans or Genoese; this is not the metaphorical slavery of the spirit alluded to in Serapion's sermons. The very subject matter of the tale, of course, precludes the possibility of its having to do with Russia's liberation.

Although the Expanded Redaction explains some of the political and military difficulties that prompted Donskoi to leave the city before the khan arrived, it remains respectful toward the legitimate Chingisid khan, Tokhtamysh.[93] Indeed, the motif of respect for Chingisid legitimacy takes on greater proportions in the Expanded Redaction, for it underlies one of the most interesting added episodes. In the Short Redaction there is a passing reference to the deceptive speeches that led the city to surrender. From this allusion, the author of the Expanded Redaction invented the speeches made before the walls by the Tatar and Suzdalian princes.[94] It is clear that these speeches were meant to sound plausible to the readers of Moscovite chronicles and to offer an acceptable explanation of the city's surrender. It is also clear that the speech put into the mouths of Tatar princes by the Muscovite bookmen is an authentic statement of Chingisid doctrine as it was perceived in Russia. Tokhtamysh was the legitimate *tsar'*, and as such was equivalent to the *tsar'* at Constantinople, the *basileus*. The speech of the Tatar princes credits Tokhtamysh with the *philanthropia* to be expected from the *tsar'/basileus*.[95] The redactor recognizes that this in itself would not fool the people of the city, and that narrative realism demands the additional deceit of their fellow Russian Christians, the Suzdal' princes. Yet the fact remains that the premise of the entire episode is that the people of Moscow would not find assertions of imperial Chingisid virtue, virtue like that of the *basileus*, incredible. Unless this fact is recognized, the story is historically unintelligible. Respect for Chingisid legitimacy, then, was an integral part of the world-view of both the redactor and his elite Russian audience. The Expanded Redaction, even more than the Short Redaction, manages to combine into its ideology both a hatred for the Tatars and a respect for their imperial clan.

Salmina has attempted to show that the Expanded Redaction of the tale of Tokhtamysh was deliberately designed to mirror analogous events of the 1440s and that it reflects the political and ideological tendencies of the "compilation" of 1448. There was a somewhat similar occurrence in the 1440s, when the Tatars harassed the outskirts of the city in the absence of Prince Vasilii II, generating a panic and a *veche* meeting. In Salmina' view, in the Expanded Redaction Donskoi is meant to represent Vasilii II, and Oleg of Riazan' is meant to represent his cousin and rival Dmitrii Shemiaka. This theory finesses the ambiguous assignment of identities which Salmina had previously attributed to the Expanded Redaction of the chronicle tale of 1380. In addition, Salmina's analysis depends upon the tenuous "fact" that Shemiaka promised the grandson of Dmitrii Konstantinovich of Suzdal' that he would restore the Suzdal' principality if he were grand prince of Moscow and Vladimir. In fact the effects of the Tatar visits to Moscow in 1382 and in the 1440s were very different, and in any case any interpretation of the tale of Tokhtamysh must address the relationship of the two main protagonists, Donskoi and the khan, rather than exaggerating the secondary roles of Oleg of Riazan' and the Suzdal' princes. This allegorical approach to the Expanded Redaction strikes me as forced.[96] The text could easily have been a product of the 1380s, reflecting the Russian princely relations, ecclesiastic politics, and Tatar relations of that time, particularly during the interval when Vasilii I, Donskoi's son, was still a hostage at the Horde.

The Chingisid material in the tale of Tokhtamysh changes very little in later chronicles. In the Tverian Chronicle, the princes of the Horde refer to Moscow as part of the *ulus* of the *tsar'*.[97] The *Stepennaia kniga* mitigates the sordid role of the Suzdal' princes by explaining that they too were deceived by the Tatars. Thus they look foolish rather than vicious.[98]

As we have seen, both redactions of the tale of Tokhtamysh explain the actions of Dmitrii Donskoi and the people of Moscow in terms of respect for the legitimacy of Chingisid khans. Throughout its history, the authors, redactors, and copyists of the tale believed that the articulate Russian elite would find such motivations plausible. Again we are confronted with the extraordinary ability of Russian ideologues to manipulate the Chingisid principle for their own purposes while simultaneously rejecting the historical and political realities that lay behind this respect.

The *Troitskaia letopis'* contains, under the year 1389, the Short Redaction of the so-called vita of Dmitrii Donskoi.[99] An Expanded Redaction appears in the chronicles which derive from the hypothetical "compilation" of 1448, the Novgorod Fourth and the Sofia First Chronicles.[100] It follows from this, so most scholars believe, that the short entry in the *Troitskaia letopis'* was probably not written until 1408, and that the complete text of the longer variant was not written until the 1440s. If this is the case,

Donskoi's *"vita"* has a textological history analogous to that of the two chronicles' tales about Donskoi for 1380 and 1382.

However, the Donskoi entry in the *Troitskaia letopis'* for 1389 is far shorter than the entries for 1380 and 1382. Entitled "On the death of Grand Prince Dmitrii Ivanovich,"[101] the text is only one paragraph long. It is concerned with Donskoi's funeral and his will and does not so much as mention the Battle of Kulikovo. The text holds ideological interest only because of what it does not contain. While the author had access to Donskoi's will, he quotes only the part relating to the allocation of the Muscovite patrimony. The author of the entry omitted the following very restrained provision regarding the Tatars: "If God should change the Horde, then my children will not have to give tribute to the Horde, and each son will take the tribute for his own appanage, as it is" (*A peremenit bog Ordu, deti moi ne imut davati vykhoda v Ordu, i kotoryi syn moi vozmet dan' na svoem udele, po tomu i est*).[102] This is anything but a trumpet call for the overthrow of Mongol rule, but its meaning is perfectly clear. If the Horde's power over Russia should weaken, Donskoi's sons can start keeping the tribute for themselves. The formula concerning the reallocation of the tribute later became standard in wills and treaties of Muscovite grand princes.[103] (Eventually the day arrived, in the reign of Ivan III, when the princes were able to stop sending these revenues to the steppe, and Moscow's economy burgeoned as a result.) The circumlocutory formulation of this proposition attests to the need for delicacy in describing Russo-Tatar relations. Yet the *Troitskaia letopis'*, in omitting even this mild allusion to Russia's status with regard to the Horde, proved even more cautious than Donskoi's will.

The Expanded Redaction has an expanded title as well: "On the life and death of Dmitrii Ivanovich, Russian *tsar'*" (*Slovo o zhitii i o prestavlenii velikogo kniazia Dmitriia Ivanovicha, tsar'ia rus'skago*).[104] The remarkable thing, of course, is the use here of the imperial title. Its meaning is neither *basileus* nor khan, but something akin to the Western European doctrine that "the king is emperor in his own realm" or Rex-Imperator. In Cherniavsky's formulation, the ruler-myth of the saintly prince/princely saint was superceded by that of the monk-*tsar'* in Muscovite Russia, and in the Expanded Redaction Donskoi has become such a monk-*tsar'*.[105] No interpretation of this text which fails to take into account the importance of the use of the imperial title and the importance of the ruler-myth of the monk-*tsar'* can do it justice.[106] The imperial conception of the so-called *vita* of Dmitrii Donskoi is quite different from both the pre-Florentine Tverian aspirations of Boris Aleksandrovich[107] and the post-Florentine *translatio imperio* of the Muscovite texts which eventually reached fruition in the doctrine of Moscow as the Third Rome.[108]

Whereas the Short Redaction made no allusion whatever to Donskoi's victory at Kulikovo, in the Expanded Redaction the triumph over Mamai is integral to Donskoi's glory and piety. In this version, the "*tsars* of the lands" (*zemskie tsari*) heard of Donskoi and feared him. His neighbors denounce him to the "unclean" Mamai, saying, "Grand Prince Dmitrii calls himself *tsar'* of the Russian Land, (claiming) more honor than your glory, and stands in opposition to your *tsarstvo* (empire)." Mamai believes his evil counselors, who pretend to be Christians but perform evil deeds. He tells his princes and soldiers that they will ride against the Russian Land, destroy its churches, trample its faith, and make the Russians bow to their Makhmet instead.[109] He further intends to install *baskaki* in the Russian cities and to kill the Russian princes. Mamai first sends Begich against the Russian Land, but when Begich is defeated Mamai rides out himself. In the face of this threat, Donskoi turns to prayer, and *boyare* express their willingness to die as martyrs on his behalf. But Mamai is defeated and perishes in unknown parts (*vez vesti*). In his death-bed speech to his *boyare*, Donskoi claims to have "laid low the infidels" (*poganye nizlozhikh*).

Donskoi's dying words do not reflect pretensions of having shattered the Tatar Yoke.[110] As in all of the literary monuments of the Kulikovo cycle, there is no mention of any ramifications beyond the simple military victory. Indeed such a reference would make no sense in a work which says nothing whatever about the political relationship between Russia and the Horde, and to do so would have violated the hyperbole of the panegyric.[111] And in any case, of course, conceptualizing Russia's relationship with the Horde in political terms was virtually unknown in medieval Russian thought.

Mamai's role in the Expanded Redaction of Donskoi's "*vita*" is noteworthy in several particulars. First of all he is accorded no title of any kind, neither "prince" nor "khan," and the issue of *lèse-majesté* is never raised. Second, Mamai's motives recall those of Chol Khan in the mid-fifteenth-century redactions of the tale of the Tverian uprising of 1327.[112] Like that earlier villain, Mamai plans to kill the Russian princes and impose Islam on Russia. In addition, he intends to revive the *baskak* system. None of the works of the Kulikovo cycle contain the suggestions that the emir meant to install *baskaki* or undertake forcible conversion. (Of course, such claims enchance Donskoi's accomplishment in foiling such schemes; indeed in this version, by preventing the imposition of Islam, Donskoi has saved the souls of all Russians.) The third deviation from tradition is the assertion that Mamai met his death in parts unknown, in spite of the stories in all other texts that he died at the hands of either Tokhtamysh's Tatars or the Genoese. In a variety of ways, then, the author of the Expanded Redaction seems to have disregarded the information of other texts. It is difficult to imagine this happening if the text were written in a scriptorium or chancellery as part of a "group project" of compiling the *svod* of 1448. It is also difficult to believe that the treatment of Mamai reflects the anti-Tatar atmosphere of the Muscovite civil war. Not even then were the Tatars accused of wanting to impose Islam on Russia or to revive the hated *baskak* system. Nor is there any need to search the text for allegorical connections to the events of the Muscovite civil war; contemporary texts were quite explicit enough.

Despite the differences between Donskoi's "*vita*" and other texts that recount his exploits, the work resembles those of the Kulikovo cycle in its avoidance of the topic of Russia's political relations with the Golden Horde. The reasons for this are obvious, since the ethos of the text's political mythology is that Donskoi is a monk-*tsar'*, and politics are extraneous to such a conception. The work neither violates Chingisid doctrine by calling Mamai a *tsar'*, nor exploits it to denigrate him, which might have been unseemly.[113] The "*vita*" of Dmitrii Donskoi is not really about Russo-Tatar relations, but its narrative of the Battle of Kulikovo uses the standard ideological and intellectual devices of all medieval Russian texts in portraying such relations.

There is one more medieval Russian text that recounts the Battle of Kulikovo, namely the *vita* of St. Sergius of Radonezh.[114] St. Sergius, who played a prominent and noble role in the *Skazanie o Mamaevom poboishche*, proves even more important in his *vita*, naturally enough. According to this text,[115]

> For our sins, the prince of the Horde (*ordynskii kniaz'*)
> Mamai moved a great force, the whole horde of godless
> Tatars, and came against the Russian Land. The
> puissant and reigning prince, who held the scepter of all
> *Rus'*, great Dmitrii, having a great faith in the saint,
> came to ask him if he counseled him to go against the
> heathen. The saint bestowed upon him his blessing,
> and strengthened by prayer, said to him: "It behooveth
> you, Lord, to have a care for the lives of the flock
> committed to you by God. Go forth against the
> heathen and, upheld by the strong arm of God,
> conquer, and return to your country sound in health
> and glorify God in loud praise.

On the eve of battle, Sergius bolsters Donskoi's courage with a
timely message predicting great losses but a Russian victory (as in
the *Skazanie*). Donskoi, upon his triumphant return, makes a
donation to the Trinity monastery.

The author of the *vita* of St. Sergius is interested only in
enhancing the role of his hero, and does not concern himself with
political matters. For him, Donskoi's victory is important as proof
of the profound wisdom behind Sergius's advice, and of the saint's
influence with the heavenly powers. The text honors medieval
Russian fastidiousness concerning the titles of Mongol rulers, and
describes Mamai only as a "prince."[116]

We have seen, then, that every narrative of the Battle of
Kulikovo—the three works of the Kulikovo cycle as well as the
vitae of Dmitrii Donskoi and St. Sergius—presents the battle only
as a great Russian victory without further political ramifications.
The success at Kulikovo is frequently described as a religious
triumph but never as an act of liberation.

Tokhtamysh had come to power as the client of the great
sultan from Samarkand, Timur (Tamerlane; in the Russian sources,
Temir-Aksak). In the 1380s and 1390s, however, the khan tried to
free himself of this relationship. He was unsuccessful. Timur
invaded the territory of the Golden Horde, smashing Tokhtamysh's
armies, ravaging both Old and New Sarai, and driving his former
client into exile. Timur's campaigns against the Horde were only
one step in his grand scheme of conquest, but his ambitions lay in
the east, not in the west. In Moscow, however, the sultan's
depredations caused great concern, and when at one point Timur

and his army appeared to be moving toward Moscow, the city was thrown into a panic. To protect the city, the famous Vladimir Icon of the Virgin (*Bogoroditsa*) was brought to Moscow. When Timur proved instead to be heading off to the steppe again, a miracle was declared and the Virgin was credited with saving the city. It is a good example of the pervasive role of religion in Russian perceptions of Russo-Tatar relations.[117]

The Russians recorded Timur's exploits in the "Tale of Temir-Aksak." The textological history of this text has not been well studied. Whether the *Troitskaia letopis'* contained the full tale is open to question; Priselkov thought not. Neither the tale nor the legendary biography that accompanies it can be attested before the middle of the fifteenth century, when they appear, respectively, in the Tverian Chronicle and the Sofia First Chronicle. In the absense of any dated manuscripts outside the chronicle tradition from the first half of the century, earlier datings based on substantive or textological arguments remain plausible but not conclusive.[118]

The full tale[119] begins by noting the regnal years of Khan Tokhtamysh—the fifteenth year of his *tsarstvo* and the thirteenth year after the Tatar campaign (*tatarshchina*) and the taking (*vziatie*) of Moscow. The arithmetic is quite correct. "Some (*nekii*) say that Temir-Aksak was not a *tsar'* by birth, nor the son of a *tsar'*, nor of the imperial family (*ne plemeni tsarska* or *ne ot roda tsarska*), nor of princely rank, nor of *boyar* rank, but simply the son of shabby people, of *Zaiatskii* Tatars (from beyond the Yaik river in the Urals), of the Samarkand Horde which is beyond the Iron Gates (Derbend in the Caucasus) ...." The text goes on to say that Timur was merely a runaway slave and the son of a blacksmith. After he was lamed by raiding bandits, he received the name Temir-Aksak, which means "Iron Lame" in the Polovtsian tongue, because of his father's profession. Temir-Aksak gathers about him a band of cutthroats of his own (*razboinitsi* and *khishchnitsi*) and begins a successful career as a bandit. "And when he had a hundred robbers, he called himself a senior thief (*stareishii razboinik*), when a thousand, they called him prince. And when their numbers had increased beyond number, and he had captured (*plenil*) many cities and countries and taken (*vzial*) *tsarstva*, then he even began to call himself *tsar'*." The text says that Temir-Aksak plundered (*plenil*) the following lands: Chagatai, Korsun', Golustan, Kitai, *Siniaia Orda* (the Blue Horde), Shiraz,

Isfahan, Ornach, Gulian, Siz, Shirben, Shamikhi, Savas, Arzunnut', Tiflis, Gurzustan, Obrezin, Gruzii (Georgia), Badabat, Temir Bab (the Iron Gates), Assyria, Babylonia, Sebastae, Armenia, Damascus, and Great Sarai. He plundered (*plenil*) Tokhtamysh in his nomadizing grounds (*kochevishche*), and like Batu, he wanted to plunder (*plenil*) the Russian Land and take (*vzial*) it. But God saved the Russians from his campaign (*nakhozhdenie*).

That the tale begins by citing the regnal years of the legitimate Chingisid khan, Tokhtamysh, is hardly an accident. When this is followed by the story of Timur's origins, the contrast between Russia's respectable ruler and the low-born slave and bandit could scarcely be more explicit.[120] Although Timur was in fact an aristocratic (albeit Turkicized) Mongol of the Burlas tribe, the scurrilous story of his base parentage and beginnings was widespread in the lands of his enemies. However, the Russian variation of this legendary biography contains a uniquely Russian element in that it accuses the sultan of usurping the title of *tsar'*, that is, of claiming the status of a Chingisid khan. Timur in fact was not a Chingisid, though he had married a Chingisid princess. His only official titles were sultan and *gurkan* (in-law). Although popular accounts usually fail to mention it, Timur paid scrupulous attention to the Chingisid rules of imperial politics, and always maintained Chingisid puppets for propriety. He did find it useful to sponsor a fictitious genealogy tracing his ancestry to Chingis Khan, extant in funerary inscriptions and panegyric necrologues, but he carefully restricted its use.

There is no reason to believe that the Russian accusation of *lèse-majesté* was based in ignorance. The tale's list of Timur's conquests is somewhat chaotic, with no discrimination between cities, provinces, and nations, and in addition some of the names are undecipherable, unidentifiable, or biblical adulterations like Assyria and Babylonia. Nonetheless the list is basically accurate and shows considerable familiarity with the sultan's career.[121] Russians in the armies of Tokhtamysh had first-hand experience with him, and the Russian chronicles accurately record his victories over the khan. The Russians had a detailed knowledge of Timur's exploits and had lived in great fear of his pretentions and ambitions. That they could have been unaware of his circumspection with regard to the Chingisid issue is most implausible.

The deliberately contrived accusation of *lèse-majesté* against

Timur is most interesting. The unfavorable comparison with Tokhtamysh certainly was not designed as a defense of the khan, who was no friend to the Russians. Yet the contrast of the Chingisid Tokhtamysh with the non-Chingisid challenger offered an opportunity that the Russian bookman could hardly ignore. Drawing upon the tradition of castigating Emir Mamai for commiting *lèse-majesté*, he used the same weapon to attack the sultan, fully aware that the claim was untrue. Since the function of the tale of Temir-Aksak was to defend Russian actions and give courage to Russian hearts, and since such tales were produced by and for Russia's political and ecclesiastical elite, it is evident that such a strategem could only be effective if Russia's upper classes had thoroughly assimilated the principles of Chingisid ideology.

The tale of Temir is of a piece with all the other texts concerning Russo-Tatar relations during the Kulikovo era, from 1380 to 1408, and could easily have been written at that time. It describes the accomplishments of both Tokhtamysh and Timur with the standard vocabulary; they launch campaigns, take, and plunder.[122] It even takes a tip from the texts about Mamai and says that in his intention to invade the Russian Land, Timur was like Batu. Timur, who hoped to emulate not Batu but the great Chingis Khan himself and to recreate the great Mongol Empire, would probably have been insulted by the comparison.

After Timur had defeated Tokhtamysh's forces, the deposed khan and his men sought refuge in Lithuania. Here they were welcomed by Grand Prince Vitovt, who had his own designs on Eastern Europe and the Pontic steppe and could see the advantage of having his own Chingisid pawn. In 1399, Vitovt and his new client Tokhtamysh led their armies into battle with the forces of two of Timur's clients, Emir Edigei and Khan Temir-Kutlui, on the river Vorskla. The Lithuanian and his allies were disastrously defeated. The Russian chronicles, beginning with the *Troitskaia letopis'*, contain a brief narrative about the battle.[123] According to this account, Vitovt's plan was to "sit" (*posazhu*) or "install" Tokhtamysh on the (Volga) *tsarstvo* and then to have Tokhtamysh "sit" Vitovt in Moscow, the Russian Land, the grand principality.[124] First, however, Vitovt must be victorious in battle. This fails to happen, and after the battle the triumphant Temir-Kutlui and Edigei ride to Kiev, extract a ransom (*okup'*), and proceed to plunder (*plenisha*) many cities and villages in the

"Lithuanian Land" (i.e., the Ukraine, which was under Lithuanian control).

Vitovt, who had settled Tokhtamysh's Tatars in Lithuania (where their Islamic faith and Tatar language created an ethnographic and linguistic curiosity for centuries), was well acquainted with both the practices and principles of Horde politics. Although he had told the Pope that he was invading Eastern Europe in a crusade against Islam, the ostensible reason for the campaign with Tokhtamysh was the restoration of the rightful khan of the Golden Horde! This expedition was a failure, but Vitovt continued, in the opening decades of the fifteenth century, to meddle in Horde affairs through the use of Chingisid pawns (though for a time his instrument was his former foe, Emir Edigei, who had fallen upon hard times). Thus the Russian bookmen were justified in seeing Vitovt's plans in Chingisid terms.

The bookmen, however, did not and could not spell out the logic of the grand prince's scheme. What Vitovt has in mind is a double investiture—he will give the Volga Horde back to Tokhtamysh, and the khan will award him the Muscovite principality. The political reality underlying this plan is not difficult to perceive; evidently whoever sat on the Horde throne ruled Russia and could award it to whomever he chose. The only texts containing such explicit notions of suzerainty are those in which the would-be conqueror fails, as Vitovt and Mamai did. Nonetheless, the argument behind Vitovt's program for a double investiture is most revealing of Russian perceptions of Russo-Tatar relations at the turn of the fifteenth century.

The text describes Tatar activities in the Ukraine in the usual terms, i.e., plundering. The Sofia First Chronicle contains a variant passage in which Vitovt says he will plunder the Tatar Land (*pleniti Tatarskuiu zemliu*).[125] He had originally intended to rule the steppe through Tokhtamysh; since there is no indication plundering involves suzerainty, he has apparently scaled down his plans. The Nikon chronicler[126] invents a fascinating dialogue between Vitovt and Edigei at the river Vorskla on the subject of political seniority, giving solid substantiation of Russian appreciation of the importance of numismatic iconography.[127] In this version, Vitovt's ambitions have extended to include, besides the Horde, Kaffa, Azov, the Crimea, Astrakhan', the Yaik Horde, and Kazan', and he intends also to seize Novgorod, Pskov, Riazan', Tver' and many Russian principalities. With typical Nikon hyperbole, the list of Vitovt's objectives in the steppe is padded with an anachronistic geography of the Horde, and his plans for Russia embellished with additional Russian cities, many of which, during the fourteenth and fifteenth centuries, were under Lithuanian political pressure. Yet despite the extensive interpolation in the Nikon Chronicle, Vitovt's manipulation of the Chingisid principle still underlies his schemes.[128]

The "Tale of the Battle on the River Vorskla," perhaps even more than previous texts, shows how thoroughly the Chingisid principle was integrated into Russian ideological vision. For this was a case not merely of manipulating it to defame Russia's enemies, but of perceiving it as an element of the political programs of a ruler who was neither a Russian nor a Tatar. Although in the "Tale of Temir-Aksak" the Chingisid principle was used mendaciously to slander Timur, while in the account of Vitovt's adventuring it probably constitutes a historically accurate analysis of that ruler's plans, its significance with regard to Russian perceptions remains the same. Finally, the tale is especially interesting in that it ventures dangerously near to admitting that whoever ruled the Horde ruled Russia.

It was nine years before Emir Edigei, the real victor of the battle on the Vorskla, could turn his full attention to Moscow. This hiatus was due in part to the necessity of reuniting the Horde and in part to the interference in Horde politics of his patron, Timur. In 1408, with Timur dead, Edigei was at last able to take complete control of his own affairs. He led his forces to Moscow and besieged the city. The events of that year are recorded in three Russian texts—a narrative tale, a theoretical treatise, and an epistle. Each of these textologically unrelated works has a unique perspective, and all of them appear to be contemporary.[129]

The narrative tale is obviously the work of a Muscovite eyewitness and its reliability is assured. It appears as the concluding annal of the *Troitskaia letopis'*.[130] According to this rather sparse account, Edigei attacks Moscow with the permission of *Tsar'* Bulat. His army includes four *tsarevichi*, Buchak, Tegrii-Berdii, Altimir and (a different) Bulat; five princes (*kniazi*), Makhmet, son of Isup Siulemen, Tegrinia, son of Shikh, Sarai, son of Uruskhan, Obriagin, son of Temiria, and Yak'shibii, son of Edigei himself; and three additional notables, Sietialibii, Burnak, and Erikliberdii. The grand prince of Moscow, Vasilii I, leaves the defense of the city in other hands and is chased, unsuccessfully, by Tegri-berdii, Yak'shibii, and Sietialibii with thirty thousand men (an obviously inflated figure which must be the result of a scribal error). The Tatars "took" Pereiaslavl' and headquartered in Kolomenskoe, but Edigei could only burn the suburbs and outskirts of Moscow, unable to storm the city. Meanwhile a revolt breaks out in the Horde against the rule of *Tsar'* Bulat, who is vulnerable in the absence of Edigei and his troops. The *tsar'* sends swift messengers (*skoroposol'niki*) to the emir, who terminates his siege for a ransom (*okup'*) of three thousand rubles. Facing no military opposition, Edigei is able to seize innumerable captives (*polony*) as he rides back to the steppe. Although Christian Russians pray to God to be saved (*izbaviti*) from the Tatar campaign (*nakhozhdenie*), each Tatar leads forty captives into the steppe to be sold. The Russian Land is plundered (*plenena*) from Galich to Beloozero, all because of Russian sins.

The second text about Edigei's siege of 1408 is a theoretical treatise of a type rather rare in Old Russian literature. It is definitely not a Muscovite text, and although it first appears in the Tverian chronicles, it may or may not be of Tverian authorship.[131] The treatise discusses the relations between the Russians and the deceitful, godless Ishmaelites. Prince Edigei, the "eldest" (*stareishii*) of all Horde princes, installs and deposes *tsari* at his will (*volia*). He incites trouble between the grand princes of Lithuania and Moscow, Vitovt and Vasilii I, just as the Polovtsy turned the Russian princes against one another. Edigei, who deceitfully claimed to be Vasilii's father, promises to aid him against Vitovt, then besieges Moscow himself. Edigei plunders (*plenil*) and takes (*vzial*) many Russian cities. The Christians should have known better than to trust him; Sil'vestr' warned of such things in the "Primary Chronicle" (*Nachal'naia letopis'*).

The third text concerning the events of that year is an epistle from Edigei to Vasilii I. Since it is found in the Novgorod Fourth Chronicle, among others, it can safely be dated to no later than the first half of the fifteenth century.[132] In this letter Edigei lodges a series of complaints against Moscow's prince. Vasilii shelters the sons of Edigei's enemy, Tokhtamysh, in particular Zeleni-Saltan. He has sent no tribute (*vykhod*) for twelve years, and no longer respects envoys and merchants from the Horde. His patrimony was once the "*ulus* of the *tsar'*" (*tsarev ulus*), but no longer. Vasilii used to cooperate with the Horde and listen to the

advice of his elders, especially his deceased treasurer (*kaznachei*)
and "favorite" (*liubovnik*), Fedor Koshka. Unless Vasilii reconsiders
his rash policy, his *ulus* will suffer Tatar wrath. The two hundred
rubles Edigei has received are absurdly inadequate.

I have thought it best to summarize the texts back-to-back
to bring out the contrasts between them.[133] The brief Muscovite
narrative, though it describes the sad fate of the enslaved Russians,
is virtually an apologia for Edigei, who is personally accused of
nothing. The text accurately describes him as a prince, but
carefully points out that he is acting with the permission of the
khan and that his army is replete with Chingisids and other Tatar
aristocrats. When the emir leaves Moscow, it is to save the throne
of his rightful lord. Edigei is treated as gingerly as if he were the
legitimate khan. The text shows just how much information
Muscovite bookmen could acquire about the enemy even in the
midst of a Tatar siege: the personnel, their Chingisid status and
family relationships, and the course of events in the distant Horde.
With the exception of the amount of the ransom, which may be
exaggerated, there are no suspicious details in the narrative. The
vocabulary of Russo-Tatar relations is catholic; the invocation of
Russian sins is orthodox. When one considers that the bookman is
relating an attack on his city by the hated infidel oppressors, the
passivity of this text is remarkable. It surely reflects the
resurgence of Horde power under the leadership of Edigei. The
Horde's revival reduced the number of viable ideological options for
Muscovite bookmen, and the energy of the anti-Tatar ideology
generated by the victory at Kulikovo thirty years earlier seems to
have dissipated.

The theoretical treatise on Russo-Tatar relations proves that
this is not the whole story. This text exploits all of Edigei's
ideological weaknesses, though its attack seems largely aimed at
Vasilii I. Whether the text originated in Tver', in the
metropolitanate in Vladimir, or elsewhere, the author clearly
advocates peace between Lithuania and Muscovy. This policy looks
similar to that of Metropolitan Kiprian, who was already deceased.
The text is vehement in its distrust of Tatar intentions, Edigei's in
particular. There is no evidence for its claims that Edigei ever
called himself Vasilii's father or that Vasilii considered himself
Edigei's son. The implied relationships are of course political,
indicating that Edigei considered Vasilii his subordinate. Ironically,
Vasilii did have such a relationship with Vitovt. He had married

Vitovt's daughter, and Vitovt was the most powerful ruler in Eastern Europe. The author of the treatise seems to be distorting political history to strengthen his case.

Whereas the author of the narrative in the *Troitskaia letopis'* did not take advantage of Edigei's non-Chingisid status, the author of the treatise does. Indeed he draws upon the *Troitskaia letopis'* itself, or at least to the "Tale of the Battle on the river Vozha" found in that chronicle. The author uses the same language as was used against Mamai to accuse Edigei of the crime of *lèse-majesté*: Edigei, too, is a "senior" prince who arbitrarily plays khan-maker in the Horde. Historically, of course, the link was justified. Mamai and Edigei were alike in that both were powerful rulers, barred by Chingisid tradition from actually occupying the throne of the Horde. Both resorted to ruling through puppet khans. (And while the treatise attacks Edigei for this, the narrative obsequiously upholds the pretense that the emir came to the khan's rescue out of loyalty rather than because the Chingisid was too useful a tool to lose.) In the treatise of 1408 the charge of *lèse-majesté*[134] against Edigei is not carried to the extremes of the attacks on Mamai in the Expanded Redaction of the chronicle tale of 1380, but it is still a powerful indictment. It is especially noteworthy in comparison with the exaggerated caution of the narrative of 1408.

The treatise also deals with Russo-Tatar relations as if Russia and the Horde were entirely independent states that might or might not make alliances and treaties depending on their needs. There is no hint of Muscovite political subjugation to the Horde or of Russia's conquest by the Mongols.[135] Vasilii is Edigei's son by his own foolish consent. Furthermore, the Tatars are accused of pursuing the same divide-and-exploit policy as the Polovtsy. The flaw in the analogy, of course, is that the Tatars had conquered Russia and the Polovtsy had not. Despite this crucial difference, the conceptual framework of the relations between Kievan *Rus'* and the steppe is imposed onto Russo-Tatar relations. The treatise gives the impression that Moscow's relations with Lithuania and with the Tatars were carried out on roughly the same basis, but this does not reflect a new era of Russo-Tatar relations inaugurated at Kulikovo. Whatever political capital Moscow had acquired in that triumph had certainly been liquidated two years later when Tokhtamysh sacked the city. Russia's apparent independence in this text is a sign not of new found liberty but of the continuing power of the Russian intellectual tradition of rejecting the fact of the Mongol conquest and its enduring consequences. The discrepancies between historical reality and the picture of Russo-Tatar relations painted in the text are more than usually evident because this is one of the rare cases in which the medieval bookmen directly addressed the theoretical aspects of Russia's status with regard to the Horde. Since the text is an attack on Vasilii I as well as on the Tatars, the third-party perspective may also help to bring this aspect of medieval Russian attitudes into focus.

The third text is something else entirely. It is not, of course, a genuine letter from Edigei to Vasilii. If it were it would be in Turkic, it would conform to the diplomatic forms of the Golden Horde's chancellery, and it would probably bear the name of Edigei's puppet-khan. Rather, it is the creation of a Russian bookman, apparently working for a faction of Muscovite society that was both pro-Edigei and pro-Tatar. Judging from style and contents, it was meant to be taken seriously. The epistle's first accusation is historically verifiable; Vasilii was indeed sheltering Tokhtamysh's son, Zeleni-Saltan, who eventually became khan of the Golden Horde. Whether it was true that Moscow's prince had not paid tribute in twelve years cannot be ascertained. It is quite possible that the Horde was in no condition, in the aftermath of Timur's invasion, to compel Moscow to pay tribute, and that this state of affairs obtained until Edigei had restored order on the Volga. It is also true that as the conflict with Timur loomed closer, Tokhtamysh became increasingly solicitous of Moscow's desires. He probably went so far as to give his official approval to Donskoi's testament, in which, in direct violation of the khan's formal prerogatives, Donskoi willed the grand principality of Moscow and Vladimir to his son and heir, Vasilii I. Tokhtamysh also awarded the principality of Nizhnii Novgorod to Vasilii in 1393, perhaps to protect his northern flank when Timur launched his invasion. However, since from 1396 on the situation in the Pontic and Caspian steppe was completely chaotic, it seems more likely that it was disorder rather than Mongol concessions that allowed Moscow to withhold tribute.

The epistle of Edigei presents a marvelously distorted vision of Moscow's relations with the Horde before 1395. In decrying the present state of affairs, Edigei depicts the good old days, when respectful, friendly, and mutually beneficial relations obtained.

Princes, envoys, and merchants travelled between Moscow and the Horde without tension or disagreement. This is a fantasy, of course, but not an idle fantasy. The text's ideological message is that when Russians acted like members of the *ulus*, Russia was immune from harm. Vasilii I, in disregarding this tradition, has imperiled the safety and security of his domain. The sponsors of this text wished Vasilii to submit to Edigei, but one can only wonder what group of people would have been willing to take so public a stance in favor of reconciliation with the hated Tatars. Another puzzle is the allusion to the collaborationist policies of Fedor Koshka. Although the epistle is sympathetic to him, it certainly manages to compromise his reputation. Koshka was an influential *boyar*, but nothing else is known of his attitude toward the Tatars. Despite the epistle, his descendants had successful careers in Muscovy.[136]

Clearly the epistle of Edigei was not considered genuinely treasonous or it would not have been repeated in the chronicles as it was without adulteration, emendation, or comment. Its position was sufficiently credible to merit the attention of the Russian elite, and it shows a profound insight into the Horde's perspective on Russian affairs. The attitudes toward Russo-Tatar relations expressed in the epistle are utterly irreconcilable with those found in the theoretical treatise of 1408. In some ways they resemble those of the Muscovite narrative of that year. Yet the remarkable thing about the epistle is that it goes even further than either of those texts in casting a veil of silence over any hostility in the past between Russians and Tatars. For a medieval Russian bookman to use this intellectual device is extraordinary.

As a set then, the three Russian texts concerning Edigei's siege of 1408[137] are quite different from the five literary monuments that immortalized the Battle of Kulikovo. They are, among other things, far less homogeneous in their approach to Russo-Tatar relations; while there is no ambiguity in the Kulikovo texts concerning Mamai's villainy, the same cannot be said of Edigei in the texts about his siege of Moscow. The siege of 1408, then, seems to mark the end of the Kulikovo era, and the difference between the two sets of texts is due perhaps to the altered nature of Russo-Tatar relations. By 1408 the ideological inspiration of Donskoi's victory was exhausted, and from then on there were no events in Russo-Tatar relations to spark new ideological responses until the decades of the great Muscovite civil war.

The Kulikovo era stands out as a distinctive phase of medieval Russian intellectual thought about the problem of Russia's relations with the Mongol conquerors. In recording the great events of their time, the mostly Muscovite bookmen depended for historical context upon earlier Russian texts. As a natural consequence the conceptual framework of Kievan *Rus'*-steppe relations, which did not include concepts of conquest or articulation of changes in sovereignty, continued to be employed. There was simply no place in such a vision for the idea of liberation from a political subjugation that had never been acknowledged. The preponderance of scholarly opinion notwithstanding, the texts that celebrate the manifestations of Moscow's growing strength do not do so in terms of Russian emancipation. The texts from the Kulikovo era do, however, further develop existing themes of Russo-Tatar relations. The mutual chivalric respect between Russian and Tatar warriors that was evident in the Evpatii episode of the "Tale of the Destruction of Riazan'" becomes the leitmotif of the later epic, the *Zadonshchina*. The religious aspects of earlier narratives developed into a full crusading ethos in the *Skazanie o Mamaevom poboishche*. Yet the most striking feature of Russo-Tatar ideology in the Kulikovo era, that which sets it apart from the periods before and after, is the sensitivity to and manipulation of the principle of Chingisid legitimacy. The assiduous attention to Tatar sensibilities reflects in part the recognition of the bookmen that the Horde still remained a potent factor on the political scene. It is also in part a function of accident. During this comparatively brief period, Russia faced three great Tatar adversaries, none of whom, by Tatar tradition, had the right to rule. It is one of the great ironies of the texts from this time that the Russian bookmen, in seeking ways to defame their Tatar (and Russian) enemies, should do so in terms that show a thorough assimilation of the Tatars' political precepts.

Chapter V:

Civil War in Muscovy

The victor of the Battle of Kulikovo, Grand Prince Dmitrii Donskoi, was succeeded on the throne of Muscovy by his eldest son, Vasilii Dmitrievich, Vasilii I. Before his death, however, Donskoi had taken a step which, while designed to ensure the security of his realm, was to result in disaster. In making out his will Donskoi stipulated that since Vasilii had as yet no heir, the throne should pass from him to his younger brother, Yurii Dmitrievich. When Vasilii I later fathered a son, Vasilii Vasilievich, the stage was set for a classic medieval Russian dynastic succession dispute between direct and collateral heirs. It was inevitable that upon the death of Vasilii I there would be a contest between the patrimonial claims of the direct descendent still in his minority and the "seniority" rights of the elder uncle. The result was violent civil war within the Muscovite house that lasted for most of the second quarter of the fifteenth century. Upon the death of Yurii Dmitrievich, his cause was taken up by his two sons, Dmitrii Krasnii and Dmitrii Shemiaka, whose court, the *Shemiakin sud*, became synonymous in Russian folklore with corrupt justice. In the brutal internecine struggle, two Riurikids had their eyes put out, many *boyare* were ruined, and untold damage was done to property and countryside.

If the war was inevitable, so was its involvement of the Tatars, for the power to award the throne of the grand prince of Vladimir lay with the khan of the Golden Horde. The actual role of the Horde in the eventual resolution of the conflict remains unclear and is not the concern of the present work. Rather, we shall examine how the Russian chroniclers and the society they spoke for perceived the contribution, so to speak, of the Tatars to the development of the civil war in Muscovy. The chronicle entries about the war that deal with Tatar activities underwent almost no textological variation. They were either included in a chronicle or they were not, and in our present state of knowledge about the relationships among the chronicles in the second half of the fifteenth century, it is not possible to draw any obvious

conclusions from which entries appear in which chronicles. It is
possible, of course, that a pattern may emerge in the distribution
of the entries which will allow us to correlate particular chronicles,
social groups, and points of view, and to illuminate the varieties of
social response to the war.

The Muscovite civil war was so confused that there is
disagreement about the course of political events.[1] (Each stage of
the conflict was marked by the ratification of a series of treaties
among the princes, but these tell us little about Russo-Tatar
relations other than who, at a given moment, was permitted direct
communication with the Horde.)[2] In 1425, Vasilii II and his uncle
and rival, Yurii Dmitrievich, agreed that the *tsar'*, i.e., the Mongol
khan, would choose the next grand prince,[3] though legally, of
course, the khan's prerogative to do this had never been abrogated.
For a time, nothing further happened. Vasilii was then enjoying
the powerful protection of two men, his grandfather and guardian,
Grand Prince Vitovt of Lithuania, and Metropolitan Fotii. While
these two lived, Yurii could not act with any expectation of
success. Then, in 1432, with both Vitovt and Fotii dead, the
struggle for the throne began in earnest.[4]

Vasilii II and Yurii Dmitrievich both travelled to the Horde,
though it is not known if they went together, or, if not, which of
them went first. In the chronicle, Vasilii is greeted there by Min
Bulat, a supporter of his who is the *ulus doroga Moskovskii* (the
title implies that Min Bulat had administrative responsibility for
the Muscovite principality). Yurii also has an ally, Prince of the
Horde Taginia of the Shirin clan, one of the most powerful Tatar
clans in the Crimea. As soon as Yurii arrives at the Horde,
Taginia escorts him to the Crimea for the winter. This action
obviously served two purposes in that it clearly demonstrated
Taginia's political support for Yurii while also guaranteeing the
Russian's safety. However, it also gave Vasilii's *boyare* an
opportunity to advance their claimant's case without opposition.
The *boyare* try to persuade the princes of the Horde, including
Aidar, to influence the *tsar'* (khan) in favor of Vasilii. They warn
the Tatar princes that if the *tsar'* heeds Taginia and awards the
throne to Yurii, Moscow will be dangerously friendly with
Svidrigailo of Lithuania. This argument, according to the chronicle,
"pierces the hearts" of the Tatars, and the princes of the Horde
elect to back Vasilii. Their influence with the khan proves
decisive, for he renders judgement in favor of Vasilii.

Taginia returns to the Horde in the spring, and is warned by his cousin (*bratanich*), Usein, the "*tsar*"'s gentleman of the bedchamber" (*postel'nik tsarev*), of the khan's decision. Taginia's influence was apparently great enough to reopen the debate, for both sides continue lobbying and the khan takes no action to implement his decree. According to the chronicle, the grand prince, Vasilii II, relies upon the principle of patrimony (*otechestvo i dedstva*), while Yurii Dmitrievich cites chronicles (*letopistsy*), "old manuscripts" (*starye spiski*), and the testament (*dukhovnaia gramota*) of Dmitrii Donskoi. Vasilii's spokesman at the Horde was the *boyar* Ivan Dmitrievich Vsevolozhskii.[5] In his argument for the prince, he describes Vasilii as the "slave" (*kholop*) of the *tsar'*, one who legitimately wants to retain the grand principality, the khan's *ulus* (*tsarev ulus*), and his census (*devter'*) and patent (*yarlik*). Vsevolozhskii asserts that Ulu-Muhammed is a "free *tsar'*" (*volnii tsar'*, actually a Byzantine epithet) whose free choice should not be hindered by the charter (*gramota*) of a dead prince (i.e., Donskoi). He adds that Vasilii I had left his throne to his son Vasilii II with the khan's grant (*zhalovanie*).

These arguments apparently proved effective, for the khan once again concludes that Vasilii should have the throne. He orders Yurii Dmitrievich to lead his nephew's horse around the Tatar camp in a symbolic gesture of submission. Vasilii, however, is mindful of Taginia's continued opposition and does not wish to dishonor his uncle so greatly. Prudently, he leaves the Horde.

At this point centrifugal tendencies within the Horde take the upper hand. Kichi Akmed seizes the throne from Ulu-Muhammed and partially reverses the decree of his predecessor, leaving open the question of the grand principality. Yurii Dmitrievich does receive some satisfaction, for Kichi Akmed sends his envoy Akmed to install Yurii in Dmitrov, thus adding that city and territory to the Russian's Galich appanage and increasing his power and prestige. Vasilii II continues to hold Moscow. Several months later Mansyr' Ulan mysteriously arrives to install Vasilii as grand prince.

This Kremlinological analysis of the Russian political struggle at the Horde in 1432 was undoubtedly the work of a well-informed eyewitness. He appears to have been an adherent of Vasilii, since he calls Vasilii "grand prince" and records only the speech in favor of him. Though the author discreetly avoids mentioning bribery, he leaves little question that influence-peddling was the name of

the game, and he shows a clear understanding of how the Horde's
own internal divisions influenced the Tatars' Russian policy.   The
1432 entry is an insider's account, written by someone who knew
the names, origins, families, factions, and policies of all of his
characters and everything they said and did.

One of the most striking aspects of this account is its
remarkable neutrality with regard to the Tatars.   It contains none
of the standard repertoire of anti-Tatar epithets and none of the
usual passages devoted to denouncing them.   True, the Tatars in
this narrative happen not to be plundering or murdering, but
Russian bookmen had always found ways to excoriate the infidels
regardless of the circumstances, and for that matter to attack when
necessary any Russian prince who sought Tatar assistance.   The
author of this narrative had neither the motive nor the opportunity
to do this, for the entire narrative revolves around the attempts of
the hero as well as the villain to curry favor with the Horde.   The
result is one of the most unprejudiced descriptions of Mongol
politics in the medieval Russian sources.

The arguments put forward by the two rivals are of great
interest, though it must be kept in mind that they are not
necessarily reliable.   This is, after all, campaign propaganda.
Vasilii's supporters begin with the damaging slander that Yurii
Dmitrievich is pro-Lithuanian.   Now in 1380, Mamai had allied
himself with Lithuania, and in 1480, the Great Horde, seeking aid
against a pro-Muscovite Crimea, would establish an alliance with
Poland-Lithuania.   On the whole, though, Lithuania and the
Golden Horde were enemies, and whether the accusation against
Yurii was true or not, it would certainly have been effective.   If
Yurii had entangling alliances with powers hostile to the Horde, he
would be politically unreliable, and the Horde would be acting
against its own interests if it favored him over Vasilii.

Next, the chronicle says, Vasilii invokes the principle of
patrimonial succession, while Yurii cites various written texts and
documents.   This contrast is curious, since Yurii could have
invoked the right of inheritance with as much justice.   He was,
after all, the son of Grand Prince Dmitrii Donskoi and the
grandson of Grand Prince Ivan II.   The chronicle implies, however,
that Yurii's claims were weaker in this regard, though it does not
say how.   It is natural that he should turn to Donskoi's testament
to back his claim to the throne.   Whether the actual manuscript
was among the documents that Yurii brought to the Horde is an

open question; certainly Vasilii would have worked to prevent this. The other written works, the chronicles and old manuscripts, are not identifiable, and nothing could have made Yurii's case more powerfully than Donskoi's will. Perhaps Yurii was padding his portfolio, or perhaps the otherwise scrupulous chronicler exaggerated a bit here.

By far the most significant aspect of the mention of Yurii's written evidence, however, is the premise that underlies it. For it follows from the fact that Yurii brought objective written evidence to substantiate his case, that such evidence was respected in political disputes subject to Horde authority. The implication is that the Horde reached its decisions with at least some consideration for justice and legality, though this is not entirely consistent with the rest of the narration. It is also worth noting that Yurii's manuscripts would have been written in Slavic, and it is doubtful that any of the scribes in the khan's chancellery would have been able to translate them. As usual, our Russian source makes no mention of linguistic barriers and how they were overcome.

The same holds true for the speech of Vasilii's spokesman, Vsevolozhskii, which, to be understood by the princes of the Horde, had to be either delivered in Tatar or translated. Whichever it was, the chronicler found it too obvious to note. The record of Vsevolozhskii's peroration is probably accurate in substance. He begins with protestations of loyalty designed to win sympathy for Vasilii, who, Vsevolozhskii says, conceives of himself as the "slave" of the khan. This is a potent declaration, which I believe to be a rhetorical excess, but it was certainly what the Tatars wanted to hear. He goes on to say that Vasilii wishes only his patrimony, the grand principality, the *tsarev ulus*. Alluding to Russia as part of the *ulus* of the khan was clearly a ploy to emphasize the joint interests of Vasilii and the Tatar khan. Russia was probably not a formal part of the *ulus*, but for the time being it served everyone's interests to pretend otherwise. Vsevolozhskii continues his use of Tatar political terms as he claims that Vasilii wants to keep both the census, the record on the basis of which tribute was determined,[6] and the *yarlik*, the khan's patent for the grand-princely throne.

Having established Vasilii's loyalty, and done so in terms meant to show how thoroughly Vasilii's political vision corresponded with that of the Horde, Vsevolozhskii seeks to

undermine Yurii's case.   He asserts that a free and autonomous
khan like Ulu-Muhammed cannot be constrained by the mere
documents of a dead prince.   Besides, succession from Vasilii I to
Vasilii II had been ratified by a khan.   The logic of this argument
is at best confused.   Donskoi's testament, naming Yurii as the
successor of Vasilii I, had also been ratified by a khan.   Why the
testament of one dead Russlan was worthless and that of another is
sacrosanct is not clear.   Vsevolozhskii does not rest his case on the
fact that the testament of Vasilii I was more recent.   Actually, it
is probable that Vasilii I had his will ratified not by the Mongol
khan but by Vitovt, who was the designated guardian of Vasilii II,
still a minor.   If this is true, it is not surprising that Vsevolozhskii
omits to mention it, especially considering that Vasilii's partisans
were slandering Yurii as a Lithuanian sympathizer.

Vsevolozhskii's speech can be reduced to the simple claim
that Vasilii was both a loyal servant of the Horde and the rightful
heir to the throne.   But the way in which the chronicler has
Vasilii's spokesman make his case is most informative.   The
chronicler clearly expects his readers to find it plausible that a
cogent speech in defense of a just claim tipped the balance of
opinion at the Horde in Vasilii's favor.   Therefore, the Tatar
grandees are amenable to logic and good sense.   This is a
remarkable admission for a medieval Russian author to make.
Equally unusual is the eagerness of a Russian prince to present
himself as a slave to an infidel.   On this subject, the chronicler,
who is one of Vasilii's partisans, has no comment.

When Kichi Akmed expelled Ulu-Muhammed from the Horde,
the latter's judgement in the suit between Vasilii II and Yurii
Dmitrievich was rendered null and void.   Strangely, however, it
was the refugee khan, rather than his successor, who figured most
during the next dozen years in Russian politics and the civil war.
Ulu-Muhammed moved along the frontier between Russia and the
steppe until, in 1437-1438, he encountered Russian forces at Belev.[7]
After his troops turned to looting at an unpropitious moment in
the battle, Ulu-Muhammed was defeated.   He opened negotiations
by sending a distinguished group of envoys to the Russian
commanders, who were the western appanage princes of Muscovy.
According to the chronicle, the delegation consisted of
Ulu-Muhammed's brother-in-law (*ziat'*) El'berdei, *daraga* prince
Usein Saraeva,[8] and Usein-khozia.   They bring from the defeated
khan the following proposal: he will give his son, Mamutek, and

other relatives as hostages (*zaklad*) to the Muscovites, protect the Russian Lands (from other Tatars?), and cease to ask for tribute (*vykhod*). In return for peace, in other words, he agreed to be "in the will" (*volia*) of the Russian princes.[9] Ulu-Muhammed had in effect offered to renounce his former pretensions to suzerainty over Russia and to become a Muscovite client or vassal. There is no reason whatever to doubt the reliability of this report. Such details in the chronicle as the names of the envoys and the terminology reinforce the narrative's credibility. The chronicler makes no remark about the former khan's offer, not even to say that as a refugee, Ulu-Muhammed was hardly able to collect tribute anyway, or that having lost the battle, he wasn't in much of a bargaining position. The Russian princes, however, were apparently thinking along these lines for they reject Ulu-Muhammed's suggestion. The Tatar commander responds with a surprise attack which proves successful. The chronicler criticizes the Muscovite princes for their stubbornness, in part because in their arrogant reliance on their own prowess they failed to accept an offer that would have forestalled the later Russian defeat. The two princes involved in the Belev incident were Vasilii's cousins, Dmitrii Krasnii and Dmitrii Shemiaka, sons of the now deceased Yurii Dmitrievich. Since this pair was not at the moment actively opposing Vasilii, the Muscovite civil war was in a temporary lull. However, the princes' failure to either contain Ulu-Muhammed or accept him into Muscovite service was to have profound consequences for their rival.

Following his defeat-turned-to-victory, Ulu-Muhammed moved eastward, though his exact route is not known. He appears to have threatened Moscow en route to Nizhnii Novgorod, where he found suitable winter quarters; there was adequate water and the abandoned buildings offered shelter from the wind and cold. The chronicle says that in 1445, Vasilii II challenged Ulu-Muhammed at Nizhnii Novgorod, and the Tatars gave ground, retreating to Murom. Vasilii went in pursuit, and Russian and Tatar forces met in battle outside Suzdal'. In a complete reversal of fortunes, Ulu-Muhammed was able to capture Vasilii. The Tatar commander immediately dispatched two envoys, Achisan and Bigika, to take word of this development to Moscow and Dmitrii Shemiaka, respectively. Bigika, however, carrying news of Vasilii's capture to his great enemy, was intercepted by soldiers loyal to Vasilii. When his envoy did not return, Ulu-Muhammed assumed that Shemiaka had killed or incarcerated him and was not amenable to terms. Hence, the former khan reached an agreement with Vasilii instead. In accordance with this arrangement, Vasilii was released after having sworn to pay a ransom (*okup'*). The prince returned to his capital accompanied by five Tatar envoys—Prince Seit Asan, Utesha, Kuraisha, Dylkhozia, and Aidar.[10]

Ulu-Muhammed's wisdom in releasing Vasilii on such terms has been questioned, but it is difficult to imagine what other advantage could have been extracted from the situation.[11] The ransom appears to have been much higher than usual, judging from the conspicuous presence of Tatar envoys to guarantee payment, and from the displeasure of the Muscovite populace. The ransom was expected to anger the Muscovites, and it did. The chronicle says that Vasilii was told that the Christians did not like the Tatars and would not pay. Dmitrii Shemiaka, the elders of the Troitse-Sergiev monastery, and the Muscovite *gosty* (merchant elite) found themselves in unanimous agreement: the ransom should not be paid.

According to several chronicles, the Devil moved Shemiaka, who wanted to be grand prince, to spread the following message: "The *tsar'* (Ulu-Muhammed) released the grand prince (Vasilii II) because the grand prince swore that the *tsar'* could sit in Moscow and in all Russian cities in our patrimonies, and (Vasilii) himself wished to sit in Tver'" (*Tsar' na tom otpustil velikogo kniazia, a on k tsariu tseloval, chto tsar' sideti v Moskve a na vsekh gradekh Russkikh i na nashikh otchinakh, a sam sochet sesti na Tferi*).[12]

Note that Ulu-Muhammed, a renegade without a throne, is still titled *tsar'* because he is a Chingisid. This entire accusation against Vasilii is sheer fantasy. He had not agreed to renounce his throne, and Grand Prince Boris Aleksandrovich of Tver' would have had something to say about Vasilii relocating in his city. It is the claim of Shemiaka's message that Vasilii has forsaken Russian sovereignty, and that as a result the Tatars under Ulu-Muhammed will directly rule in the Russian cities. This annal makes no mention of the ransom; to interpret the claim that Ulu-Muhammed would sit in Moscow as a distortion of the role of the Tatar envoys sent to collect the ransom is stretching a point.

Vasilii escapes the rising opposition to his settlement with Ulu-Muhammed by a timely pilgrimage to the Troitse monastery. Here he is warned that his enemies are coming to seize him. The description of his behavior in the chronicles is modeled on that of the passion-suffering Russian saints like Boris and Gleb. He declines to flee, accepts his fate, and awaits his capture in prayer. Vasilii II was blinded, deposed, and exiled.

The chronicles record the charges against him as made by the appanage prince Ivan of Mozhaisk.[13]   "Why did you bring the Tatars into the Russian Land and give them cities and districts in *kormlenie* (i.e., governorships)?   You love the Tatars and their speech beyond measure and without mercy, and you give gold and silver and property to the Tatars" (*Chemu esi Tatar privel na Russkuiu zemliu, i gorody dal esi im i volosti podavil esi v kormlenie? a Tatar liubish i rech' ikh pache mery, a krest'ian pomish pache mery bez milosti, a zlato i srebo i imenie daet Tatarom*).   Parts of this indictment are just the inevitable exaggeration of the facts. Vasilii had brought Tatars into the land (albeit five envoys) and although he hadn't given them gold and silver yet, he planned to. Some of the other charges are less easily explained.

What cities and districts could Vasilii have given to the Tatars in *kormlenie?*   Holders of these governorships (literally, "feedings") were expected to remunerate themselves from the fees and revenues collected in office. Certainly no infidel nomad could ever have been given a Russian city to rule, but in some cases the incomes from cities were assigned to Tatars. The question is whether Vasilii II had done this, as accused. The chronology of the founding of Moscow's client khanate of Kasimov is highly controversial,[14] but the essential facts are these: Ulu-Muhammed's son Mamutek murdered his father and founded the khanate of Kazan'.   His other two sons fled their patricidal brother and entered Muscovite service, as their father has proposed in 1437-1438, founding the Muscovite serving khanate of Kasimov. It is possible that the founding of Kasimov panicked the Muscovite citizenry and contributed to the rise of Shemiaka, but this is an inference only, since the chronicles never mention the establishment of that client state.[15]   Also, it is unlikely that the grant of the *Meshcherskie mesta*, the lands of the Finno-Ugric peoples of the Volga and the abandoned city of Gorodets, would have worried the Muscovites at all.   Russian cities were eventually assigned in *kormlenie* to Kasimov *tsarevichi*,[16] but this would not have happened until sometime after the founding of the Kasimov khanate, and cannot justify the accusations against Vasilii II. It seems clear that Ivan of Mozhaisk's charge that the grand prince had given cities to the Tatars in *kormlenie* was as false as Shemiaka's claim that the grand prince meant to give Moscow to Ulu-Muhammed.

Vasilii's enemies invented and manipulated these fantastic rumors and accusations because they were powerful political weapons, given the mood of the populace.[17] The sight of Vasilii II and his Tatar entourage collecting an onerous ransom was transformed rhetorically into the imposition of Mongol rule, into the idea that Tatars would "sit" in the Russian cities or be granted *kormlenie*. It is quite possible that the perpetrators and disseminators of these claims were fully aware of their falsehood. Finally, there is no confirmation that Vasilii even knew the Tatar language, much less "loved" it. Ulu-Muhammed was Vasilii's enemy, captor, and blackmailer. It is doubtful that the grand prince loved the Tatars. In the long run, of course, Vasilii was ruined by the size of the ransom and perhaps by the heavyhanded way in which it was extracted from his people. The outcome of the civil war was determined by politically sophisticated classes who could hardly have been deceived by the wild accusations, even if they found them useful.

Only in the midst of a vicious civil war could a grand prince have been subjected to such ideological attacks on the Tatar issue. It is interesting what the chronicles have retained. Shemiaka's speech is inspired by the Devil and thus by definition a lie, yet the chroniclers judged it meet to include it in their record. Similarly, though the account of Vasilii's fall casts the grand prince as an imitator of Christ and a martyr, the bookmen still thought it best to record Ivan of Mozhaisk's indictment. Perhaps the fluid political atmosphere during the civil war, when Moscow changed hands more than once, prompted the chroniclers, almost as a defensive measure, to tell the story the way it was.

A measure taken in defense of Vasilii shows that in Russian politics of the day, the Tatar issue was a two-edged sword that might be turned against anyone. Vasilii's supporters in the Russian Orthodox Church organized a council of bishops[18] which composed a circular letter ostensibly addressed to Shemiaka but intended to reach a broader audience. This letter blamed Shemiaka for bringing Tatars into the Russian Land and for the fact that they had not left. At the same time, it accused him of failing to recognize the authority of the khan and of engaging in

treasonous dialogues with Kazan'.[19] This epistle attests to both the
seriousness of the Tatar issue at the time and the opportunistic
way it was manipulated even by the hierarchs of the Russian
church.

During Vasilii's exile, a group of Tatar *tsarevichi* who were
loyal to the grand prince, Kaisim, Yakup Makhmetovich, and
Berdodat' Kudurdatovich, fled to Lithuania in the company of
like-minded Russian *boyare*. None were willing to serve a traitor,
i.e., Shemiaka.[20] Upon their return to Muscovy, they encountered
a local group of Vasilii's Russian supporters but nearly came to
blows before discovering that all were on the same side.[21] These
Tatars are the future minions of Kasimov, who served in Vasilii's
armies at Novgorod and Kazan' in the later years of his reign.
This annal validates the suspicion that the founding of Kasimov
was somehow precipitated by internal Russian politics—namely the
civil war—rather than purely as a result of such external concerns
as the need for defense along the southern and southeastern
frontiers against the Tatars, in particular those of Kazan'. It also
indicates that despite the importance of anti-Tatar public opinion
in Vasilii's overthrow, his reinstatement was due in part to Tatar
assistance.

The anti-Tatar rhetoric chracteristic of texts from the time of
the Muscovite civil war is especially striking in contrast with the
neutral account of the Horde's role as arbitrator in 1432. It is
tempting to infer that this change reflects the waning power of the
Golden Horde as it fragmented, producing the khanates of Kazan'
and Kasimov, as well as Astrakhan' and the Crimea.
Unfortunately, I doubt that this is a justifiable conclusion. The
change in tone in the chronicles is sharp and precisely dated, while
the disintegration of the Horde was an almost imperceptibly
gradual process. To attempt to correlate the two seems most
problematic.

Instead, the vehemence of anti-Tatar expressions in
manuscripts of the 1440s is a symptom of the turmoil within
Muscovy rather than a sign of any abrupt change in Russo-Tatar
relations or in Russian perceptions of these relations. Attacking
rivals with accusations of Tatar dealings was a time-honored
tradition in Russia, and the extreme circumstances of the civil war
simply resulted in extreme indulgence in this sort of opportunistic
progaganda. And for such charges to have force, the Tatars

themselves must be made to look particularly bad. The vicious and unscrupulous political attacks from this era make it very hard to accept the theory that some redactions of texts about Kulikovo and Donskoi are mid-fifteenth century allegories designed to subtly criticize the actors in the Muscovite civil war. (Furthermore, the alleged allegories contain accusations—such as the claim that Mamai desired to impose Islam and *baskaki*—which find no echo in the annals of the civil war.) Subtlety had no place in the atmosphere of the time.

        Despite the extensive discussion of the Tatars in texts from this period, the chronicles do not address the actual nature of the relationship between Russia and the Horde. The account of the debate at the Horde relates the facts without comment and maintains a cautious neutrality with regard to the Tatars. Clearly it was impossible for the author, a partisan of Vasilii, to engage in anti-Tatar rhetoric when both villain and hero were so thoroughly compromised. The accounts of Russia's misadventures with the renegade Ulu-Muhammed were able to ignore the question of Russia's relationship with the legal khan. In any case, Vasilii II and Shemiaka and their supporters dealt in anti-Tatar sloganeering only in pursuit of short-term political advantages. Any polemic concerning Russian aspirations for libertion from the Tatar Yoke would have been incomprehensible to them.

Chapter VI:

Liberation

For Muscovy, 1480 was certainly both the best and the worst
of times. The once invincible Golden Horde was but a shadow of
its former self, fragmented into several warring khanates, yet the
nomadic core, the Great Horde under Khan Akhmat, was still
capable of agressive action against Russia. And while the Crimean
khanate and the Nogai Tatars were powerful allies of Muscovy, the
Great Horde had cast in its lot with the Polish-Lithuanian
Commonwealth, and the Livonian Knights were always willing to
join an anti-Muscovite coalition. Within Russia, Muscovy was
successfully uniting under its aegis all of the northeast, but Grand
Prince Ivan III was hamstrung by the political opposition of his
brothers. (Ivan, though a shrewd statesman, was cautious to a
fault, and many of his actions give the appearance of cowardice.)
In the midst of such complex and contradictory times, the high
drama of Russia's liberation from the Tatar Yoke occasionally
seemed a comedy of errors.

Indeed, historians have disagreed about the significance of the
events of 1480, some minimizing their importance, while others
have extolled them as having world-wide implications.[1] But
neither skeptics nor eulogists have taken serious note of what the
Russian sources themselves say or do not say regarding the
meaning of 1480 for Russo-Tatar relations. Even those who have
been highly critical of the tendentiousness of the texts, and pointed
to late origins, have been largely concerned with domestic
Muscovite politics and in evaluating the performance of Ivan III.
The significance for Russo-Tatar relations of the "Stand on the
Ugra River" has been taken for granted but not explored. This
discussion will slight other aspects of the texts and concentrate on
the treatment of the events of that year in terms of Russia's
relationship with the Mongols. The diversity of the sources
concerning 1480 is greater than for any other event in Russo-Tatar
history. The only way to appreciate this heterogeneity as well as
the evolution of Muscovite opinion is to analyze the material text
by text.

Just when Muscovy ceased paying tribute to the Great Horde cannot be established, in part because the grand prince continued to collect it from his people. No chronicle ever mentions that the payments to the Horde had stopped. Embassies, in any case, continued to be exchanged, though the sources do not usually explain their purposes. The actual course of Russo-Tatar diplomacy in preparation for the confrontation of 1480 remains a matter of conjecture.[2] In 1476, Khan Akhmat sent his envoy Bochiuk to Moscow, summoning Ivan III to the Great Horde. Ivan did not go.[3] From their efforts to organize coalitions and forge alliances, it is obvious that both sides were anticipating a military show-down.

Of all the factors that have been considered as causes of the conflict between Ivan III and Akhmat, the one that need be taken least seriously is the role of the grand princess, Sofia Paleologina. Sofia was the niece of the last Byzantine emperor. The Pope had arranged her marriage to Ivan III in the hope that Ivan would launch a crusade against the Ottoman Turks to reclaim the throne of Constantinople; this hope was not fulfilled. Sofia, according to the travel account of Sigismund von Herberstein, envoy of the Holy Roman Empire to the court of Vasilii III, complained to her spouse of the ignominy of marriage to a servitor of the barbaric Tatars. When Ivan was obliged to greet mounted Tatar ambassadors on foot, Sofia persuaded him to feign illness and avoid the disgrace. In a vision, Sofia received instructions to build a church on the site of the house in Moscow used by the Tatars as an intelligence center. Ivan, always sympathetic to the wishes of his exalted bride, granted her request and never again gave the Tatars a house in the city. Whether this legend has the least validity is open to dispute. Certainly Sofia's revulsion at Ivan III's tenuous subservience to the Tatars is fanciful,[4] and would have had no bearing on the Stand on the Ugra. (In any case, Sofia's behavior in 1480 should have dispelled any belief in her deep-seated opposition to the Tatars. She became a controversial figure in Muscovy because of her role in the dynastic crisis at the turn of the sixteenth century.)

Scholars have disagreed over which narrative about 1480 is most authoritative and whether the various chronicle accounts are contemporary or reflect the political tensions of the Muscovite dynastic crisis that took place a score of years later.[5] The limitations of the fundamental chronicle accounts have not been fully appreciated, in part because the events themselves are almost too well known.

This is the story the chronicles tell.[6] The godless *Tsar'* Akhmat of the Great Horde (*Bol'shaia orda*) wishes to imitate Batu and destroy and "plunder" (*pleniti*) all Orthodox Christians. To this end he concludes an alliance with King Casimir of Poland, but waits in vain for Polish military assistance. This is because Mengli-Girei, the khan of the Crimea, in accordance with his pact with Ivan III, attacked Podolia and distracted the Polish forces. (Although the narrative does not mention it, a revolt under Prince Belskii of the East Slavic population of Lithuania-Ukraine also helped to keep Casimir's attention elsewhere.) The Muscovite and Tatar armies stare at each other from either side of the Ugra river. The armies exchange arrows and insults, but the river, not yet frozen, remains impassible. Two of Ivan's courtiers, Grigorii Andreevich Mamon and Ivan Vasil'evich Oshchera, are evil and avaricious, traitors to Christianity and accomplices (*ponorovniki*) of the Muslims. They counsel caution but cannot persuade Ivan to retreat from his position on the river. Then the river freezes but neither Russians nor Tatars advance. Instead a miracle occurs, and both sides simultaneously retreat. Later *Tsar'* Ivak of the Nogais, along with his brothers-in-law Murza and Yamgurchii, attacks the Great Horde. Ivak slays Akhmat in combat. Thus, the chronicler piously concludes, did God "save" (*izbavi*) the Christians from the infidel Tatars.[7]

The constraints underlying Ivan III's caution in 1480 are well known. His brothers, unhappy with Ivan's distribution of lands, refused to commit their troops pending a settlement more to their liking; there may well have been connivance with Akhmat, Casimir, or both. In addition, the threat from Muscovy's western neighbors must also have been a factor. Finally, Ivan's reputation for indecisiveness was not undeserved. His wife, Sofia, does not seem to have had great confidence in Moscow's forces, for during the stand on the river, at a time when she was in no immediate danger, she followed the example of Donskoi's wife, Evdokiia, in 1382 and made off for safer climes with her children and the treasury. This probably did not endear her to the citizens who had to stay behind. The personal courage of both Ivan III and Sofia is a sensitive point in Russian history.

The Tatars' intentions in the chronicle account are the customary ones. *Tsar'* Akhmat wishes to imitate Batu and destroy

Russian Christians by "plundering" Russia. The connection between Batu and Akhmat is not one of inheritance or reclaiming a lost possession. The latter merely wishes to emmulate the legendarily successful raids of the former. Two hundred and forty years after Batu, a khan of the Horde is simply continuing a tradition of "plundering" Russia—*pleniti* can hardly mean "conquer." Furthermore, the antagonism between Ivan III and Akhmat in the chronicle is not political, but religious. Thus, the two *boyare* who try to dissuade Ivan from meeting the Tatar threat are religious more than political traitors.

The religious cast of the narrative carries through to the very end, when the chronicler, without the least sense of irony, explains that Christianity triumphed over the infidels, and Akhmat got his just desserts when he was killed by Ivan's Muslim allies, the Nogai Tatars. So God saved the Christians from another "plundering."

In fact, after 1480, the Great Horde never again launched an attack directed at Moscow, and the Stand on the Ugra had been a last-ditch attempt to restore its influence over Muscovy. Yet while it is apparent from the attention the chronicler devotes to the incident that he considered it important, the concept of the liberation of Russia from the Tatar Yoke is nowhere to be found in the narrative. Nor is there any hint, apart from the stereotypic reference to Batu as a role-model, that there had ever been a political relationship between Russia and the Mongols, much less one that hung in the balance in 1480. In keeping with the practice in Russian texts ever since 1237, the chronicler avoids the concepts of conquest and its inverse, liberation. While aware of the significance of the events of 1480, the bookman has adhered to the ideology of silence in shunting aside questions of political suzerainty in favor of hostile religious rhetoric. Thus in contemporary writings on the battlefield, the two and a half centuries of the Tatar Yoke ended with a wimper.

That the later chronicles that incorporated this account did not alter its content or lexicon with regard to Russo-Tatar relations makes the significance of this observation more apparent. With the passage of time the "Tatar scare" of 1480 would have worn off. More important, it would have become increasingly obvious in retrospect that the Stand on the Ugra marked the Great Horde's last major offensive against the Russian forest zone. Yet the ideology of silence rigidly excluded these perspectives from the narrative of 1480.

A number of later chronicles did append to the essential narrative a lament concerning the fate of the South Slavs, which touched upon the historical implications of the Stand on the Ugra. The ethos of this text seems most consistent with that of the *Khronograf* of 1512, which sought to integrate Russian, South Slavic, and Byzantine history in a Christian and teleological vision of the world.[8] Despite the actual behavior of the Russian armies in 1480, this text lauds their bravery in standing up to the Tatars[9] to protect the "fatherland" (*otechestvo*) from looting and to defend women and children. Its intent is to contrast Russia, where men are brave, with the lands suffering under the Ottoman Turks. In Bulgaria, Serbia, Greece, Trebizond, the Morea, Arbonasy (Albania?), Croatia, Bosnia, Mankup (in the Crimea), and Kaffa, cowards fled to strange (*chuzhye*) lands rather than fight the infidel. The Orthodox Christians of Russia, thanks to the protection of the Virgin, were spared the fate of the other lands.

Much has been made of the Russian perception of a parallel between the fate of the Balkans under the Ottomans and the fate of Russia under the Tatars. And in later centuries, however cynically this feeling may have been manipulated by Russia's rulers, some segments of the Russian population were genuinely sympathetic with the plight of their fellow Slavs. However, this passage bespeaks a slightly different perspective. First, the list of oppressed peoples is not restricted to Orthodox Christians. Croatia was Catholic; "Kaffa" may be an anachronistic reference to the Genoese, and "Mankup" could be an allusion to the Crimean Goths. Second, the author is not at all sympathetic with the fate of these Ottoman subjects. He accuses them of cowardice and irresolution, and there is no suggestion that they deserve any help. It should be noted that many of the South Slavic intellectuals, all of them clerics, had showed up in Muscovy as refugees.

The ideational framework of this text suggests what became known as the ideology of Moscow, the Third Rome, and in keeping with that ideology, his concerns are religious rather than political. Russian bravery and success arise from the true Russian Orthodox faith, which has earned Russia the protection of the Virgin. The Christians who have fallen before the Ottomans have simply suffered the inevitable consequences of errant faith. The contrast is between the fates of good and bad Christians, not between a Russia liberated from the Tatar Yoke and a Balkan peninsula under Ottoman suzerainty. Nor does the author take a messianic

view of things. He does not propose that Russia spread her brand
of Orthodox Christianity into the stricken areas, or that the Balkan
and Anatolian peoples improve their faith and dispose of their
oppressors. He does not even adjure the enumerated peoples to
imitate Russian bravery, since the text is not addressed to them
anyway. Given the author's evident distaste for emigres, it does
not appear that Greeks or South Slavs seeking military, political, or
even eleemosynary assistance would have received a sympathetic
hearing from him.

In order to engage in this exercise in self-congratulation, the
author of this text had to make a very generous interpretation of
the Russian action on the Ugra river. He did so, however, without
departing from the apolitical conceptual framework of Russo-Tatar
relations found in the main narrative.

The bishop of Rostov and father-confessor (*dukhovnii otets*) to
Ivan III in 1480 was Vassian Rylo. Vassian was a militant
member of the Josephan faction of the Russian Orthodox Chruch
and the most outspoken advocate of an offensive policy against
Akhmat. The Russian chronicles contain an epistle allegedly
written by Vassian to Ivan during the Stand on the Ugra and
designed to strengthen Russia resolve in the face of the Tatar
threat. If Vassian was the author of the "Epistle to the Ugra
river" (*Poslanie na Ugru*), then the text is indeed contemporary,
for the bishop died in 1481. There is, however, a school of
thought which holds that the epistle is a product of the infighting
in the Muscovite court early in the next century. With regard to
this question, the image of Ivan III in the text is crucial.[10] At
least as interesting is what Vassian says about Russo-Tatar
relations.

The epistle "travels" in the Russian chronicles with its own
contextual material, an introduction and a sort of epilogue about
what happened after the epistle was written. Both the text of the
epistle and the accompanying material are quite stable in the
chronicles.[11] The introduction explains that the people of Moscow
are terrified by Akhmat's campaign (*nakhozhdenie*). They spend
their time in prayer, which is the most effective defense against
infidels. Although Ivan III has intended to fight, evil-doers
discourage him. He removes his family and treasury from Moscow
and seems on the verge of abandoning his army on the Ugra. At
this point, Vassian's epistle begins. You are an Orthodox *tsar'*,
thunders the bishop. Do not listen to evil advice; be brave and

fight. Follow the examples of Igor' and Sviatoslav and Vladimir, who took tribute from the Greek *tsari*, of Vladimir Monomakh, who fought the Polovtsy, and of Dmitrii, who fought on the Don. You do not need to worry about your oath. It was extracted by coercion, and men of the church can release you from it. It was not an oath to a *tsar'* but to a brigand and savage and iconoclast (*razboinik i khishchnik i bogobortsa*). They call themselves *tsari*, but you are the Orthodox *tsar'*. Batu arrived and behaved like a brigand; he plundered (*plenil*) all our land, enslaved (*porabotati*), and took the title *tsar'* (*v"tsarisia*), but he was not a *tsar'* nor from an imperial clan (*ne ... ot tsarska roda*). This was only God's punishment for Russian sins, just as the Israelites were given in slavery (*rabota*) to Pharoah and foreigners (*inoplemenniki*). Rely on the *Tsar'* of Heaven and the Heavenly Host. The epistle ends with this exhortation, and the narrative continues. The people of Moscow complain that the grand prince rules mildly (*v drotosti i v tikhosti*). They fear they will be turned over to the Tatars of the *tsar'*, who is angry because the tribute (*vykhod*) has not been paid. The grand prince sends an envoy to the *tsar'* with gifts, asking that he not invade the *ulus* of the *tsar'* (*tsarev ulus*), and pointing out that the *tsar'* should not make war on (*voevati*) his own domain. The khan suggests that Ivan come to him and make obeisance, but the grand prince is afraid. He offers instead to send his son or his brother, but his counter-proposal is declined. Fedor Basenkov's embassy to the Horde accomplishes nothing, but the Tatars become afraid and depart. As in the regular narrative, the conclusion is anticlimatic, and there is no battle. Ivan III returns to Moscow and offers his thanks to God.

Although at the beginning of the entry the people of Moscow are behaving well, i.e., praying, their morale is not laudable. They fear the Tatar campaign (*nakhozhdenie*—the term for Tatar incursions ever since the time of Batu). After this the narrative is fairly consistent with other annals. The epistle itself is a literary *tour de force*, and its author was adept at the stentorian rhetoric of Byzantino-Slavic epistolary prose. Although the obvious purpose of the letter is to shore up Ivan's morale, it is clearly a highly partisan publicistic text not addressed to Ivan alone. Vassian rejects the argument that prudence is patriotic; to him, extremism in the defense of the Orthodox faith is no vice. But the full annal and the epistle cannot be simplistically categorized as patriotic, populist nationalism.[12]

Vassian begins by regaling Ivan with the deeds of the prince's glorious ancestors, reaching back to Kievan and even pre-Christian times. The list starts with Igor' and Sviatoslav, both of whom campaigned against the Byzantines, and includes St. Vladimir, citing the fact that he extracted tribute from the Greek *tsari*, i.e., the Byzantine *basilei*. In an image reminiscent of the "Tale of the Destruction of the Russian Land" (*Slovo o pogibeli russkoi zemli*), Vassian lauds Vladimir Monomakh for defeating the Polovtsy. The last hero alluded to is of course Donskoi, though Vassian does not mention whom he fought at the Don. The omission from this list of Aleksandr Nevskii, despite his successes against schismatic Catholic Germans and Swedes, is both curious and noteworthy. This edifying pantheon of Russian heroes draws no distinction between fighting Muslim Tatars, pagan Polovtsy, or Orthodox Christian Greeks. Russia's enemies, regardless of who they are, must be defeated.

Vassian turns now to the core of the matter, the Mongol khans and how much respect they deserve. Ivan III can consider himself absolved from any loyalty oath he has given the khan, because Akhmat is unworthy to receive such an oath. Using terms from the "Tale of Temir-Aksak," Vassian describes him as a criminal. In any case, for a non-Christian to call himself a *tsar'* is meaningless. Batu usurped the title when he ravaged the Russian Land, but he was not a real *tsar'*, and he succeeded only because God was using him to punish Russians for their sins. Vassian describes Batu's exploits with both the normative vocabulary—he "plundered" Russia—and the exaggerated didactic vocabulary that came into use in the sixteenth century—he "enslaved" Russia just as Pharoah enslaved the Hebrews. Cherniavsky offers the following analysis of Vassian's approach to Russo-Tatar relations:

> The archbishop is trying here to destroy the image of the khan-tsar by raising the image of the tsar-basileus; only one tsar is possible, the orthodox Christian one, and the other is an imposter. Yet in order to fight this imposter it is necessry, Vassian felt, to raise the Grand Prince to the role of tsar himself. What Vassian was trying to do was to solve an ideological problem. Ivan III's reluctance to face the khan in battle was caused by political and military fears, not by his awe before his sovereign. Yet, politically and militarily, the Tatars

remained a most serious danger for Russia not only during the fifteenth but also during the sixteenth century. Vassian's problem, the ideological problem, was not just to defeat the Tatars in battle—it was to destroy the image of the khan as tsar'.[13]

Vassian meant to resolve the ideological confusion between the tsar'/basileus and the tsar'/khan by deleting the latter factor from the equation.

To fight the false tsar', Ivan must be elevated to the status of true tsar'. (This Josephan tactic is not atypical; to exterminate the Judaizer heretics and protect ecclesiastical landholding, the Josephans would similarly imitate Byzantine imperial panegyric, cribbed from Agapetus.) Indeed, the Muscovite ruler will be the only tsar', since the Byzantine Empire had ceased to exist. To this end the epistle, while critical of Ivan, must exalt the grand prince as the God-crowned, God-chosen, God-given basileus.

Vassian's remarks about Batu are unprecedented. The bishop accuses Batu of usurping the title tsar', which no infidel can carry. Not even Cherniavsky appreciated the significance of Vassian's insistence that Batu was not of the imperial clan (rod). The bishop was not rejecting Batu's Chingisid status, but the very concept of a non-Christian imperial clan. Though this extremist statement is somewhat obscured by its rhetorical baggage, it is unique in medieval Russian history, for it is nothing less than a rejection of the principle of Chingisid legitimacy. Other Russian texts had castigated such non-Chingisids as Mamai and Timur as usurpers, but the very premise of such attacks was acceptance of the Chingisid principle. In Vassian's vision, the very founder of the Golden Horde was a usurper, and so too were all of his descendents down to and including Akhmat. Despite the development of the Muscovite autocracy and the use in Muscovy of Byzantine imperial doctrines in the sixteenth century, Vassian's claims were never echoed during the reign of Ivan IV. In raising the status of Ivan III, Vassian had gone too far in denigrating the dynasty of Chingis Khan. He had confronted the Chingisid issue too squarely, and his solution gathered intellectual dust in subsequent decades.

For all the revolutionary ramifications of Vassian's epistle, the bishop does not call for the liberation of Russia from the Tatar Yoke. He sticks with the customary lexicon of Russo-Tatar relations which finesses any political theory. Vassian's political framework is that of Exodus: the Russians are the Israelites, Ivan III is Moses, and Akhmat is Pharoah. Ivan can prevent the enslavement of the Russians by stopping Akhmat. The apparent logical contradiction between the fact that Akhmat is about to enslave Russia and the fact that Batu has already done so is unimportant. The slavery alluded to here is metaphorical, not political. Vassian merely urges Ivan to prevent further Tatar outrages, and there is no room in the bishop's *Weltanschauung* for such political terminology as conquest or liberation.

Whether or not the epistle was really written during the Stand on the Ugra, the text contains no hint of the outcome of the confrontation between Ivan III and Akhmat. Even if it were written after the event, it could not do so without undercutting its apparent authenticity. Thus there is no "pay-off," no declaration that Russia had been liberated from slavery, even within the ideational pattern of the text. The narrative that follows the epistle properly completes the emasculation of Vassian's polemic. The text repeatedly alludes to Akhmat as *tsar'*, without qualification, implicitly relegating Vassian's diatribe on Chingisid legitimacy to the rubbish heap of history. Furthermore, the Russian *tsar'* whom Vassian has exalted is considered weak by his people, who doubt his ability to protect them from Akhmat. (The connection between Ivan's "mildness" and the non-payment of tribute is unclear. Ivan continued to collect the tribute from his people; he simply had stopped forwarding it to the khan, beginning perhaps in 1476.) Far from acting the part of the fearless Orthodox Christian *tsar'*, Ivan seeks a compromise, even going so far as to call Russia a part of the *tsar''s ulus* (a tactic his father, Vasilii II, had successfully used with Ulu-Muhammed). Following the failure of this rather servile attempt at diplomacy, God's sure hand delivers Russia from the Tatars anyway.

In spite of the uneasy relationship between the narrative epilogue and the Epistle to the Ugra, the former appears in the chronicles only in the company of the letter. Yet, the account of the communications between Ivan III and Akhmat is historically plausible. The author was fully conversant with the lexicon and nuances of Russo-Tatar relations, and was obviously entirely uninfluenced by the epistle for which he had composed a frame.

In the Epistle to the Ugra, Vassian demonstrates once again that medieval Russian intellectuals conceived of Russo-Tatar relations in religious rather than political terms. Yet the text is most interesting for its attack on the Chingisid doctrine: it is the remarkable exception that proves the rule that the Russian bookmen avoided questioning the political principle upon which rested the empire of their conquerors.

Additional readings or passages concerning the Stand on the Ugra can be found in a variety of texts that appeared later than the basic narrative text and Vassian's epistle. These include several chronicle accounts, a tale, and another epistle. The first of these is in the *Vologodsko-Permskaia letopis'*. This chronicle contains both the regular narrative and Vassian's epistle, but adds some interesting details. Akhmat's envoy to Ivan III, who is named Temir, tells the prince that no tribute has been paid in eight years (which would date the termination of payment to 1472 rather than 1476). Akhmat's message contains an offer to give Ivan a grant (*pozhalovati*), presumably of a *yarlik*, if only the prince will petition properly. This account also develops further the analogy with Exodus, hailing Ivan III as the "emancipator" (*svoboditel'*) of the new Israel from the new Pharoah. The redactor is aware of the irony of the analogy, admitting that Ivan's victory over the godless Hagarenes was bloodless.[14]

The Ustiug chronicler, because of his geographical position, was well placed to gather intelligence concerning steppe affairs. Although the new material in the Ustiug chronicle contains nothing of an ideological nature, the additional factual detail is so complete that it deserves our attention, particularly with regard to the death of Akhmat. According to this annal, *Tsar'* Ivak Shabanskii takes one thousand Cossacks (*kazaki*) with him when he joins the Nogais. (This is most illuminating, since it explains that Ivak was from the Shibanid khanate in Siberia, and shows how the Nogais, who had no khanate or regular dynastic line, happened to be led by a Chingisid in 1480.) Ivak and his brother-in-law, the Nogai Musu mirza, along with Yamgurchei and fifteen thousand *kazaki*, cross the Volga and chase Akhmat as far as the Don. There, at Bela Vezha on the Donets at Malom near Azov, they launch a surprise attack, catching Akhmat in his sleep. Ivak personally kills the khan. After spending five days looting the Great Horde, Ivak and his men recross the Volga. Ivak's envoy, Chiumgura, bears the good news to Ivan and receives gifts and honor in return.[15] There seems no reason to doubt the accuracy of this supplementary narrative.

Further elaboration appears in a newly-discovered brief tale about 1480 which embellishes the diplomatic exchange between Ivan III and Akhmat. The grand prince tells the khan, "my predecessors were under oath not to raise their hands against the *tsar'*." The Tatar replies with questions: Why has Ivan neither paid tribute nor addressed Akhmat as *tsar'*? Why has he raised his sword and spear, forgetting the assistance he has received from the Tatar princes and lords? Akhmat predicts that Ivan will meet the fate of the *tsari* of Kazan'; Akhmat will bring the Russians under his sword, like his father.[16] This dialogue draws upon the Tale of Tokhtamysh, *sub anno* 1382, and apparently from the Epistle of Edigei of 1408. In Lur'e's opinion, it contributed to the fantasies of the *Kazanskaia istoriia* for 1480.

The *Stepennaia kniga* also makes a contribution to the lore of 1480. This "Imperial Book of Degrees," written in the time of Metropolitan Makarii, is replete with religious bombast, prophecy, and pretension and represents sixteenth-century Muscovite ideology at its zenith. It records, in addition to the regular narrative of 1480 and Vassian's epistle, a prophecy attributed to Saint Iona, archbishop of Novgorod. The prophecy says that "the Russian autocrats will not be under the region of the *tsari* of the Horde" (*Rus'stii samoderzhtsy ne imut byti pod oblastiiu Ord"skikh tsarei*). This passage as it stands would seem to mean that Russia would not remain "within the region" or "as part of the sphere of influence" of the Horde, awkward constructions at best. Probably a scribe made an error in copying *pod vlastiiu*, i.e., "under the authority" of the Horde. It is typical of the *Stepennaia kniga* in that it refers to all Russian grand princes since Riurik as autocrats. The passage does not reflect Vassian's rejection of Chingisid legitimacy; the khans of the Horde are *tsari*. The narrative explains in greater detail that both the Russian and the Tatar forces on the Ugra were waiting for the river to freeze but withdrew when it became possible to cross. In this version, Ivak, having slain Akhmat, sent this message to Ivan III: "Thus will all perish who wish to harm the God-chosen Russian tsardom!" (*Tako bo pogibnet vziak, khotia ozlobiti bogoizbrannoe i Rosiiskoe tsarstvie!*). This is a ludicrous thing for a Muslim to say, as well as being an obvious anachronism. It was no doubt meant to flatter Ivan IV following his imperial coronation.[17]

The last step before the *Kazanskaia istoriia* in the evolution of accounts of the events of 1480 is another epistle, this one written in the 1550s and addressed to Ivan IV in connection with the campaign against Kazan'. It is variously attributed to Ivan IV's father confessor, Sil'vestr, or to Metropolitan Makarii. In a biblical reference, the epistle claims that "all the *tsari* of the earth and all peoples will bow down" in subservience to Ivan IV, the Orthodox Christian *tsar'*. The epistle accords cosmic significance to four events in world history: the victory at Jerusalem of the Hebrew Judge Ezekial, the defense of Constantinople against the infidels by Emperor Constantine IV Pogonatus in 674–678, the similar defense by Emperor Leo III in 717, and the Stand on the Ugra river. As the epistle describes this event, *Tsar'* Akhmat of the Great Horde attacked the Russian Land in 1480, intending to plunder (*plenil*) it. Although he desired to be ruler (*vlastets*) over the land, he failed. All of his *tsarstvo* and clan (*rod*) perished, his places (*mesta*) became empty, and God freed (*osbodi*) *Rus'* from the unclean infidels. The realm (*derzhava*) and glory (*slava*) of Akhmat were eliminated.

Although this epistle[18] is supposedly derived from that of Vassian, it does not endorse his anti-Chingisid ideology. It is also conventional in its treatment of Akhmat's motives. As we have observed before, Russian texts were willing to deal with the concept of suzerainty when the infidels who desired it failed. Hence the epistle asserts that Akhmat wanted to become the ruler of Russia, though of course it associates his invasion with his desire to *plunder* the Russian Land, the standard neutral verb. (The epistle does not mention Batu, the Tatar Yoke, or any Mongol conquest.) After Akhmat's failure, the Russians were freed, though it is not clear from what. The Great Horde no longer poses a threat to Russia because it no longer exists. Indeed it is this latter aspect of the epistle that is interesting. The text telescopes the punitive expedition of Ivak and his Nogais in 1480 with the final destruction of the Great Horde at the hands of the Crimeans in 1502. In fact, the epistle omits Ivak's role entirely, as it equates the Stand on the Ugra with the end of the Tatar problem. At last, three quarters of a century after the fact, the Stand on the Ugra had acquired its ideological importance as the demise of the Great Horde.

Yet the greatest revision of Russian perspectives on the Stand on the Ugra was not to appear in the texts until another milestone in Muscovite history, the annexation of the khanate of Kazan'. When this triumph was followed by the acquisition of the khanate of Astrakhan' at the mouth of the Volga, Muscovy assumed mastery of the entire Volga artery, increasing her wealth from international commerce and opening vast territories of Slavic colonization. Although the Tatar threat was far from over—the Crimean khanate remained dangerous until the eighteenth century—Russian influence extended deeply into the steppe. As the first step in this expansion, the conquest of Kazan' was much glorified in Muscovite literature and thought, and nowhere more so than in the lengthy and vivid narrative tale, the *Kazanskaia istoriia*. While most scholars acknowledge that this text's literary history, manuscript tradition, and textological evolution require further study, it is generally thought to be a product of the 1560s.[19] The *Kazanskaia istoriia* contains a narration of the events of 1480 which is crucial to an analysis of Muscovite retrospective evaluations of that so-called "liberation from the Tatar Yoke."

This text[20] begins with recapitulation of the exploits of Batu. Batu plundered (*plenil*), took (*vzial*), and enslaved (*porabotal*) *Rus'* and collected tribute for the Golden Horde (*Zlataia orda*, the earliest recorded usage of the name). The text says that Batu exacted *vykhod, dan'*, and *obrok*. *Vykhod* and *dan'* were commonly used to refer to the Tatar tribute, but *obrok* commonly meant the dues that serfs owed to their masters. The bookman explains that Batu gave power (*vlast'*) in *Rus'* to whomever he chose, illegally and not by generation, not by clan (*ne po kolenu, ni po rodu*). From Batu's time until the *tsarstvo* of Akhmat, son of Zeleni Saltan, and the reign of Ivan III, the barbarians held a great and evil and proud authority (*vlast'*) over the Russian Land. During that epoch the beauty (*krasota*) of *Rus'* vanished (*pogibsha*), and there was oppression (*nasilie*). Then the blessed Ivan III "took and enslaved under him Great Novgorod." Because he could no longer endure Tatar oppression, he ceased paying tribute and purchasing authority over *Rus'* in the Golden Horde (*vlasti ruskiia kupiti*).[21]

Akhmat sends envoys to Ivan III, demanding obedience according to the old custom. They have brought with them a "physical portrait of Akhmat's person" (*basma parsunu*), expecting Ivan to bow down before it. Enraged, Ivan tramples the image underfoot and orders all but one of the envoys executed for making such an insulting suggestion. The survivor brings the news of Ivan's refusal and the manner of it to Akhmat. Akhmat in turn becomes furious at the slaying of his envoys and the insult to his honor; he wants to destroy Moscow the way his grandfather, Tokhtamysh, had done. The khan brings his entire army (*vsia sila*; literally, entire strength) to the Ugra river, and is amazed that his "false slave" (*mnimago raba*; disloyal slave?) has mustered the courage to oppose him. Ivan dispatches the Gorodets *tsari* to attack Akhmat's rear. They plunder (*plenil*) the Tatar Land and desire to destroy (*razoriti*) the *yurt* of Batu. Once in Sarai, however, Ulan Obliaz' reminds the Kasimov khans that they are of the same clan (*rod*) as the rulers of the Great Horde (i.e., Chingisids), dissuading them from carrying their mission to its logical conclusion. In the meantime, Akhmat abandons his position on the Ugra and meets his end at the hands of Ivak and the Nogais. "And thus ended the *tsari* of the Horde, and by such divine intervention the *tsarstvo* and great power of the Golden Horde perished (*pogibe*). And then in our Russian Land we were freed from the burden (*yarmo*) and submission (*pokorenie*) to the Muslim (*busurmanskogo*) and began to recover, as if from winter to clean spring." Ivan III justly won glory like that of St. Vladimir, the baptizer of *Rus'*, for Moscow, the second Kiev, the third Rome.

Although Tatishchev accepted the historical accuracy of the *Kazanskaia istoriia*'s narrative of 1480, historians have debated it even since.[22] That Ivan III ordered the serving Tatars of Kasimov/Gorodets to invade the Horde's territory and perhaps even to attack Sarai is not implausible. It at least offers a more historically satisfying explanation for Akhmat's abrupt withdrawal than divine intervention.[23] Although the dialogue with Ulan Obliaz' in Sarai is probably literary intervention, its premise makes sense in suggesting that the Kasimov *tsarevichi* might have been susceptible to an invocation of their Chingisid ancestry. It is unlikely, however, that such an argument would have had enough force to deter them from ravaging Sarai, for the Kasimov khans had no lost love for the Great Horde, which had expelled their ancestor, Ulu Muhammed. The most historically controversial detail in this narrative is Akhmat's *basma*. Of course, the scene of Ivan III trampling the khan's portrait underfoot makes for high drama (Eisenstein adapted it for the confrontation between Ivan IV and the envoys of Kazan' in his film, "Ivan the Terrible"). Yet, it is surely fantasy. First, Akhmat was a Muslim and such a portrait would have been forbidden.[24] Second, the episode is entirely inconsistent with Ivan III's known comportment at the time. Even the narrative that accompanies Vassian's epistle notes Ivan's

continuing desperate attempts at a negotiated settlement. It was
not Ivan's style to burn his bridges behind him, and such an
outrage to diplomatic immunity as putting envoys to the sword
would have guaranteed the war he was frantically trying to avoid.
The famous incident of the *basma* must be historical fiction.

However, for our analysis of Russian perceptions of
Russo-Tatar relations, the account of 1480 in the *Kazanskaia
istoriia* is an extraordinary document. Much of it is of course
conventional; Batu plundered, took, and extracted tribute. Too, he
is said to have "enslaved" *Rus'*, the common sixteenth-century
Muscovite extravagance that resonated with the imagery of Exodus
for 1480 and with the larger system of metaphors and ideas of
Russia as the New Israel. The imagery of Russia's sad state after
Batu is also commonplace, reviving the notion of "oppression"
(*nasilie*) found in Russian texts from the thirteenth and fourteenth
centuries. Yet this text has some striking new elements. The
term *obrok* for tribute has connotations of the relationship between
serf and master. The accusation that Batu disregarded genealogical
legitimacy in awarding political power in Russia, though quite
untrue, does elucidate the real nature of Russia's relationship with
the Horde. And the text goes further than any other in
conceptualizing the period from Batu to Akhmat as one of Tatar
sovereignty, *vlast'*, over Russia. In the *Kazanskaia istoriia*, 1480
was the year when Russia's burden (*yarmo*) and submission
(*pokorenie*) came to an end. The latter term explicitly denotes
political suzerainty. The verbal form appeared in the *vita* of
Alexandr Nevskii—Batu had *pokoril* (conquered? reduced to
submission?) many lands. The term *yarmo*, while it must be
differentiated from *igo*, "yoke," clearly has a similar sense.
Sil'vestr's epistle to Ivan IV had taken the step of equating the
events of 1480 with the end of the Great Horde. The author of
the *Kazanskaia istoriia*, drawing upon the epistle, found it possible
to present the Stand on the Ugra as the end of an era of Tatar
suzerainty. The *Kazanskaia istoriia* articulates a historical
conception of the period of Tatar dominion and recognizes, at the
intellectual level, the political relationship between Russia and the
Horde.

It would be going too far to say that the author of this
account presents a historically accurate picture of the end of the
Mongol period. As in Sil'vestr's epistle, the *coup de grace*
administered by the Crimeans in 1502 is conflated with the deeds

of Ivan III and Ivak in 1480. The author has manipulated the chronology so as to inflate the importance of the earlier episodes. It is difficult te escape the suspicion that the confusion of dates concerning the final destruction of the Great Horde was not a mistake, but deliberate strategy. The author was clearly familiar with Mongol history, as indicated by such details as the references to Chingisid ideology, Akhmat's genealogy, and the *yurt* (i.e., *ulus*) of the Great Horde. But while every Muscovite bookman after 1505 (when the last *"tsar'* of the Horde," Shaikh Akhmat, died) knew that the Great Horde was gone, only the author of the *Kazanskaia istoriia* voiced a historical perspective concerning Russia's genuine political status under the Mongols, its beginning and its end.[25] He did so in violation of the conceptual framework that Russian intellectuals had applied to Russo-Tatar relations for more than four hundred years. The widespread and long-held belief that the Stand on the Ugra was the definitive moment in the liberation of Russia from the Tatar Yoke owes much to the author of the *Kazanskaia istoriia.*

Finally, the most enigmatic of the sources on the Stand on the Ugra is the so-called "charter" (*yarlik*) of Akhmat to Ivan III.[26] The putative purpose of this document, actually an epistle, appears to be extortion, with Akhmat attempting to bully Ivan into submitting and paying the tribute. However, the language is so convoluted that it is difficult to extract any coherent political message. The epistle begins by invoking the sun, moon, stars, and so forth, an animistic *invocatio* which the Muslim Akhmat could never have used. Akhmat announces (absurdly) that he commands seventy hordes and alludes to an otherwise unattested "emblem" of Batu. He demands an astronomical amount of tribute, and, as if recognizing the fact, offers a plan for gradual payment.

Keenan has proposed that this text is a forgery and that the unique manuscript, dating from the seventeenth century, may be the original. In his view it is a pseudo-historical exercise in *turcica* by someone in the *Posol'skii prikaz* (Bureau of Foreign Affairs), a historical ballad in epistolary form, intended to satirize Tatar hauteur and bombast.[27] Certainly it is true that attempts to perceive any meaningful political message in the text have proven unsatisfactory.[28] The demand for tribute is more plausible if the epistle is considered a product of 1476 rather than 1480, but dating the epistle to four years before the Stand on the Ugra does not make its content any more coherent.[29] In any case, the epistle cannot be considered the product of Akhmat's chancellery by any stretch of the imagination. Although meant to seem of Tatar provenance, it was written in Muscovy for a Muscovite audience. Attempts have been made to interpret it as a garbled record of an oral message from Akhmat[30] or to compare it to the Mameluke model for correspondence with the Ilkhanid state,[31] but these do little to clarify the substance of the text. I think it is a mistake, however, to assume that because the text is not what it purports to be and survives only in a seventeenth-century manuscript, that it is necessarily a product of the seventeenth century. For example, the "epistle of Edigei" of 1408 was also a "forgery" and cannot be attested earlier than the 1440s. Nonetheless it remains a contemporary ideological work. While the *yarlik* of Akhmat does seem to have a hint of parody, it may have been written much closer in time to the Stand on the Ugra. It represents the literary/historical effort of an unknown author writing at an unknown time. So far, unfortunately, it has proved impenetrable.

As we have seen, the medieval Russian sources reveal that the importance of the Stand on the Ugra in Russian ideology underwent profound evolution during the three quarters of a century following Ivan's and Akhmat's confrontation. Innovations came gradually, and could be rejected when mistimed. An example of this was Vassian's attempt to discard Russian concern for Chingisid legitimacy. Long after the demise of the Great Horde, Muscovy had to deal with the often powerful Chingisid dynasties of Kasimov, Kazan', Astrakhan', and the Crimea.[32] The Chingisid principle remained so important in Russian politics and diplomacy that it would have been impractical to reject it. Vassian's epistle was recopied, but its anti-Chingisid content ignored. Despite such missteps, the pattern of changing Russian perspectives on 1480 is clearly discernible. Originally celebrated as just a successful episode in the resistance to the Tatars, the incident became increasingly laden with religious significance to emerge as an epoch-making clash between the forces of Christian truth and those of Muslim barbarism. Finally, through the conflation of the Stand on the Ugra with the liquidation of the Great Horde, the events of 1480 became synonymous with the emancipation of Russia from the "Tatar Yoke."

Chapter VII:

Conclusion

Any extended study structured around the detailed analysis and interpretation of each of a series of texts runs the risk of losing sight of the forest for the trees. Unfortunately, it is only by examining each tree with great care that one can be confident that one's conclusions about the shape of the forest will withstand criticism. Balancing micro-analysis of the trees with macro-analysis of the forest is always difficult and carries no guarantee of success.

But the task cannot be ignored. Conclusions about the Mongol impact on Russian history rest upon studies of Russo-Tatar relations during the thirteenth to fifteenth centuries. These studies rest in turn upon conclusions about what the medieval Russian sources have to say about such relations. The sources themselves can only be meaningfully interpreted in the light of the conceptual framework that determined how medieval Russia's scribes, redactors, and intellectuals thought and wrote about the Tatars. Failure to appreciate the perceptual approach of the medieval Russian bookmen, to analyze the world-view of our informants, can only result in erroneous conclusions concerning the Russian reaction to the Mongols, the nature of Russo-Tatar relations, and ultimately the entire impact of the Mongols on Russian history.

That the Russians were hostile to the Tatars during the Mongol period is a conclusion so obvious that it can easily lead us astray. The Tatars, after all, laid waste the Russian cities and countryside at an incalculable cost in lives and property. They then settled in for centuries of ruthless economic exploitation interspersed with further military incursions as needed. The medieval Russian narrative sources graphically describe the cruelty of Tatar oppression, and it is natural to assume that the Russians hated their Mongol conquerors. But to go no further than this in analyzing Russian attitudes toward the Tatars would be a mistake. First of all, this conclusion is too vague. We must explore for exactly what reasons and in exactly what ways the Russians were hostile to the Tatars, no matter how obvious such an inquiry may seem.   Second, by looking no further than Russian animosity we overlook several essential aspects of medieval Russian perceptions of the Mongols.   Only a comprehensive social and intellectual approach to Russian reactions to the conquest and the enduring Tatar presence can provide a solid basis for historical conclusions.

Russian hostility toward the Mongols took a very specific form.   With the exception of the fifth sermon of Serapion, the medieval sources unremittingly castigate the Tatars in religious terms.   In all of the Old Russian literature concerning the Mongols there is not a single racial epithet.   The Mongols are never attacked as "filthy Asiatics" or anything of the sort.   It was not until the nineteenth century that Russia became infected with the racist ideology of the Yellow Peril, a concept imported from Western Europe.   Nor are the Tatars lambasted as primitive pastoral namads, and indeed references to the Tatars' nomadic way of life are few and far between.   Though the Russians knew that the Mongols were not Occidentals and that they were by and large nomadic, they never attacked them on ethnic or cultural grounds. The Tatars were hateful because they were not Orthodox Christians, but infidels, pagans, Muslims, Ishmaelites, Hagarenes, *Besermeny*.   In the medieval devotional and confessional universe relations among peoples were defined in religious terms, and the fact that the Tatars were unbelievers outweighed all other considerations.   The implications of the medieval Russian religious perception of the Tatars have not been fully appreciated.

Religious exclusivism was the motive force of the ideology of silence characteristic of the medieval ethno-religious frontier.   The pragmatic realities of existence required considerable peaceful cooperation between religious enemies.   Yet at the same time ideological exigencies made it impossible to acknowledge any interactions other than hostile ones.   The concept of peaceful cooperation with infidels called into question the militant religious values forming the very foundations of these societies. Consequently, Russian bookmen generally recorded only the incidents of hostility between Russians and Tatars, passing over in silence such common phenomena as trading and military alliances between the two peoples, and downplaying the familiarity with Tatar affairs and customs which would betray an unseemly intimacy.   The bookmen spoke of the Tatars with hostility or not at all, and religion provided the vituperative vocabulary.   This gambit for avoiding the awkward ideological problems of occasional peaceful cooperation with religious enemies was commonplace along the medieval ethno-religious frontier, and Russian bookmen had become accomplished at it during Kievan times.

But the medieval Russian bookmen raised the ideology of silence to a a second and higher level. Russia had never before been subjugated by an alien, infidel power and lacked a historical theory to account for it. That God should allow the conquest of Russia posed an even thornier ideological problem than non-hostile interactions with unbelievers. Hence Russian intellectuals continued to describe Russo-Tatar relations using the vocabulary of the Kievan era, despite, or perhaps because of, its inappropriateness. The medieval sources present Russo-Tatar relations as they had presented, for example, Russo-Polovtsian relations—as a series of military clashes without consequences for political sovereignty. Russian intellectuals avoided the ideological problem of the Mongol conquest by effectively denying that it had occurred.

This conclusion about the perspective of the Russian texts is so fundamental to an unbiased interpretation of them that I have harped upon it while analyzing every text which is presumed to allude to changes in Russia's political status. If I have fallen into redundancy or even monotony it has been worth the price to make the point that when the Russian sources describe the Tatars' intention for two and a half centuries *pleniti* Russia, the verb implies not endlessly repeated conquest, but plundering. This is not to say the Mongol conquest and Russia's liberation were not realities, of course, or even that the Russian elite did not fully grasp the fact that Russia was part of a Mongol empire. The Russians were neither blind nor stupid, and the sources present the *realia* of Tatar rule *in extenso*—the vassal-like trips of princes and ecclesiastics to the Horde or even to Karakorum, the presence in the Russian forests of Tatar administrators and tax collectors, and Tatar expeditions sent to punish disloyalty or quell disorder. But while the Russian bookmen did not omit from their narratives the signs of the Tatar presence, they never addressed the issue of Russia's true status under the Horde or articulated any ideology of either conquest or liberation.

The Russian refusal to deal intellectually with the problem of the Mongol conquest was not the result of intellectual poverty. Indeed the monuments of Old Russian literature display in their narratives impressive flexibility and imagination. Nor is the "failure" of Russian thinkers to deal in political theory attributable to the lack of a "secular" tradition, since Arabo-Persian authors, operating completely within the Muslim religious framework, did acknowledge infidel rule even while loathing it as an abomination. It was simply not within the Russian historical experience to achieve equivalent perspectives on Russo-Tatar relations. Russia had never before been conquered from the East (and never would be again); for a unique historical experience there was no ready-made or easily acceptable theory. Russian authors had long rationalized Russian defeats as punishments for Russia's sins, but they were not willing to go so far as to imagine a God who would deliver them utterly into the hands of the infidels. The intellectual trick lay in maintaining the status quo in literature if not in life, recording the events of both conquest and liberation as discreet victories and defeats without consequences for political suzerainty.

Religion, which was the cause of the ideology of silence, also provided the means to sustain it. Since the Tatars, as unbelievers, were by definition evil, there was never any need to analyze their motives. Infidels were servants of the Devil whose only wish was to do harm to Christians. The political motives or strategic concerns of Mongol military expeditions in the Russian forest zone, which might have required dangerous explanation, could be ignored. Hence, Chol Khan's mission to Tver' in 1327 was to exterminate Christians. Similarly, Mikhail of Tver', in the previous century, was not executed for his part in an anti-Tatar rebellion, but instead was a martyr for the Orthodox Christian faith. By casting all Russo-Tatar relations in a religious context, the bookmen avoid discussing the political context that actually determined Horde actions. Of course, the medieval narratives do contain exceptions to this rule: we find that in Kursk *Baskak* Akhmat acted to squash opposition to his administration, and that in 1380, Mamai was seeking to avenge the death of his comrade Begich. Yet even in such cases the larger political picture is missing, and the essential fact that Russia had been conquered remains hidden.

The Russian bookmen were of course well aware that Russia had been subjected to the Mongols since the campaigns of Batu in the thirteenth century, and an occasional glimmer of this historical consciousness comes through. There is an implicit sense of history in the texts about Kulikovo or the Stand on the Ugra in which Mamai and Akhmat desire to repeat the exploits of Batu. It was not until the mid-sixteenth century, long after the collapse of Horde power, that a Russian author went so far as to establish the *termini* of a Mongol period stretching from Batu to (with a little manipulation) Akhmat. The forthrightness of this historical conception was absolutely revolutionary. Yet, even then there was no explicit articulation of the idea that these historical markers designated an era of Mongol suzerainty in Russia.

One of the most remarkable aspects of the ideology of silence as it was practiced in Russia during the Mongol period is the respect the bookmen show for the Mongol khans. Expertise in Chingisid dynastics was a *sina qua non* for Russia's princes and ecclesiastics, who had to enter into personal relationships with the khans if they hoped for successful careers. Russian assimilation of Chingisid doctrine is consistently apparent in the sources where other indications of Russia's peaceful or subservient relations with the Horde have been excluded. While the texts never acknowledge that the khans are Russia's rulers, they still betray the fact implicitly in the narratives. In many of the accounts, a khan's behavior only becomes intelligible once we have grasped the importance to the Russians of Chingisid legitimacy. Perhaps most striking are the texts from the Kulikovo epoch which accuse Mamai or Timur of *lèse-majesté* and actually present Moscow as the defender of Chingisid legitimacy. Bishop Vassian's "Epistle to the Ugra river," which was an attempt to undermine Chingisid legitimacy, only emphasizes the importance of the concept in medieval Russian political thought. Unable to reconcile respect for the khan/*tsar'* with the blanket condemnation of Tatars required by religious ideology, the Russian bookmen carefully discriminated between the actions of the khan, often presented as good or neutral, with the actions of the Tatars in general, which were uniformly heinous. On top of this, Russian ideologues achieved the extraordinary feat of exalting the rulers of the Horde without admitting that the khans were also the rulers of Russia. When we consider the complex and often contradictory effects of the Mongols on Russian political, social, economic, and cultural life, it is not surprising that the Russian intellectual response was often equally ambiguous.

The medieval ethno-religious frontier was inherently a transient phenomenon. The proximity of religious enemies was tolerated only as a necessary evil, and when changing circumstances made it possible to exterminate or expel them, the frontier disappeared or at least relocated. Thus, after many years of coexistence, the Spanish Catholics abruptly expelled the Moors and even the Moriscoes. The Abassids did away with the Byzantine institutions and bureaucratic personnel used by the Ummayad Empire, and the Ottoman Empire became far less tolerant of Orthodox Christianity in the sixteenth century than it had been in the fifteenth. In Russia, the frontier, which had existed long before the Mongols appeared, endured for some time after the collapse of Horde power. From 1480 to the 1550s, although Muscovy did not neglect its relations with such western powers as the Polish-Lithuanian Commonwealth, its primary foreign policy concerns were with the successor states of the Golden Horde, particularly Kazan'. Russia was independent but still within the Inner Asian pastoral nomadic universe. Not yet able to exercise its own power effectively in the steppe, Muscovy had to remain pragmatic about the infidel presence. The Muscovite *yam* (the postal system adopted from the Mongols) respected Muslim prohibitions against pork and alcohol, and Muslim envoys could take oaths upon the Koran in legal and business transactions, pray to Mecca within the Kremlin, and pronounce the name of the Ottoman sultan in the *hutba*. Respect for Chingisid legitimacy remained of paramount importance in dealing with the Horde's successor khanates and with such Mongol-influenced tribes as the Nogais. Indeed, when Ivan IV abdicated, his successor was Symeon Bekbulatovich, a baptized Chingisid.

With the annexation of Kazan' and Astrakhan' and the Livonian War, Muscovy turned its attention to the West. The steppe peoples were no longer the most serious threat, and Muscovite concern for Mongol or Muslim sensibilities rapidly faded. Muscovy's reorientation toward the West was accompanied by a surge of religious intolerance under Metropolitan Makarii characterized by forcible conversion, as the Russian Orthodox Church transformed Kazan' into a Christian city. As Muscovy evolved into an early modern European nation-state, its relations with Muslim or pagan steppe peoples became increasingly brutal and exploitative, a situation only exacerbated by the westernization of the Russian elite in the seventeenth and especially the eighteenth centuries.

In the middle ages the disintegration of the ethno-religious frontier usually resulted in an increase in religious diatribe in contemporary texts. Ideologues who had previously felt constrainted by the unacknowledged realities of pragmatic cooperation with the infidel, released the full flood of religious hostility when these limitations were removed. Among the major cultural activities undertaken in Moscow in the sixteenth century was the rewriting of Russian history. One would expect, following the elimination of the Tatar threat and forced accommodation, a total revision of the rather restrained and ambivalent presentations of Russo-Tatar relations in the sources from the Mongol period. Remarkably, this did not occur. It is true that in the great anthologies and chronicles written and assembled under Metropolitan Makarii's sponsorship the level of rhetoric and sheer verbiage rose dramatically, but there was little apparent change in Russian perspectives on Russo-Tatar relations during the Mongol period.

Texts from this time not only perpetuate the tradition of avoiding the concept of Tatar suzerainty, but they treat with some embarrassment those *realia* of Mongol power which bookmen of the Tatar period had mentioned without comment. Such phenomena were now declared to have been the custom (*obychai*) at the time. In literary analysis I believe this would be called a distancing device, a way of establishing psychological distance between what was done then and what one thinks should be done now. Also, *obychai* was a generic with a usage as varied as that of "custom" in modern English. There was no distinction between customs that were social or religious and those that were political. Thus in 1237, Vasil'ko was martyred for refusing to submit to Tatar "custom,"[1] and Mikhail of Chernigov met the same fate for refusing to observe the Tatar "custom" of walking between two fires.[2] At the same time, the texts say that Novgorod had the "custom" of feuding with the grand prince,[3] ringing a bell to summon the *veche*,[4] and expelling its own princes.[5]

The Sofia First Chronicle of the mid-fifteenth century says that when Mikhail of Tver' went to the Horde to receive his patrimony, he was following the custom of the Russian princes of his time. The chronicle also mentions that it was the custom of the Tatars to sow discord (*vrazhda*) among the Russian princes.[6] The *vita* of Metropolitan Alexei, recorded *sub anno* 1377 in the Moscow compilation of 1479, contains a similar sentence: Ivan II went to the Horde "because it is the custom to receive the grand principality there" (*iako zhe est' obychai vziati tamo velikoe kniazhenie*).[7] Other chronicles recording this Russo-Tatar interaction create even further distance either by changing the verb to the past tense or by adding the phrase that this was done "at

that time" (*v to vremia*).[8]   Though I could not find this sentence
in any form in the Nikon Chronicle's version of Alexei's *vita*, the
Nikon chronicler was clearly familiar with and even fond of this
construction with the term "custom."   He habitually uses the
device for explaining that things were done in a certain way during
the Mongol period (we have already discussed his interpolations in
the tale of *Baksak* Akhmat of Kursk and in the *vita* of Mikhail of
Tver').   In addition, the Nikon chronicler adds a new sentence *sub
anno* 1277 to set the stage for the rivalry between Andrei and
Dmitrii Yaroslavovichi for the grand princely throne: "They went
to the Horde to receive *yarliki* in their names from the *tsar'* for
the principality of Yaroslav because it was then the custom"
(*obychaia zhe radi byvshago togda*).[9]

Given the Nikon chronicler's propensity for historical and
literary excess and his violent prejudices against the hated infidels,
this is a rather modest remark about such a hateful "custom."
The expression is almost noncommittal.   There is no attempt to
draw   attention   to   the   odious   political   circumstances   that
necessitated this custom, or even to applaud the fact that those
circumstances   no   longer   existed.   This   is   a   most   restrained
rewriting of the past.   The basic redaction of the Nikon Chronicle
was compiled, probably at the Joseph of Volokolamsk monastery,
by the 1530s.   Muscovy had yet to launch its major offensive
against Kazan', but was already an ambitious and arrogant society.
It is remarkable that its political, social, and religious pretentions
inspired no greater revision of the historical annals on Russo–Tatar
relations than the almost polite formula that such had been "the
custom in those days."

Under Metropolitan Makarii, virtually all of medieval Russian
literature was brought together into a gigantic anthology, the
"Great Menology," an encyclopedia designed to extol the virtues of
Russian tsardom.   The "Book of Degrees" (*Stepennaia kniga*)
embodied a new approach to Russian history, structured around a
dynastic   succession   stretching   from   Kievan   times   through   the
sixteenth century, and stressing the unity of Church and State and
the continuity of the Russian autocratic tradition.[10]   Some purging
of the historical record is to be expected, but there is remarkably
little.   By the 1550s and 1560s, before the *oprichnina* of Ivan IV
brought most chronicle-writing and much literary activity to a
grinding halt, Muscovite bookmen could have taken advantage of
the removal of the threat from Kazan' to take greater liberties

with the record of Russia's Tatar period.   But even as the ideological necessities of the frontier evaporated in the bright sunshine of Muscovite military and political expansion, new ones appeared to hold the ideology of silence firmly in place.   The major themes of the new Muscovite ideology depended on a vision of the sustained and harmonious power of Orthodoxy and autocracy from Kievan times to the present.   Russia alone possessed true Orthodoxy, and its autocrat alone inherited the eschatological responsibilities of the Byzantine basileus.[11]   The most ambitious formulation of this creed was of course the theory of Moscow as the Third Rome.   According to this concept, the Muscovite ruler was responsible for the maintenance of pure Christianity in Muscovy, the last remaining *tsarstvo* on earth, on whose survival the very possibility of salvation depended.

The Mongols had no place in this schema.   They represented a historical discontinuity, an interruption of the tradition of independent glory stretching from Kievan *Rus'* to Muscovite *Rus'*. For the ideologues of sixteenth-century Muscovy to admit not only that the Mongols had conquered Russia, but that they had remained its masters for nearly two and half centuries, was simply out of the question.   The bookmen of autocratic Muscovy thus had not the least desire for a revision of the perspectives of their predecessors concerning Russia's relationship with the Horde from the time of Batu to the time of Akhmat.   It was enough to translate the vague "Tatar oppression" alluded to in the earlier texts into a calculatedly metaphorical "yoke of slavery" on the model of the Hebrews in Egypt.   The anti-Tatar passages of earlier texts could be enhanced, and the martyrdoms of Russian princes at the hands of Tatars further dramatized.   On the whole, however, the major response of sixteenth-century Muscovite bookmen to the Mongol period in their history was to pretend that it had never occurred.   Thus, the reluctance of Russian intellectuals during the Mongol period to confront the actual nature of Russia's political relationship with the Golden Horde was carried over into the tsardom of Muscovy.   The ideology of silence, now serving a new purpose, acquired new life.

Indeed, it has survived to a degree into our own time. Imperial Russian historiographers adopted the historical schematization of the Muscovite bookmen, and the cautious approach to the Mongol period implicit in this conception of Russian history was transferred into the Russian historiographic

mainstream. Uncritical acceptance of this schema has continued to
result in the neglect of the study of the Mongol role in the history
of Russia.

The modern reader of the medieval Russian sources, aware
that he is reading the records of the Mongol conquest and the
Tatar Yoke, may have one of two reactions. If he believes that
the medieval bookmen share his conception of a Tatar Yoke, he
will find his expectations confirmed. But the more critical reader
who concentrates without preconceptions on the actual content of
the texts will gradually have the impression of a vast conspiracy of
silence. He will not be able to reconcile historical reality with the
picture of Russo-Tatar relations in the texts. Reading the sources
in terms of political suzerainty gives the effect of a mirage, as if
the Russians were unable to perceive the reality of the situation.
But the vision of the texts is at least two removes from our own
perspectives. First, what the Russians "knew," they knew in terms
of their own world-view. Second, the bookmen did not reveal all
of their knowledge in their writings. The treatment of
Russo-Tatar relations in the medieval texts makes sense once it
has been analyzed on its own terms.

The Russian intellectual response to the Mongol conquest is
an indication neither of hypocrisy nor of any weakness of "national
character." While Russia's particular permutations of the ideology
of silence were unique, they were only variations on a phenomenon
characteristic of the entire ethno-religious frontier. Russian
intellectuals during the Mongol period were confronted with a
reality that simply could not be reconciled with the religious
foundations of their society. Their response, a very human one,
deserves the serious attention of scholars.

Notes

Introduction

[1]Charles J. Halperin, "The Russian Land and the Russian Tsar: The Emergence of Muscovite Ideology, 1380–1408," dissertation, Columbia University, 1973, revised and published under the same title in the *Forschungen zur osteuropaischen Geschichte*, 23 (1976), pp. 7–103.

[2]Michael Cherniavsky, "Khan or Basileus: An Aspect of Russian Medieval Political Theory," *Journal of the History of Ideas*, XX (1959), pp. 459–476, reprinted in Cherniavsky, ed., *The Structure of Russian History* (New York, 1970), pp. 65–79.

[3]Halperin, "A Chingisid Saint of the Russian Orthodox Church: The 'Life of Peter, *tsarevich* of the Horde,'" *Canadian-American Slavic Studies*, 9:3 (Fall, 1975), pp. 324–335.

[4]Halperin, "Sixteenth-Century Foreign Travel Accounts to Muscovy: A Methodological Excursus," *The Sixteenth Century Journal*, VI:2 (October, 1975), pp. 89–111.

[5]Halperin, "Russia and the 'Mongol Yoke': Concepts of Conquest, Liberation and the Chingisid Idea," *Archivum Eurasiae Medii Aevi*, II (1982), pp. 99–107.

[6]Halperin, "Bulgars and Slavs in the First Bulgarian Empire: A Reconsideration of the Historiography," *Archivum Eurasiae Medii Aevi*, III (1983), pp. 183–200.

[7]Halperin, "Medieval Myopia and the Mongol Period of Russian History," *Russian History*, 5:2 (1978), pp. 188–191.

[8]Shakhmatov's reputation, like that of other "hold-overs" from the Imperial academic establishment, has fluctuated. His most vehement and prolific defenders have been Likhachev and Lur'e; his most active detractors, Azbelev, Pashuto, and especially Kuz'min. Buganov and Shapiro take moderate positions, and Zimin is basically favorable to Shakhmatov. Essentially the debate is over how much of Shakhmatov's methodology can be accepted and how much of a contribution he made to the study of chronicles. Soviet articles frequently respond to polemics in previous publications. To give an idea of the course of this debate, this bibliography is chronological: D. S. Likhachev, "A. A. Shakhmatov kak issledovatel' russkogo letopisaniia," in *A. A. Shakhmatov 1864–1920. Sbornik statei i materialov*, ed., akad S. P. Obnorskii (Moscow-Leningrad, 1947), pp. 253–293; Likhachev, *Russkie letopisi i ikh kul'turno-istoricheskoe znachenie* (Moscow-Leningrad, 1947), pp. 10–34; V. T. Pashuto, "A. A. Shakhmatov—burzhuaznyi istochnikoved," *Voprosy istorii*, 1952, #2, pp. 47–73; Likhachev, *Tekstologiia (na materiale russkoi literatury X–XVII vv.)* (Moscow-Leningrad, 1962), especially pp. 44–49, 357–389 *et passim*; A. L. Shapiro, *Russkaia istoriografiia perioda imperializma. Kurs lektsii* (Leningrad, 1962), pp. 99–107 (p. 106, no. 13 on the *Skazanie o Mamaevom poboishche* is quite wrong); A. G. Kuz'min, *Riazanskoe letopisanie. Svedeniia letopisei o Riazani i Murome do serediny XVI veka* (Moscow, 1965), pp. 3–5; S. N. Azbelev, "Tekstologiia kak vspomogatel'naia istoricheskaia distsiplina," *Istoriia SSSR*, 1966, #4, pp. 81–106; V. I. Buganov, "Russkoe letopisanie v sovetskoi istoriografii," *Voprosy istorii*, 1966, #12, pp. 143–144; Likhachev, "Po povodu stat'i S. N. Azbeleva, 'Tekstologiia kak vspomogatel'naia istoricheskaia distsiplina,'" *Istoriia SSSR*, 1967, #2, pp. 230–235; Ia. S. Lur'e, "Izucheniia

ruskogo letopisaniia," *Vspomogatel'nye istoricheskie distsipliny*, I (Leningrad, 1968), pp. 4–32; A. A. Zimin, "Trudnye voprosy metodiki istochnikovedeniia Drevnei Rusi," in *Istochnikovedenie. Teoreticheskie i metodicheskie problemy* (Moscow, 1969), pp. 427–449; Lur'e, "Problemy izucheniia russkogo letopisaniia," in *Puti izucheniia drevnerusskoi literatury i pis'mennosti* (Leningrad, 1970), pp. 43–48; Lur'e, "K izucheniiu letopisnogo zhanra," *Trudy otdela drevnerusskoi literatury*, XXVII (1972), pp. 76–93; Lur'e, "O nekotorykh printsipakh kritiki istochnikov," *Istochnikovedenie otechestvennoi istorii*, I (Moscow, 1973), pp. 78–100; Kuz'min, "Spornye voprosy metologii izucheniia russkikh letopisei," *Voprosy istorii*, 1973, #2, pp. 32–53; D. S. Likhachev, V. L. Ianin, and Ia. S. Lur'e, "Podlinnye i mnimye voprosy metologii izucheniia russkikh letopisei," *Voprosy istorii*, 1973, #8, pp. 194–203; Lur'e, "Problema rekonstruktsii nedoshedshikh svodov pri issledovanii letopisei," in *Tekstologiia slavianskikh literatur* (Leningrad, 1973), pp. 137–144; Pashuto, "Nekotorye obshchie voprosy letopisnogo istochnikovedeniia," *Istochnikovedeniia otechestvennoi istorii*, I (Moscow, 1973), pp. 64–77 (which is milder than his 1952 article); Buganov, *Otechestvennaia istoriografiia russkogo letopisaniia. Obzor sovetskoi literatury* (Moscow, 1975), pp. 7–48, 321–327; Lur'e, "O shakhmatovskoi metodike issledovaniia letopisnykh svodov," *Istochnikovedenie otechestvennoi istorii. sb. st. 1975 g.* [=II] (Moscow, 1976), pp. 86–107; Lur'e, *Obshcherusskie letopisi XIV–XV vv.* (Leningrad, 1976), pp. 3–16; and Kuz'min, *Nachal'nye etapy drevnerusskogo letopisaniia* (Moscow, 1977), pp. 5–54.

For an interpretation of the influence of Shakhmatov on Soviet textology, see the review by Donald G. Ostrowski of Lur'e, *Obshcherusskie letopisi XIV–XV vv.* and A. G. Kuz'min, *Nachal'nye etapy drevnerusskogo letopisaniia* in *Kritika*, XVI:1 (Winter, 1980), pp. 5–23. I would not assent to all of Ostrowski's conclusions.

[9]Riccardo Picchio applied this concept to Old Russian literature: manuscripts of a single "text" were rarely identical since each scribe made conscious or unconscious alterations, therefore, it is more proper to speak of the history of "works" than of "texts." For a brief adumbration of this and his other theories of Old Russian literature, see Riccardo Picchio, "Models and Patterns in the Literary Tradition of Medieval Orthodox Slavdom," *American Contributions to the Seventh International Congress of Slavists. Warsaw, August 21–27, 1973*, volume II, *Literature and Folklore*, ed., V. Terras (The Hague, 1973), pp. 439–467.

[10]Halperin, *Russia and the Golden Horde: The Mongol Impact on Medieval Russian History* (Bloomington, Indiana, 1985).

[11]Halperin, "The Ideology of Silence: Prejudice and Pragmatism on the Medieval Religious Frontier," *Comparative Studies in Society and History*, 26:3 (July, 1984), pp. 442–466.

[12]Halperin, "Russia in the Mongol Empire in Comparative Perspective," *Harvard Journal of Asiatic Studies*, 41:3 (June, 1983), pp. 239–261.

[13]Halperin, "Soviet Historiography on Russia and the Mongols," *Russian Review*, 41:3 (July, 1982), pp. 306–322; Halperin, "George Vernadsky, Eurasianism, Russia and the Mongols," *Slavic Review*, 41:3 (Fall, 1982), pp. 477–493.

[14]Of his numerous publications expounding this concept, see D. S. Likhachev, "Literaturnyi etiket drevnei Rusi (k probleme izucheniia)," *Trudy otdela drevnerusskoi literatury*, XVII (1961), pp. 5–16, and *Poetika drevnerusskoi literatury* (Leningrad, 1967).

[15]Likhachev, "Literaturnyi etiket drevnei Rusi," pp. 12–16, and *Poetika drevnerusskoi literatury*, pp. 104–107.

Likhachev's comments concern the violation of the literary etiquette of

Russo–Tatar relations in the *Kazanskaia istoriia*, one issue in the polemic between Keenan and Pelenski on the dating of the text.

[16]O. Miller, "O drevnerusskoi literature po otnosheniiu k tatarskomu igu," *Drevniaia i novaia Rossiia*, 1876, tom II, #5, pp. 49–60, is very episodic; M. V. Shakhmatov, "Otnoshenie drevne–russkikh knizhnikov k tataram," *Trudy IV S" ezd Russkikh Akademicheskikh Organizatsii za granitsi v Belgrade, 16-23 Sent. 1928*, ch. I (Belgrade, 1929), pp. 165–173, reduces all texts to two opinions, active hatred of the Tatars and passive hatred of the Tatars. I disagree with his interpretation of every text he cites.

[17]Halperin, "Know Thy Enemy: Medieval Russian Familiarity with the Mongols of the Golden Horde," *Jahrbücher für Geschichte Osteuropas*, 30 (1982), pp. 161–175, "*Tsarev ulus*: Russia in the Golden Horde," *Cahiers du monde russe et soviétique*, 23:2 (April–June, 1982), pp. 257–263; "The Defeat and Death of Batu," *Russian History*, 10:1 (1983), pp. 50–65; "The Tatar Yoke and Tatar Oppression," *Russia Mediaevalis*, 5:1 (1984), pp. 20–39.

Chapter I

[1]Denis Sinor, "The Barbarians," *Diogenes*, 18 (1957), pp. 47–60.

[2]Though outdated, the best surveys of the historiography are B. D. Grekov and A. Iu. Iakubovskii, *Zolotaia orda i ee padenie* (Moscow–Leningrad, 1950), pp. 247–261, and V. V. Kargalov, *Vneshnepoliticheskie faktory razvitiia feodal'noi Rusi. Feodal'naia Rus' i kochevniki* (Moscow, 1967), pp. 219–255.

[3]For example, B. Szczesniak, "A Note on the Character of the Tartar Impact upon the Russian Church and State," *Etudes slaves et est–européens*, 17 (1972), pp. 92–98; Oscar Halecki, *The Limits and Divisions of European History* (New York, 1950); and Tibor Szamuely, *The Russian Tradition* (New York, 1975).

[4]Karl A. Wittfogel, *Oriental Despotism. A Comparative Study of Total Power* (New Haven, 1957), especially pp. 201-203, 219-225, on Russia, and Wittfogel, "Russia and the East: A Comparison and Contrast," and "Reply," *Slavic Review*, 22:4 (Dec., 1963), pp. 627–643, 656–662.

[5]Otto Böss, *Die Lehre der Eurasier: Ein Beitrag zur russischen Ideengeschichte des 20 J.* (Wiesbaden, 1961); Nicholas V. Riasanovsky, "Prince N. S. Trubetskoy's 'Europe and Mankind,'" *Jahrbücher für Geschichte Osteuropas*, XIII (1964), pp. 207–220, and "The Emergence of Eurasianism," *California Slavic Studies*, 4 (1967), pp. 39–72; G. E. Orchard, "The Eurasian School of Russian Historiography," *Laurentian University Review X:1* (Nov., 1977), pp. 97–106.

[6]George Vernadsky, *The Mongols and Russia* (= volume 3 of *A History of Russia* by George Vernadsky and Michael Karpovich; New Haven, 1953), a work that has been misunderstood for too long. See also Halperin, "Russia and the Steppe: George Vernadsky and Eurasiansim," *Forschungen zur osteuropaischen Geschichte*, 36 (1985), pp. 55–194.

[7]Robert Ignatius Burns, S. J., *Islam under the Crusaders: Colonial Survival in the Thirteenth–Century Kingdom of Valencia* (Princeton, 1973) and "Spanish Islam in Transition: Acculturative Survival and its Price in the Christian Kingdom of Valencia," in Speros Vryonis, Jr., ed., *Islam and Cultural Change in the Middle Ages* (Wiesbaden, 1975), pp. 87–105.

[8]Speros Vryonis, Jr., "Byzantium and Islam, Seventh–Seventeenth Centuries," *East European Quarterly*, 2 (1968), pp. 205–240, and "The

Byzantine Legacy and Ottoman Forms," *Dumbarton Oaks Papers*, 23–24 (1969–1970), pp. 253–308.

[9]Joshua Prawer, *The Latin Kingdom of Jerusalem. European Colonialism in the Middle Ages* (London, 1973).

[10]Owen Lattimore, *Inner Asian Frontiers of China* (1940; Boston, 1962), and *Studies in Frontier History. Collected Papers 1928–1958* (London, 1962).

[11]Herbert Franz Schurmann, *Economic Structure of the Yüan Dynasty. Translation of Chapters 93 and 94 of the Yüan shih* (Cambridge, Mass., 1956); Jung-pang Lo, "The Controversy over Grain Conveyance during the Reign of Qubilai Qaqun, 1260–1294," *Far Eastern Quarterly*, 13 (1954), pp. 262–285; Paul Heng-chao Ch'en, *Chinese Legal Tradition under the Mongols. The Code of 1291 as Reconstructed* (Princeton, 1979).

[12]Salikh Zakirov, *Diplomaticheskie otnosheniia Zolotoi Ordy s Egiptom (XIII–XIV vv.)* (Moscow, 1966).

[13]Perry Anderson, *Passages from Antiquity to Feudalism* (London, 1974), p. 227, recognizes this point.

[14]Kargalov, *Vneshnepoliticheskie faktory razvitiia feodal'noi Rusi*, pp. 167–172, 185–188, *et passim*.

[15]*Gramoty Velikogo Novgoroda i Pskova*, ed., S. N. Valk (Moscow–Leningrad, 1949), #30, p. 57.

[16]Janet Martin, "The land of darkness and the Golden Horde. The fur trade under the Mongols. XIII–XIV centuries," *Cahiers du monde russe et soviétique* XIX:4 (1978), pp. 401–422.

[17]Much of this analysis is taken from the unpublished monograph by Michel Roublev, *The Scourge of God.* I am grateful to him for providing me with a typescript of this study.

[18]The most extensive if somewhat outdated survey of the historiography is in L. V. Cherepnin, *Obrazovanie russkogo tsentralizovannogo gosudarstva v XIV–XV vv.: Ocherki sotsial'no-ekonomicheskoi i politicheskoi istorii Rusi* (Moscow, 1960), pp. 15–144. Cf. Cherepnin, *passim*, with A. E. Presniakov, *Obrazovanie velikorusskogo gosudarstva. Ocherki po istorii XIII–XV stoletiia* (Petrograd, 1918) and John L. I. Fennell, *The Emergence of Moscow, 1304–1359* (Berkeley and Los Angeles, 1968).

[19]See no. 17.

[20]Gustave Alef, "Origin and Development of the Muscovite Postal Service," *Jahrbücher für Geschichte Osteuropas* XV (1967), pp. 1–15.

[21]Peter Olbricht, *Das Postwesen in China unter der Mongolenherrschaft im 13. und 14. Jh.* (Wiesbaden, 1954).

[22]N. I. Veselovskii, "Tatarskoe vliianie na posol'skii tseremonial v moskovskii period russkoi istorii," *Otchet Sv. Peterburgskago Universiteta za 1910*, pp. 1–19, and separate publication, St. Petersburg, 1911. Cf. Alan W. Fisher, "Muscovite–Ottoman Relations in the Sixteenth and Seventeenth Centuries," *Humaniora Islamica*, 1 (1973), pp. 207–213.

[23]Edward L. Keenan, Jr., "The *Yarlik* of Axmed-khan to Ivan III: A New Reading—A Study in Literal *Diplomatica* and Literary *Turcica*," *International Journal of Slavic Linguistics and Poetics*, 11 (1967), pp. 33–47.

[24]*Novgorodskaia pervaia letopis' starshego i mladshego izvodov*, ed., A. N. Nasonov (Moscow–Leningrad, 1950), s.a. 1269, pp. 88–89; *Polnoe sobranie russkikh letopisei*, V, s.a. 1371, p. 228; *Gramoty Velikogo Novgoroda i Pskova*, #15, p. 26, and #3, 1270, p. 13.

[25] *Troitskaia letopis'. Rekonstruktsiia teksta*, ed., M. D. Priselkov (Moscow–Leningrad, 1950), pp. 327–328.

[26] *P.S.R.L.*, XV, pp. 42–44, IV, pp. 50–51.

[27] M. D. Poluboiarinova, *Russkie liudi v Zolotoi Orde* (Moscow, 1978).

[28] *Voinskie povesti drevnei Rusi*, ed., V. P. Adrianova-Peretts (Moscow–Leningrad, 1949), pp. 13–14.

[29] *Povesti o Kulikovskoi bitvy*, ed., M. N. Tikhomirov, V. F. Rzhiga and L. A. Dmitriev (Moscow–Leningrad, 1959), pp. 9–17. See the discussion in Halperin, "The Russian Land and the Russian Tsar," pp. 9–22.

[30] Likhachev, *Poetika drevnerusskoi literatury*, pp. 11–13.

[31] Thomas S. Noonan, "Medieval Russia, the Mongols and the West: Novgorod's Relations with the Baltic, 1100–1350," *Medieval Studies*, 37 (1975), pp. 316–339.

[32] D. S. Likhachev, *Kul'tura Rusi vremeni Andreia Rubleva i Epifaniia Premudrogo (konets XIV–nachalo XV v.)* (Leningrad, 1962), and Riccardo Picchio, "On Russian Humanism: The Philological Revival," *Slavia*, 44:2 (1975), pp. 161–171.

[33] Cherniavsky, "Khan or Basileus," and Halperin, "The Russian Land and the Russian Tsar," especially Chapter III, "Moscow, the Defender of Chingisid Legitimacy," pp. 38–57.

[34] To discuss every reference to the Tatars in the sources, every chronicle entry or passage, would necessitate an intensive review of two hundred and forty years of Russo–Tatar relations and is impractical; this survey will be selective.

Chapter II

[1] On this text, see John L. I. Fennell, "The Tatar Invasion of 1223: Source Problems," *Forschungen zur osteuropaischen Geschichte*, 27 (1980), pp. 18–31, and his remarks in Fennell and Anthony Stokes, *Early Russian Literature* (Berkeley, 1974), pp. 81–88. See also M. B. Sverdlov, "K voprosu o letopisnykh istochnikakh 'Povesti o bitve na Kalke,'" *Vestnik Leningradskogo universiteta*, #2, seriia istorii, iazyka i literatury, vypusk I (1963), pp. 139–144, and A. V. Emmauskii, "Letopisnye izvestie o pervom nashestvii mongolo–tatar na Vostochnuiu Evropu," *Uchenye zapiski Kirovsk. gos. ped. inst. im. V. I. Lenina*, vyp. 17, t. 3, ist.–fil. fak, 1958, pp. 59–109. Fennell's textology seems compatible with that of the Soviet studies; his interpretation of the tale is quite different from mine.

See also the remarks of *Istoriia russkoi literatury*, t. II, ch. 1 (Moscow–Leningrad, 1946), pp. 77–78; V. T. Pashuto, "Kievskaia letopis' 1238 g.," *Istoricheskie zapiski* 26 (1948), pp. 286–288; V. T. Pashuto, *Ocherki po istorii Galitsko–Volynskoi Rusi* (Moscow–Leningrad, 1950), pp. 39–43, 51–55; N. V. Vodovozov, "Povest' o bitve na reke Kalke," *Uchenye zapiski Mosk. gorod. ped. inst. im. V. P. Potemkina*, kafedra rus. lit., vyp. 6, t. 67, 1957, pp. 3–77; I. U. Budovnits, *Obshchestvenno–politicheskaia mysl' drevnei Rusi* (Moscow, 1960), pp. 291–297; N. V. Vodovozov, *Istoriia drevnei russkoi literatury* (Moscow, 1962), pp. 109–111; A. N. Nasonov, "Lavrent'evskaia letopis' i Vladimirskoe velikokniazheskoe letopisanie pervoi poloviny XIII v.," *Problemy istochnikovedeniia*, XI (1963), pp. 462–463; and N. K. Gudzii, *Istoriia drevnei russkoi literatury*, 7th ed. (Moscow, 1966), pp. 189–190.

[2] *Novgorodskaia pervaia letopis'*, pp. 264–266, 61–63.

[3] *P.S.R.L.*, I, cols. 445–447.

[4] The Nikon chronicle, *P.S.R.L.*, X, p. 90, commits the inevitable howler and renders Bastii as Batyi–Batu.

[5] *P.S.R.L.*, II, cols. 740–745.

[6] It is ironic that the Mongols should be known as Tatars, since the Tatars were a different tribe, sworn enemies of the Mongols, nearly exterminated by Chingis. Even Carpini acquired this information. In Latin, "Tatars" became "Tartars," a pun on "Tartarus" = Hades, from whence, obviously, the Mongols came. The Russian sources do not use the distortion "Tartars."

[7] Some scholars have erroneously given Kotian and the Polovtsian rulers the title "khan." When accorded a title, the Polovtsian rulers appear in the East Slavic chronicles as "*kniazi*" (princes). The entirely nomadic Kipchaks (Polovtsy, Kumans) did not participate in the imperial Inner Asian tradition of the Türk, Khazar and later Mongol Empires; their rulers never took the title kagan/khan.

[8] Based upon the rewriting of the Tale of 1223 by the Nikon chronicler, Vernadsky made an unconvincing argument that the Mongol envoys were Nestorian Christians. See G. V. Vernadskii (George Vernadsky), "K voprosu o veroispovedanii mongol'skikh poslov 1223 g.," *Seminarium Kondakovianum*, III (1929), pp. 145–148.

[9] Fennell calls the rendering of the envoys' speeches in the Novgorodian chronicle too elliptical and nearly unintelligible, a result of hyperliteral translation by poorly–qualified translators.

[10] E. Voegelin, "The Mongol Orders of Submission to European Powers, 1245–1255," *Byzantion*, 15 (1941), pp. 378–413; Francis Woodman Cleaves, "A Chancellery Practice of the Mongols in the Thirteenth and Fourteenth Centuries," *Harvard Journal of Asiatic Studies*, 14 (1951), pp. 493–526; and A. P. Grigor'ev, *Mongol'skaia diplomatika*, XIII–XV vv. (*Chingizidskie zhalovannye gramoty*) (Leningrad, 1978).

[11] Likhachev, *Russkie letopisi i ikh kul'turno–istoricheskoe znachenie*, pp. 124–125, and *inter alia*, pp. 114–144.

[12] *P.S.R.L.*, IV, p. 28. Mid–fifteenth–century Russian chronicles interpolate an allusion to Alesha Popovich and his *bogatyri* into the tale of 1223, from which Likhachev has argued that the *bylina* cycle had already evolved sufficiently to influence chronicle–writing by that time. Cf. Alex E. Alexander, "The Death of the Epic Hero in the *Kamskoe poboishche Bylina*," *Slavonic and East European Review*, L, #118 (Jan., 1972), pp. 1–9.

[13] John Andrew Boyle, tr., *Juvaini, The History of the World Conqueror*, 2 vv. (Manchester, England—Cambridge, Mass., 1958), v. II, p. 640.

[14] *P.S.R.L.*, VII (*Voskresenskaia letopis'*), pp. 129–132.

[15] Grekov and Iakubovskii, *Zolotaia orda i ee padenie*, p. 203. The Tverian chronicle (*P.S.R.L.*, XV, cols. 335–343) makes Ploskynia the *voevoda* of the *brodniki* and says he gave an oath that for a ransom (*okup*) the Russian princes would be freed.
On the 1353 citation cf. Cherepnin, *Obrazovanie russkogo tsentralizovannogo gosudarstva*, pp. 537–538, and Fennell, *The Emergence of Moscow*, p. 222.

[16] European impressions of the Mongols are comprehensively surveyed in Gian Andri Bezzola, *Die Mongolen in abendländischen Sicht (1220–1270). Ein Beitrag zur Frage der Völkerbegegnung* (Bern, 1974).

[17]Russian familiarity with the Prester John legend can only be demonstrated from the fifteenth century, the dating of the earliest manuscripts of the Russian version of the legend, the "Tale of the Indian Empire" (*Povest' ob Indiiskom tsarstve*).

[18]Fennell finds the tale of 1223 "stylistically stark and unadorned" with "primitive sentence structure" and clumsy stereotypical formulas. He notes its failure to exploit potentially dramatic scenes (such as the Russian princes being crushed to death under the boards of the feasting Tatars), its "deadpan, unemotional" prose, the lack of the rich opprobrious epithets for the Tatars so ubiquitous in the Russian literary monuments of later centuries, and especially the fact that the text does not blame the Tatars for their attack, since it was the will of God.

[19]Ihor Ševčenko, "The Decline of Byzantium Seen Through the Eyes of its Intellectuals," *Dumbarton Oaks Papers*, XV (1961), pp. 167–186.

[20]Fennel goes to excessive lengths to deny original Novgorodian authorship of the tale, claiming, for example, that no Novgorodian had ever seen a *brodnik*, when any Novgorodian who had visited Kiev would be familiar with the term. He also finds the "apocalyptic resignation" of the tale of 1223 incompatible with ambience of "thriving commerical Novgorod," which strikes me as naive.

[21]*P.S.R.L.*, XXVI, p. 69.

[22]*P.S.R.L.*, X, pp. 89–92.

[23]Thomas T. Allsen, "The Mongols and the Easter Qipchaks," paper, American Association for the Advancement of Slavic Studies Convention, Philadelphia, November 5, 1980.

[24]Kargalov, *Vneshnepoliticheskie faktory razvitiia feodal'noi Rusi*, pp. 83–84. See S. A. Anninskii, "Izvestiia vengerskikh missionerov XIII veka o tatarakh i Vostochnoi Evropy," *Istoricheskii arkhiv*, III (1940), pp. 71–112 on Julian.

[25]*P.S.R.L.*, I, cols. 460–468.

[26]This usage of the concept of the "Suzdalian Land" is very helpful in the dating of the text; see Charles J. Halperin, "The Concept of the Russian Land from the Ninth to the Fourteenth Centuries," *Russian History*, II:1 (1975), pp. 29–38.

[27]*P.S.R.L.*, II, cols. 778–782.

[28]*Poruka* (surety) was the term used in medieval Russia to describe a variety of relationships of mutual obligation in law. Here *poruchniki* presumably is meant to characterize a vassal relationship between a Mongol khan and a Russian prince, were Russia subordinated to the Tatars. Such an application of the concept of *poruka* is extraordinary.

[29]*Novgorodskaia pervaia letopis'*, pp. 286–289, 74–77.

[30]This theory was first proposed on textological grounds by Komarovich; recently Prokhorov has revived it with a much more elaborate textological and codicological analysis, as well as an original historical interpretation of much late fourteenth–century Russian history. For Komarovich's comments, see *Istoriia russkoi literatury* (1949), pp. 90–96, and V. L. Komarovich, "Iz nabliudenii nad Lavrent'evskoi letopis'iu," *Trudy otdela drevnerusskoi literatury*, XXX (1976), pp. 27–59. Prokhorov's most apposite publications on this point are G. M. Prokhorov, "Kodikologicheskii analiz Lavrent'evskoi letopisi," *Vspomogatel'nye istoricheskie distsipliny*, IV (1972), pp. 77–104, and "Povest' o Batyevom nashestvii v Lavrent'evskoi letopisi," *TODRL*, XXVIII (1974), pp. 77–98.

[31] Komarovich's observations were answered in their time by Nasonov, and Lur'e has polemicized with Prokhorov. See Nasonov, "Lavrent'evskaia letopis' i Vladmirskoe velikokniazheskoe letopisanie pervoi poloviny XIII v.," pp. 438–445, and A. N. Nasonov, *Istoriia russkogo letopisaniia XI–nachala XVIII veka. Ocherki i issledovaniia* (Moscow, 1969), pp. 168–201. Of Lur'e's numerous publications, see Ia. S. Lur'e, "Lavrent'evskaia letopis'—svod nachala XIV veka," *TODRL*, XXIX (1974), pp. 50–67, and *Obshcherusskie letopisi XIV–XV vv.*, pp. 17–66.

[32] Lur'e, *Obshcherusskie letopisi XIV–XV vv.*, pp. 35–36, qualifies any dating of the tale of 1237–1238 in the Laurentian chronicle as "controversial" but clearly tilts toward 1305, where its "antagonistic attitude toward the conquerors" would, like the episode of *baskak* Akhmad of Kursk and the portrayal of the execution of prince Oleg of Riazan' in 1270, "fit" the anti–Tatar mode developing in Tver', where the 1305 *svod* was compiled, preparatory to Tverian anti–Tatar politics of the early fourteenth century. I will discuss the Tverian sources in due time, but it is appropriate to recall that Fennell (see no. 34) and Budnovnits (see no. 35) do not find the Laurentian chronicle account sufficiently anti–Tatar, compared to the Novgorodian and Hypatian accounts respectively. Fennell sees nothing in the northeastern chronicle tradition of the thirteenth century equivalent to the "oppositionist tendencies" of unoccupied and unlooted Novgorod. Cf. M. D. Priselkov, "Lavrent'evskaia letopis' (istoriia teksta)," *Uchenye zapiski L.G.U*, t. 32, seriia ist. nauk, vyp. 2, 1939, pp. 76–142, and "Istoriia rukopisi Lavrent'evskoi letopisi i ee izdanie," *Uchenye zapiski Leningr. gos. ped. inst. im. A. I. Gertsena*, t. XIX, 1939, pp. 175–197.

[33] Pashuto, "Kievskaia letopis' 1238 g.," pp. 273–305, and his *Ocherki po istorii Galitsko–Volynskoi Rusi*, pp. 288–290.

[34] John L. I. Fennell, "The Tale of Baty's Invasion of North–east Rus' and its Reflexion in the Chronicles of the Thirteenth to Fifteenth Centuries," *Russia Mediaevalis* III (1977), pp. 41–78. Cf. *Istoriia russkoi literatury* (1946), pp. 74–80, and Kuz'min, *Riazanskoe letopisanie*, pp. 154–180.

[35] Despite Budovnits, *Obshchestvenno–politicheskaia mysl' drevnei Rusi*, pp. 297–307.

[36] *Istoriia russkoi literatury* (1946), pp. 61–62; Budovnits, *Obshchestvenno–politicheskaia mysl' drevnei Rusi*, pp. 314–319; and John L. I. Fennell, "The Tale of the Death of Vasil'ko Konstantinovič: A Study of the Sources," in Hans Lemberg, Peter Nitsche and Eric Oberlander, eds., *Osteuropa in Geschichte und Gegenwart. Festschrift für Gunther Stökl zum 60 Geburtstag* (Köln, 1977), pp. 34–46.

[37] The late fifteenth century Simeon chronicle mostly follows the version of the Laurentian chronicle and the early fifteenth century (reconstructed) Trinity chronicle very accurately. However, the Simeon chronicle mentions the tithe although neither of them does; it must be following a Novgorod chronicle here, either the Novgorad First or perhaps the Novgorod Fourth—Sofia First chronicle tradition of the *svod* of 1448. See *P.S.R.L.*, XVIII, pp. 54–59.

[38] Kuz'min, *Riazanskoe letopisanie*, p. 162.

[39] *Troitskaia letopis'*, s.a. 1238, p. 39.

[40] For various circumlocutory remarks and lists, which sometimes include Rostov, Suzdal', Uglich, Tver', Yaroslavl', and Nizhnii Novgorod, see Nasonov, "Lavrent'evskaia letopis' i Vladimirskoe velikokniazheskoe letopisanie pervoi poloviny XIII v.," p. 451, and *Mongoly i Rus' (Istoriia Tatarskoi politiki na Rusi)* (Moscow–Leningrad, 1940), pp. 36–37; *Istoriia russkoi literatury* (1946), p. 59; Kargalov, *Vneshnepoliticheskie faktory razvitiia feodal'noi Rusi*, p. 96;

and V. A. Kuchkin, "Nizhnyi Novgorod i Nizhegorodskoe kniazhestvo v XIII–XIV vv.," in *Pol'sha i Rus'* (Moscow, 1974), p. 237.

[41]According to the Novgorod Fourth Chronicle, which derives from the *svod* of 1448, "from then on the Russian Land was enslaved to the Tatars" (*I ottole nacha rabotati Russkaia zemlia Tatarom*) (*P.S.R.L.*, IV, p. 32). According to the *Stepennaia kniga* (Book of Degrees) from the reign of Ivan IV, the wives of the Russian nobles (*sinklit*), who had slaves to do their manual labor, now suffered from the "yoke of slavery" (*rabotnu igu*) under the Tatars (*P.S.R.L.*, XXI, pp. 262–263). Otherwise these and other chronicles do not alter the basic narrative in a way which is germane to the problematica posed here.

[42]The most assiduous student of the Tale has been D. S. Likhachev. His fundamental publication is "Povesti o Nikolae Zarazskom," *Trudy otdela drevnerusskoi literatury*, VII (1949), pp. 257–406. Likhachev is responsible in *Voinskie povesti drevnei Rusi* for pp. 9–19 (text), 119–142 (discussion), 284–296 (commentary), and 244–255 (archeographic survey). See also Likhachev, *Tekstologiia*, pp. 249–258, "K istorii slozheniia Povesti o razorenii Riazani Batyem," *Arkheograficheskii ezhegodnik za 1962* (1963), pp. 48–51, and *Velikoe nasledie: Klassicheskie proizvedeniia literatury drevnei Rusi* (Moscow, 1975), pp. 221–239, all of which repeat his earlier conclusions. Likhachev has used this work to illustrate his concept of "convoy" analysis.

[43]Likhachev, "Povesti o Nikolae Zarazskom," pp. 282–302 (this is also the manuscript published in *Voinskie povesti drevnei Rusi*, pp. 9–19).

[44]Cherniavsky would have been delighted at this manipulation of the ambiguity between *tsarska* meaning Byzantine/basileus and *tsar'* meaning khan/Mongol when *tsar'* Batu lusts for a woman *tsarska roda*. (Batu was not called *tsar'* during his lifetime, so this passage originated after his death.)

[45]*Ocherki istorii SSSR*, tom II (Moscow, 1953), p. 832, describes Evpatii as a "*narodnii partizan*" (popular partisan), which strikes me as anachronistic.

[46]See the remarks of Likhachev in *Voinskie povesti drevnei Rusi*, p. 291, on his name and relationship to Batu.

[47]Althugh the image of a horse and rider struck in the open field by a stone from a catapult is dramatic, I cannot vouch for its historical authenticity.

[48]This Ottoman Turkish administrative term is probably taken from the Tale of Iskander about the Ottoman siege of Constantinople in 1453; see Likhachev in *Voinskie povesti drevnei Rusi*, p. 291, and "Povesti o Nikolae Zarazskom," pp. 382–387, the "military redaction" (*voinskaia redaktsiia*).

[49]See the remarks by L. A. Dmitriev in *Istoki russkoi belletristiki. Vozniknovenie zhanrov siuzhetnogo povestvovaniia v drevnerusskoi literatury* (Leningrad, 1970), pp. 289–290. In sixteenth–century manuscripts, the tale is followed by contemporary chronicle–like "notes" (*zapisi*), which does not mean the tale was composed in the sixteenth century. See V. L. Komarovich, "K literaturnoi istorii povesti o Nikole Zaraiskom," *Trudy otdela drevnerusskoi literatury*, V (1947), pp. 52–72.

[50]Likhachev, *Voinskie povesti drevnei Rusi*, p. 137.

[51]For one interpretation of the literary history of the tale and of the integration of the Evpatii episode, see Fennell in Fennell and Stokes, *Early Russian Literature*, pp. 88–97.

Putilov has argued, unconvincingly, that there is a connection between the Evpatii episode and a thirteenth–century historical song. B. N. Putilov,

"Pesnia o Evpatii Kolovrate," *TODRL*, XI (1955), pp. 118–139; "Pesnia ob Avdot'e Riazanochke (k istorii Riazanskogo pesennogo tsikla)," *TODRL*, XIV (1958), pp. 163–168; and "K voprosu o sostave Riazanskogo pesennogo tsikla," *TODRL*, XVI (1960), pp. 230–244.

[52]For a discussion of the relationship of the *Povest' o razorenii Riazani Batyem* to the account of Batu's invasion of the northeast in the *Novgorodskaia pervaia letopis'* see A. G. Kuz'min, "Letopisnye izvestiia o razorenii Riazani Batyem," *Vestnik Moskovskogo universiteta*, seriia IX, Istoriia, 1963, #2, pp. 55–70, and in his *Riazanskoe letopisanie*, pp. 154–180.

From the texts Likhachev has published, the earliest redaction of the tale to contain any mention of a shamaness is the Chronograph Redaction, which he relates to the Chronograph of 1512. Likhachev seems to try to make this detail plausible by invoking Mongol use of clerics as envoys and the importance of women in Mongol diplomacy and politics. Likhachev, "Povesti o Nikolae Zarazskom," p. 352, and *Voinskie povesti drevnei Rusi*, pp. 246, 294. However, the Mongols would hardly send a shaman as envoy to Christian rulers; usually Nestorian Christians were assigned to convey messages to Catholic kings. And no Chingisid princess could be sent to a hostile city. Could the shamaness be an invention of the Novgorodian chronicler which only later found its way into the *Povest' o razorenii Riazani Batyem*? At least this would explain the absence of this detail in the earliest redactions. N. I Veselovskii, "O religii tatar po russkim letopisiam," *Zhurnal Ministerstva Narodnago Prosveshcheniia*, tom 64 (1916), p. 84, also endorses this detail, claiming that the Mongols did have shamanesses, although shamans outranked them. A more critical attitude should be taken toward this improbable element of the narrative.

[53]Likhachev, *Voinskie povesti drevnei Rusi*, p. 294, calls these Polovtsy *amanaty* (hostages).

[54]Likhachev, "Povesti o Nikolae Zarazskom," pp. 363, 368.

[55]Compare Budovnits, "Ideinaia osnova rannykh narodnykh skazanii o tatarskom ige," pp. 174–175, and *Obshchestvenno-politicheskaia mysl' drevnei Rusi*, pp. 350–353; *Istoriia russkoi literatury*, (1946), pp. 80–85; Gudzii, *Istoriia drevnei russkoi literatury*, pp. 190–197; V. F. Pereverzev, *Literatura drevnei Rusi* (Moscow, 1971), pp. 91–96 (but see the rejoinder by Robinson in the Afterword, p. 298); and N. V. Vodovozov, "Povest' o razorenii Riazani Batyem," *Uchenye zapiski Mosk. gorod. ped. inst. im. B. P. Potemkina*, t. 48, kafedra rus. lit., vyp. 5, 1955, pp. 3–27, and in his *Istoriia drevnei russkoi literatury*, pp. 117–120.

[56]Likhachev, "Povesti o Nikolae Zarazskom," p. 371.

[57]*Ibid.*, p. 395.

[58]In its later literary history increasingly literary and rhetorical concerns motivated changes and distortion of the "Tale of the Destruction of Riazan' by Batu." This is partially why it was so popular in the seventeenth century, from which most of its manuscripts date. The historical inaccuracies and generalizations of these redactions and manuscripts are not of interest here.

[59]*P.S.R.L.*, I, col. 470.

[60]*Istoriia russkoi literatury* (1946), p. 29.

[61]*P.S.R.L.*, II, cols. 784–787.

[62]Pashuto, *Ocherki po istorii Galitsko-Volynskoi Rusi*, pp. 85–86.

[63]*P.S.R.L.*, XV, cols. 374–375.

[64]After I had realized the need for this emendation, I discovered that it

had been proposed in 1914 by N. I. Veselovskii, although his comments have been overlooked; see A. I. Ivanov and N. I. Veselovskii, *Pokhody mongolov na Rossiiu po ofitsial'noi kitaiskoi istorii Iuan'shi* (from Zapiski Razriada voennoi arkheologii i arkheografii Imp. Rus. Voenno–Ist. Obshch., St. Petersburg, 1914), pp. 11–14.

[65]Martin Dimnik, C. S. B., "Russian Princes and their Identities in the First Half of the Thirteenth Century," *Mediaeval Studies*, XL (1978), pp. 157–189, especially pp. 180–184, and in general Dimnik's work on this period: "The Siege of Chernigov in 1235," *Mediaeval Studies*, XLI (1979), pp. 287–305; "Kamenec," *Russia Mediaevalis*, IV (1979), pp. 25–34; "The Struggle for Control over Kiev in 1235 and 1236," *Canadian Slavonic Papers*, 21 (1979), pp. 28–44, and his *Mikhail, Prince of Chernigov and Grand Prince of Kiev, 1224–1246* (Toronto, 1981).

[66]I. M. Kataev, "Tatary i poraboshchenie imi Rus," in M. V. Dovnar–Zapol'skii, ed., *Russkaia istoriia v ocherkakh i stat'iakh* (Moscow, 1909), p. 574, observes that the northeastern Russian princes mostly died in combat fighting the Tatars, while southern and southwestern princes such as Mikhail of Chernigov and Daniil of Galicia–Volhynia fled before the Tatar invaders. (This is unexpected considering the later invidious contrast in Ukrainian and Ukrainophile historiography and publicistics between the "submissive" Muscovites/Russians and the "freedom–loving and independent" Ukrainians.)

[67]See no. 63.

[68]E.g., *P.S.R.L.*, V, pp. 175–176, and *P.S.R.L.*, IV, pp. 36, 177–178, 377–378.

[69]*P.S.R.L.*, X, pp. 115–117.

[70]The suggestion of N. V. Vodovozov, "Povest' XIII veka ob Aleksandrom Nevskom (k voprosu o sostave i ee avtora)," *Uchenye zapiski Mosk. gorod. ped. inst. im. V. P. Potemkina*, t. 67, vyp. 6, 1957, pp. 21–45 and *Istoriia drevnei russkoi literatury*, pp. 123–127, that Daniil *Zatochnik* (the Prisoner) wrote both the Lay and the Nevskii *vita* was adequately answered by Likhachev, *Tekstologiia*, pp. 291–292.

[71]Iu. K. Begunov, *Pamiatnik russkoi literatury XIII v. "Slovo o pogibeli russkoi zemli"* (Moscow–Leningrad, 1965). On the basis of textological analysis Begunov established definitively that the Lay was not part of a trilogy with the *vita* of Aleksandr Nevskii. Begunov had not noticed that the exclusive usage in the *vita* of Nevskii of the concept of the Suzdalian Land also distanced that work from the *Slovo o pogibeli russkoi zemli*, although Serebrianskii (see no. 74) quotes this observation from Bugoslavskii (pp. 208–209).

[72]It is all the more frustrating that the Lay breaks off when it does, since its author did employ the lexicon of political subordination, however inaccurately, when writing that "pagan lands" were "subordinated" (*pokoreno*) by the Christian God to earlier Russian princes, such as Vladimir Monomakh (Begunov, *Pamiatnik russkoi literatury XIII v.*, pp. 182–184, Reconstructed Text, quote from p. 183).

[73]With some embarrassment, this is conceded even by the great Imperial Russian church historian E. Golubinskii, *Istoriia russkoi tserkvy*, t. II, chast' 1 (St. Petersburg, 1900), pp. 1–49.

[74]N. Serebrianskii, *Drevnerusskie kniazheskie zhitiia (obzor redaktsii i teksty)* (St. Petersburg, 1915), pp. 108–141 (analysis), 49–86 (Texts); Budovnits, *Obshchestvenno–politicheskaia mysl' drevnei Rusi*, pp. 314–319; *Istoriia russkoi literatury* (1946), pp. 62–64.

[75] *Novgorodskaia pervaia letopis'*, pp. 298–303.

[76] M. Grushevskii (Mykhailo Hrushev'sky), *Ocherki po istorii Kievskoi zemli ot smerti Yaroslava do kontsa XIV stoletiia* (Kiev, 1891), p. 423, no. 1, doubts that Mikhail ordered the death of the Tatar envoys, because it is recorded not in "early" chronicles but in the "later" *vita*. He is probably correct.

[77] Michel Roublev, *The Scourge of God*, and Thomas T. Allsen, "Mongol Census-Taking in *Rus'*, 1245–1274," *Harvard Ukrainian Studies*, V:1 (March, 1981), pp. 36–38 accept the historicity of this census, perhaps because neither investigates the provenance of the text which records it.

[78] John Joseph Saunders, *The History of the Mongol Conquests* (New York, 1971), p. 22.

[79] For some possible literary sources of the name of this person, see *Istoki russkoi belletristiki*, p. 172, no. 65. The discussion of the *vita* of Mikhail of Chernigov by L. A. Dmitriev, pp. 212–216, does not deal with the problems I have posed here.

[80] N. I. Veselovskii, "O religii tatar po russkim letopisiam," pp. 84–101, goes too far in trying to avoid the conclusion that the hagiographer invented the imposition of these Inner Asian shamanist rituals on a Christian outsider. At least Veselovskii is skeptical that Vasil'ko (p. 79) would have been asked to apostacize (see above).

[81] Cherniavsky, "Khan or Basileus," p. 80.

[82] The fullest narration of Mikhail's life, by Dimnik (see no. 65), provides no evidence that Mikhail manifested exceptional religious piety before 1245–1246.

[83] Budovnits tries to picture the text as anti-Tatar, which is simplistic. Kargalov, *Vneshnepoliticheskie faktory razvitiia feodal'noi Rusi*, p. 144, sees in Mikhail's Pauline invocation a reflection of the attitude of the Russian Orthodox Church, which preferred peaceful relations between the princes and the Tatars. However, the *vita* was written at princely, not ecclesiastical, behest, and it seems incongruous for the Church to canonize someone who refused to accede to Tatar demands if it opposed his intransigence. Actually, there was no one Church attitude toward the Tatars.

[84] *P.S.R.L.*, XV, cols. 386–393.

[85] *P.S.R.L.*, VII, pp. 152–156.

[86] *P.S.R.L.*, XXVI, pp. 82–85.

[87] *P.S.R.L.*, X, pp. 130–133, 237–244. Cf. *P.S.R.L.*, XXI, pp. 268–277, and *P.S.R.L.*, XXII, pp. 400 ff.

[88] Michael Cherniavsky, *Tsar and People* (New Haven, 1961 and 1970), Chapter I, "Saintly Princes and Princely Saints," pp. 5–43.

[89] *P.S.R.L.*, II, cols. 805–808. The chronology of the Galician-Volhynian Chronicle is confused; although this annal is listed as 1250, most historians date Daniil's visit to the Horde in 1245–1246, before that of Mikhail of Chernigov. Because the author of the "1250 annal" refers to the martyrdom of Mikhail of Chernigov, I have chosen to discuss that text first.

[90] Pashuto, *Ocherki po istorii Galitsko-Volynskoi Rusi*, p. 270 (although Pashuto calls Sangor a provocateur trying to dissuade Daniil from submitting). For Carpini see Christopher Dawson, ed., *Mission to Asia. Narratives and Letters of the Franciscan Missionaries in Mongolia and China in the Thirteenth and Fourteenth Century* (New York, 1966), p. 70.

[91] George A. Perfecky, ed. & tr., *The Hypatian Codex. Part II. The*

Galician–Volynian Chronicle. An Annotated Translation (Munich, 1971), p. 137, no. 94, quoting Orlov.

[92] This did not change before the middle of the fifteenth century during the Muscovite civil war. However the late fifteenth–century Ermolin Chronicle interpolates the opinion that Vasilii I received more honor (*chest'*) from the Tatars than any previous prince (when Tokhtamysh granted him the Nizhnii Novgorod grand principality), which was intended to praise him (*P.S.R.L.*, XXIII, s.a. 1392, pp. 132–133).

[93] *P.S.R.L.*, II, s.a. 1256, col. 792. The always anonymous "Bolokhov princes" defy identification. They were not the communal elders of Grushevskii. Presniakov doubted they were of princely rank. Moreover, the pastoral nomadic Mongols did not eat bread; their diet was meat and dairy products. Why the Bolokhov princes would sow grain for the Tatars remains a mystery.

[94] *P.S.R.L.*, II, col. 829. This is a confusing annal; it also records the Tatar execution of the *boyar* Andrei, which is similarly mysterious.

[95] *P.S.R.L.*, II, cols. 849–855.

[96] See L. V. Cherepnin, "Letopisets Daniila Galitskogo," *Istoricheskie zapiski*, 12 (1974), pp. 228–253; Pashuto, *Ocherki po istorii Galitsko–Volynskoi Rusi*, pp. 17–130 and V. T. Pashuto, *Obrazovanie litovskogo gosudarstva* (Moscow, 1959), pp. 18–42; *Istoriia russkoi literatury* (1946), pp. 23–25; Likhachev, *Russkie letopisi i ikh kul'turno–istoricheskoe znachenie*, pp. 247–258 (p. 252 on this entry); Gudzii, *Istoriia drevnei russkoi literatury*, p. 224; I. P. Eremin, "Volynskaia letopis' 1289–1290 gg.," *TODRL*, XIII (1957), pp. 102–117; Vodovozov, *Istoriia drevnei russkoi literatury*, pp. 129–130; A. S. Orlov, "O Galitsko-Volynskom letopisanii," *TODRL*, V (1947), pp. 15–35; and George A. Perfecky, "Studies on the Galician–Volynian (Volhynian) Chronicle," *Annals of the Ukrainian Academy of Arts and Sciences in the United States*, XII, #1-2 (33-34) (1972), pp. 67–112.

[97] Pashuto, *Ocherki po istorii Galitsko–Volynskoi Rusi*, pp. 234–238, attributes the entry to a clerical chronicler who did not appreciate Daniil's statesmanship in taking advantage of his status at the Horde to enhance Galicia-Volhynia's position in Central and Eastern Europe, but (*ibid.*, pp. 92–101) also suggests that a publicist in the reign of Daniil's son Lev, who pursued an anti-Tatar policy, invented Daniil's submission to make his heir look better. See also V. V. Mavrodin, "Levoberezhnaia Ukraina pod vlast'iu tataro-mongolov," *Uchenye zapiski L.G.U.*, #32, vyp. 2 (1939), pp. 39–65 and V. T. Pashuto, "Galitsko-Volynskoe kniazhestvo vremen Daniila Romanovicha," *Uchenye zapiski L.G.U.*, seriia ist. nauk, #67, vyp. 7 (1941), pp. 25–82.

[98] Praising the martyrdom of a dead prince such as Mikhail of Chernigov is one thing; impugning the orthodoxy of a living prince like Daniil in the "1250" annal is something else again. The author of the entry understands that Daniil had no choice but to obey; it is incredible that in effect the chronicler criticizes a prince for not dying.

[99] Begunov, *Pamiatnik russkoi literatury XIII veka*, on the basis of textological analysis, definitively disproved the theory that there had been two redactions of the *vita*, one secular/martial, the other religious/hagiographic. On the dating and sponsorship of the text, see pp. 60–61, on its relationship to the chronicles, pp. 187–194.

The ealier standard studies are V. Mansikka, *Zhitie Aleksandra Nevskogo. Razbor redaktsii i teksty* (*P.D.P.I.*, t. CLXXX; St. Petersburg, 1913) and Serebrianskii, pp. 151–222 (Analysis), 108–137 (texts).

Gunther Stökl, "Kanzler und Mitropolit," *Studien zur Geschichte*

Osteuropas, III (1966), pp. 173–174, expresses a minority view denying any involvement by metropolitan Kiril. Most scholars have accepted D. S. Likhachev, "Galits kak literaturnaia traditsiia v zhitii Aleksandra Nevskogo," *TODRL*, V (1947), pp. 36–45 and *Russkie letopisi i ikh kul'turno-istoricheskoe znachenie*, pp. 258–267, who shows that the literary tradition of the *vita* suggests authorship by a scribe in the suite of metropolitan Kiril.

[100] Begunov, *Pamiatnik russkoi literatury XIII veka*, pp. 187–194.

[101] The author of the *vita* of Nevskii habitually uses *pleniti* (to plunder) and *vziati* (to take) in contexts suggestive of raids rather then conquests, i.e., changes in sovereignty. The "Roman King" (*korol Rimskii* = Swedish king) four times expresses his intention "to plunder" Nevskii's land. The Teutonic Knights "take" Pskov, and Nevskii "frees" (*svobodi*, a rarer usage) it from captivity. Nevskii sends his son on campaign against the German Land (= Livonia) and Dmitrii "takes" Iur'ev (= Dorpat), which he obviously did not hold/conquer.

[102] *P.S.R.L.*, I, col. 476. The uprising was against the *beserman* (= Central Asian Muslim tax-farmers), not Tatar sovereignty; its one identified victim was an alcoholic apostate priest, Zosima. (For the fate of a much later apostate [*arkheian*] from Greek Orthodoxy to Islam, sent as an Ottoman envoy to the Don Cossacks, see *Voinskie povesti drevnei Rusi*, p. 51.)

It is possible the *vita* of Nevskii did not specify the *veche* uprisings because it would have been unseemly to associate Nevskii with spontaneous mass political disorder.

[103] According to the sixteenth-century Ustiug Chronicle Nevskii sent an epistle to Ustiug with an order to kill the Tatars. K. N. Serbina, ed., *Ustiuzhskii letopisnyi svod (arkhangelogorodskii letopisets)* (Moscow–Leningrad, 1950), pp. 47–48. Relying upon this information, Nasonov, *Mongoly i Rus'*, pp. 50–51, tried to find a role for Nevskii in the uprisings. A. Iugov, "Daniil Galitskii i Aleksandr Nevskii," *Voprosy istorii*, 1945, #3–4, pp. 102–106, places him at the head of the anti-Tatar coalition comprising Daniil and Nevskii's brother Andrei. Budovnits, "Ideinaia osnova rannykh narodnykh skazanii o tatarskom ige," pp. 169–170, disputes this point; cf. his *Obshchestvenno-politicheskaia mysl' drevnei Rusi*, pp. 307–309. Fennell and Leitsch (see below) would also view the Ustiug Chronicle's later legend skeptically.

More fruitful is Nasonov's suggestion that the tax-farmers were responsible to the central Mongol administration in Karakorum, not to Batu's Golden Horde; since Batu was feuding with the Karakorum leadership, he would not have objected much to the 1262 uprisings. This would have made Nevskii's task in defusing any punitive expedition much easier.

[104] Georgii Vernadskii, "Dva podviga sv. Aleksandra Nevskogo," *Evraziiskii vremennik*, 4 (Berlin, 1925), pp. 318–337. Vernadsky never modified this interpretation of Nevskii's political perspective in his later works.

Walter Leitsch, "Einige Beobachtungen zur politischen Weltbild Aleksandr Nevskys," *Forschungen zur osteuropaischen Geschichte*, 25 (1978), pp. 202–216, tries to portray Nevskii as a practitioner of *Realpolitik*, whose service in Novgorod had left him so ignorant of the politics of pastoral nomads that he perceived the Tatars as similar to the Polovtsy, i.e., he thought that they would go away. While Leitsch's analysis saves Nevskii from the mythology of the Eurasian school, it suffers from the assumption that Nevskii was so blind as to misconstrue the significance of the power of the Mongol Empire. It also presupposes that no one disabused Nevskii of his misconceptions.

[105] Metropolitan Kiril had previously been keeper-of-the-seal (*pechatnik*) for Daniil of Galicia-Volhynia. Stökl, "Kanzler und Mitropolit," pp. 154–174, disposed of the only objection to this identification by establishing conclusively that *pechatnik* Kiril would also have been a cleric, hence would have kept the

same name as the metropolitan.

The identification of Daniil's chancellor with the metropolitan who sponsored Nevskii's *vita* does create one problem: Daniil and Nevskii did not pursue identical Tatar policies. Nasonov, *Mongoly i Rus'*, pp. 39–41, tried to resolve the contradiction by arguing that Metropolitan Kiril continued Daniil's anti–Tatar coalition with Andrei Iaroslavovich. Stökl and Joseph T. Fuhrmann, "Metropolitan Cyril II (1242–1281) and the Politics of Accommodation," *Jahrbücher für Geschichte Osteuropas*, XXIV (1976), pp. 161–172, suggest otherwise, although Fuhrmann, who does not cite Nasonov's views, simply turns Kiril into an opportunist who was bought off by Mongol immunities for the Church. It seems more plausible that Kiril changed his mind either because he objected to the pro–papal element of Daniil's anti–Tatar policy or because he observed that it just did not work. For an unusual argument that the Suzdalian princes also pursued ecclesiastical union with the Catholic church, see James T. Zatko, "The Union of Suzdal, 1222–1232," *Journal of Ecclesiastical History*, 8 (1957), pp. 33–52.

[106] *Pace* the series of debunking articles by John L. I. Fennell, "Andrej Jaroslavovič and the Struggle for Power in 1252: An Investigation of the Sources," *Russia Mediaevalis*, I (1973), pp. 49–63, and "The Struggle for Power in North–East Russia, 1246–1249; An Investigation of the Sources," *Oxford Slavonic Papers*, 7 (1974), pp. 112–121, as well as Fennell and Stokes, *Early Russian Literature*, pp. 108–121, especially pp. 115 ff., and Fennell, *The Emergence of Moscow*, pp. 34–35. I think Fennell carries the grand English positivist tradition too far, although his textological spade–work is impeccable.

[107] Pereverzev, *Drevniaia russkaia literatura*, p. 97–103 (cf. Robinson Afterword, pp. 298–299); *Istoriia russkoi literatury* (1946), pp. 50–58 (Komarovich); V. O. Kliuchevskii, *Drevnerusskiia zhitiia sviatykh kak istoricheskii istochnik* (Moscow, 1871), pp. 65–71.

[108] Werner Philipp, "Heiligkeit und Herrschaft in der Vita Aleksandr Nevskijs," *Forschungen zur osteuropäischen Geschichte*, 18 (1973), pp. 55–72, is good but would have been better had he noticed Cherniavsky's discussion of this theme (see no. 109).

[109] Cherniavsky, *Tsar and People*, pp. 18–22.

[110] Cherniavsky and Roublev both cavalierly associate Nevskii with the myth of the Russian Land because they do not pay sufficient attention to the textology of his *vita*. The reconstructed primary redaction of the *vita* refers only to the Suzdalian Land; only fifteenth–century texts and manuscripts amend the text to refer to the Russian Land; see Sofia I chronicle citation in no. 111 below.

[111] The Laurentian chronicle might have contained the full text of the *vita*, but the Batu episode would have been included on its missing folia. *P.S.R.L.*, I, cols. 477–481, s.a. 1263, has the beginning of the text. Iu. K. Begunov, "Kogda zhitie Aleksandra Nevskogo voshlo v sostav Levrent'evskoi letopisi?," *Die Welt der Slaven*, XVI (1971), pp. 111–120, argues that the monk–copyist Lavrentii in 1377 inserted the *vita* into the chronicle, the view held by Komarovich. Ia. S. Lur'e, "Troitskaia letopis' i moskovskoe letopisanie XIV v.," *Vspomogatel'nye istoricheskie distsipliny*, VI (1974), p. 92, no. 45, argues that the Trinity Chronicle did contain the Nevskii *vita*, against the view of Priselkov. If the *Troitskaia letopis'* included the full Nevskii *vita*, then probably so did the original Laurentian chronicle.

The younger recension of the Novgorod First Chronicle does contain the text. *Novgorodskaia pervaia letopis'*, p. 303 (visit to Batu).

[112] Iu. K. Begunov, "Die Vita des Fürsten Aleksandr Nevskij in der Novgoroder Literatur des 15 Jahrhunderts," (tr. W. Förster) *Zeitschrift für*

Slavistik, XVI:1 (1971), pp. 88–109.   Begunov publishes the text of this manuscript on pp. 105–109.   He argues that Nevskii was popular in Novgorod because of Novgorod's pretensions to be part of the Russian Land.   Since this manuscript employs only the concept of the Suzdalian Land this argument is weak.   This text also omits Nevskii's visit to the Horde.   The ransoming of captives echoes the Sofia I chronicle, *P.S.R.L.*, V, s.a. 1246, pp. 186–187.   See also Iu. K. Begunov, "Zhitie Aleksandra Nevskogo v sbornike iz sobranii N. P. Likhacheva," *TODRL*, XXX (1976), pp. 60–72.

I have tried to disprove any identification of the elitist myth of the Russian Land with a "national" consciousness, since I doubt that the masses of the population, i.e., the peasantry, shared this attachment to the concept. See Charles J. Halperin, "The Concept of the *ruskaia zemlia* and Medieval National Consciousness," *Nationalities Papers*, VIII:1 (Spring, 1980), pp. 75–86.

[113] *P.S.R.L.*, X, 1247, pp. 134–135; 1252, pp. 138–139.   Cf.   *P.S.R.L.*, XXII, p. 200, in the *Khronograf* of 1512 and *P.S.R.L.*, XXI, the *Stepennaia kniga*, pp. 287–288, Nevskii in the Horde, pp. 280–289 *passim*; p. 289, Andrei's gaffes leading to Nevrui's campaign are attributed to lack of governmental skill and poor advisors.

I can see no pattern in which chronicles reproduce Nevskii's *vita*, with or without his confrontation with Batu.   The Moscow Chronicle of the end of the fifteenth century, for example, contains the *vita* but without Batu's reception of Nevskii.   *P.S.R.L.*, XXV, s.a. 1247, pp. 139–141.

It would be worthwhile to trace all invocations of Nevskii as a saint for assistance in battle with the Tatars; one of the earliest might be in the Basic Redaction of the *Skazanie o Mamaevom poboishche* (*Povesti o Kulikovskoi bitvy*, p. 73).

[114] It is puzzling that the author of the primary redaction of the *vita* did not use Nevskii's role in imposing the Mongol census in Novgorod in 1257–1259 as another example of his "mediating" between Christians and Tatars to avoid further bloodshed and harm to his subjects.   It might be noted as partial explanation that the first segment of the text concerns Novgorod and Pskov, and the second Nevskii's activities in the northeast as grand prince.   Only the latter discusses Russo–Tatar relations, and in general Nevskii's contact with Novgorod does not much figure in that narrative.

Chapter III

[1] *P.S.R.L.*, I, col. 476.

[2] *Troitskaia letopis'*, p. 329.   The folio on which this entry would have been recorded in the Laurentian chronicle is missing.   I dispute the standard translation of this phrase in "The Tatar Yoke and Tatar Oppression," *Russia Mediaevalis*, 5:1 (1984), pp. 20–39.

[3] E.V. Petukhov, *Serapion Vladimirskii, russkii propovednik XIII veka* (Zapiski istoriko-filologicheskago fakul'teta St. Peterburgskago universiteta, ch. XVII, 1888), Appendix, p. 14.

[4] *P.S.R.L.*, I, col. 485.

[5] *Troitskaia letopis'*, p. 46.   On the interpretation of this passage, see Halperin, "The Russian Land and the Russian Tsar," p. 65.

[6] *P.S.R.L.*, IV, p. 63.

[7] The Nevskii *vita* was written in the 1280s, and Nevskii participated in the census in Novgorod in 1259.   Discussion of his *vita* could have been included in this, rather than the preceding chapter.   Nevertheless, since the

Novgorod census is excluded from the *vita*, and its central event concerning the Tatars is Nevskii's meeting with Batu, it seemed preferable to discuss the text in chapter II.

[8]Kargalov, *Vneshnepoliticheskie faktory razvitiia feodal'noi Rusi*, pp. 107–109.

[9]I have made liberal use of the discussion in Michel Roublev *The Scourge of God* (III), "Aspects of the New Order" (sub–chapter), "*Chislo* - the Census," which contains nearly a complete translation of the 1257 and 1259 entries. Nevertheless my conclusions differ from Roublev's.

[10]*P.S.R.L.*, I, cols. 474–475. Whether this decimal organization was of tax–payers (i.e., fiscal) or recruits (i.e., military contingents under *baskaki*) is a matter of dispute.

[11]*Novgorodskaia pervaia letopis'*, p. 82.

[12]Roublev infers that Nevskii punished the *boyare* and expelled Vasilii at the orders of the Tatars, which may be correct. Presniakov, *Obrazovanie velikorusskago gosudarstva*, p. 57, no. 4, draws the conclusion that Vasilii and his *boyare* opposed Nevskii's Tatar policy, and therefore the division of adherents and opponents of the Tatars along social lines in the 1259 entry is exaggerated. This is a sound point.
M. N. Tikhomirov, glava 20, "Bor'ba 'men'shikh' i 'viatshikh' v Novgorode serediny XIII v.," in his *Krest'ianskie i gorodskie vosstaniia na Rusi XI–XIII vv.* (Moscow, 1955), pp. 265–274, argues that the feuds between Nevskii and his son Vasilii and *boyare* had nothing to do with the Tatars. The Novgorodians did not object to the census, only to aristocratic manipulation of it, since they were willing to perform the enumeration themselves. This argument seems unconvincing: the chronicler objects to any census of Christians in order to pay taxes to infidels.

[13]*Novgorodskaia pervaia letopis'*, pp. 82–83.

[14]Andrei Yaroslavovich had been party to the anti–Tatar coalition with Daniil of Galicia–Volhynia which produced the punitive expedition of Nevrui in 1251. Andrei had fled abroad, but returned and was restored to a position of prominence by his forgiving brother. He was now loyal to Nevskii's pro–Tatar line.

[15]Boris Vasil'kovich supposedly advised Mikhail of Chernigov to submit to Batu, and hence would have been pro–Tatar. He may also have been the sponsor of the *vita* of Mikhail, which acknowledges the legitimacy of Tatar authority. Certainly Nevskii's aides in 1257–1259 had ample experience with the Tatars.

[16]This is Roublev's view, although he has successfully demonstrated, ironically enough, that the Muscovites manipulated their apportionment of the *vykhod* inequitably, which presumably violated Mongol intent; actually the Mongols cared mostly for the gross amount of the tribute, not its equity. See Michel Roublev, "Le tribut aux Mongoles d'après les Testaments et Accords des Princes Russes," *Cahiers du monde russe et soviétique*, VII (1966), pp. 487–530, translated as "The Mongol Tribute according to the Wills and Agreements of the Russian Princes," in Michael Cherniavsky, ed., *The Structure of Russian History* (New York, 1970), pp. 29–64.

[17]See Tikhomirov's view (no. 12 above) and Nasonov, *Mongoly i Rus'*, pp. 11–16, especially p. 14.

[18]E.g., Budovnits, *Obshchestvenno–politecheskaia mysl' drevnei Rusi*, pp. 321–323.

[19]D. S. Likhachev in *Istoriia russkoi literatury* (1946), pp. 114–121,

especially p. 116.

[20]The *boyare* did not succeed in becoming *tarkhan*, i.e., tax exempt, as the Church did, so they did not shirk their fiscal obligations entirely.

[21]Vernadsky, *The Mongols and Russia*, pp. 377–378. However, it must be remembered that the Russian countryside was pagan in the thirteenth century, and Russian pagans would not have found much comfort from the sermons of a Christian bishop.

[22]The standard work is Petukhov, *Serapion Vladimirskii, russkii propovednik XIII veka*, from which most of this discussion is taken. Also consult Gudzii, *Istoriia drevnei russkoi literatury*, pp. 205–208, and *Istoriia russkoi literatury* (1946), pp. 45–50. The only dissenter is Michel Gorlin, "Serapion de Wladimir, prèdicateur de Kiev," *Revue des Études slaves*, 24 (1948), pp. 21–28; see no. 29.

[23]Petukhov, Appendix, p. 2. I have striven for literal rather than literary translations of passages of Serapion's sermons; I have used Roublev's versions for comparison.

[24]*Ibid.*, p. 5.

[25]*Ibid.*, p. 8.

[26]*Ibid.*, p. 12.

[27]*Ibid.*, p. 14.

[28]Budovnits, *Obshchestvenno–politicheskaia mysl' drevnei Rusi*, pp. 335–339, describes Serapion's picture of *Rus'* as "humanist," a great concession given Budovnits's opinion of the Church's reaction to the Mongol conquest.

[29]Gorlin argues that the first four sermons were delivered in Kiev, in 1230, 1240, 1260, and 1273–1274, and only the last in Vladimir. In his fifth sermon Serapion dropped reference to "slavery" to the Tatars and praised their morality, which Gorlin sees as a reflection of the "correct if not peaceful relations" of northeastern *Rus'* with the Tatars. I am skeptical that anyone could have delivered a sermon in Kiev in the 1260s or 1270s, since the city was virtually deserted, and Tatar authority over Kiev was not in doubt. Moreover the fifth sermon does not seem to me to be entirely favorable to the Tatars. See the response to Gorlin of N. K. Gudzii, "Gde i kogda potekali literaturnaia deiatel'nost' Serapiona Vladimirskogo?," *Izvestiia otdeleniia literatury i iazyka A. N. SSSR*, vyp. 5, Moscow, 1952, pp. 450–456, who convincingly disputes Gorlin's argument.

[30]V. A. Kolobanov, "K voprosu ob uchastii Serapiona Vladimirskogo v sobornykh 'deianiiakh' 1274 g.," *TODRL*, XVI (1960), pp. 442–445.

[31]*Russkaia istoricheskaia biblioteka*, VI (2nd ed.; St. Petersburg, 1908), #6, col. 86.

[32]V. A. Kolobanov, "O Serapione Vladimirskom kak vozmozhnom avtore 'Poucheniia k popom,'" *TODRL*, XIV (1958), pp. 159–162.

[33]*Russkaia istoricheskaia biblioteka*, VI, #12, cols, 136, 138.

[34]V. A. Kolobanov, "Oblichenie kniazheskikh mezhdousobii v poucheniiakh Serapiona Vladimirskogo," *TODRL*, XVII (1961), pp. 329–333, concludes that Serapion and Metropolitan Kirill shared the same attitude toward the Russian princes: neither blamed the princes for the Mongol conquest or Russia's troubles.

[35]M. N. Tikhomirov, "Vossozdanie russkoi pis'mennoi traditsii v pervye desiatiletiia Tatarskogo iga," *Vestnik istorii mirovoi kul'tury*, 1957, #3, pp. 3–13, sees the Church Council of 1274 as a response to the Mongol census,

which would make it a very delayed response indeed. Tikhomirov logically infers that since Russian sins led to Mongol conquest, Russian repentance and moral reform would restore God's favor and lead to the overthrow of the Mongols, which may be too logical. Tikhomirov further contends that the Church, like the princes, was divided on the Tatar issue: some clerics wanted to use the Mongols to protect themselves while others sought to resist the Tatar Yoke.

[36]Cherniavsky, "Khan or Basileus," pp. 467, 468.

[37]O. Miller, "O drevnerusskoi literature po otnosheniiu k tatarskomu igu," p. 55, infers from the sermons of Serapion and the "rules" (pravila) of the 1274 council that at least the Church was not totally craven toward the Tatars.

[38]Cf. F. W. Mote, "Confucian Eremitism in the Yüan Period," in A. F. Wright, ed., The Confucian Persuasion (Stanford, 1960), pp. 202–240, 348–353.

[39]For a recent theory about the baskak system, see V. V. Kargalov, "Baskaki," Voprosy istorii, 1972, #5, pp. 212–216. Michel Roublev has prepared a different analysis and I address the question in Chapter IV, "The Mongol Administration of Russia," in Russia and the Golden Horde, pp. 33–43.

[40]The Laurentian chronicle, P.S.R.L., I, cols. 481–482, lacks the beginning of the Tale, which should have been located on its missing folia. The Troitskaia letopis', pp. 340–342, and Simeon chronicle, P.S.R.L., XVIII, pp. 79–81, contain the full stable text. Therefore we may infer the Laurentian chronicle first recorded the tale in its complete form.

[41]The tale can be found in the Moscow Chronicle of 1479, P.S.R.L., XXV, pp. 154–155; the L'vov Chronicle, P.S.R.L., XX, pp. 169–170; the Voskresensk Chronicle of the sixteenth century, P.R.S.L., VIII, pp. 176–178; and the Nikon Chronicle, P.S.R.L., X, pp. 163–165. On the Nikon redaction see below. The tale is also missing in the Tverian chronicles. I know of no textological analysis of the tale of Akhmat.

[42]M. D. Priselkov, Istoriia russkogo letopisaniia XI–XV vv. (Leningrad, 1940), p. 109, assigns the composition of the tale to Tver' in 1305 on the basis of oral sources. Istoriia russkoi literatury (1946), p. 100, mentions Rostov-Suzdal' or Novgorod the Great as places of origin of the tale. V. A. Kuchkin, Povesti o Mikhaile Tverskom. Istoriko-tekstologicheskoe issledovanie (Moscow, 1974), p. 4, believes someone in Vladimir recorded the story of a refugee from Kursk. Finally Lur'e, Obshcherusskie letopisi XIV–XV vv., p. 35, follows Priselkov and states that the "anti-Tatar" redactor in Tver' in 1305 wrote the tale.

[43]Nasonov, Mongoly i Rus', pp. 70–71, and "Lavrent'evskaia letopis' i Vladimirskoe velikokniazheskoe letopisanie pervoi poloviny XIII v.," p. 450.

[44]Nogai's Chingisid status is a matter of dispute, but in any event for him to have become involved in a backwater banditry episode was hardly consistent with his grand political endeavors. See Saunders, History of the Mongol Conquests, pp. 160–163; Grekov and Iakubovskii, Zolotaia orda i ee padenie, pp. 84, 86. The classic study of Nogai is N. I. Veselovskii, "Khan iz temnikov Zolotoi ordy Nogai i ego vremia," Zapiski Rossiisskoi Akademii Nauk, otdelenie istoricheskikh nauk i filosofii, tom XIII, #6 (Petrograd, 1922), pp. 1–58.

[45]Troitskaia letopis', s.a. 1297, pp. 347–348; Nasonov, Mongoly i Rus', pp. 71–77.

[46]The Nikon chronicle redaction of the Tale, P.S.R.L., X, pp. 163–165, contains much re-writing. A new introduction declares that it was the

custom of the Horde *tsari* and princes to take tribute (*dan'*) from the Russian Land (a phrase absent from the original tale) either directly or by farming it out to Russian princes or *gosty* (merchants) from the Horde. Muslim tax–farmers were not called merchants, and Russian princes did not begin to collect tribute until after the elimination of the *baskak* system. The Nikon chronicler says that among the tax–farmers assigned to *Rus'* was *baskak* Akhmat. This generalization cannot be trusted as a theory of Mongol tribute–collection.

The Nikon chronicler also alters the "merchant pilgrims," an odd phrase since the two categories of merchants and pilgrims should have been kept separate. He changes them to German and Byzantine (*Tsaregradskie*) merchants, a detail repeated uncritically in S. M. Soloviev, *Istoriia Rossii s drevneishikh vremen* (Moscow, 1963), II, pp. 213–215.

This redaction, which is padded in typical Nikon fashion with speeches and verbose didactic asides, closes with a diatribe excoriating divisions among the Russian princes. Even this short version of a much longer tale, the Nikon chronicler declares, should arouse tears and mourning in the reader.

[47] N. M. Karamzin, *Istoriia gosudarstva Rossiiskago* (St. Petersburg, 1892), IV, Notes, p. 56, no. 167, disposed of some fantastic remarks on this problem by Boltin.

[48] Despite Lur'e's views (see no. 42).

[49] V. V. Kargalov, "Osvoboditel'naia bor'ba Rusi protiv mongolo–tatarskogo iga," *Voprosy istorii*, 1969, #4, p. 128, writes that Akhmat's inability to return to *Rus'* demonstrates that Russia had already recovered from the Mongol conquest and was resisting Mongol rule, an optimistic assessment of the situation.

[50] This is the conclusion of Kuchkin in *Povesti o Mikhaile Tverskom*, the most extensive study of the text. See the favorable review by John L. I. Fennell in *Ruscia Mediaevalis*, III (1977), pp. 93–98.

[51] *P.S.R.L.*, V, pp. 207–215.

[52] Fourteenth– and fifteenth–century Russian sources usually do not specify that the *velikoe kniazhenie* (grand principality) was "of Vladimir," although that is clearly the meaning.

[53] This is an anachronism. No Tverian author of the fourteenth century would use the phrase this way. Kuchkin, *Povesti o Mikhaile Tverskom*, pp. 219–220, argues that the "Suzdalian Land" (*Suzdal'skaia zemlia*) was the original reading.

[54] This sentence might be an interpolation from the "chronicle tale" of the battle of Kulikovo from the "compilation" of 1448, found in both the Sofia I and Novgorod IV chronicles, concerning Dmitrii Donskoi, whom it better fits.

[55] I suspect that according Yurii the title of "grand prince" is also an interpolation; I doubt the original Tverian author would be so respectful.

[56] See Kliuchevskii, *Drevnerusskiia zhitiia sviatykh kak istoricheskii istochnik*, pp. 71–74; Nasonov, *Mongoly i Rus'*, pp. 84, 87; *Istoriia russkoi literatury* (1946), pp. 101–103; Cherepnin, *Obrazovanie russkogo tsentralizovannogo gosudarstva*, p. 467; Budovnits, *Obshchestvenno–politicheskaia mysl' drenvei Rusi*, pp. 369–377; and L. A. Dmitriev in *Istoki russkoi belletristiki*, pp. 216–219.

[57] *P.S.R.L.*, XV, s.a. 1317, col. 36, s.a. 1318, cols. 36–40.

[58] *P.S.R.L.*, XXV, pp. 161–166.

[59]Kuchkin, *Povesti o Mikhaile Tverskom*, pp. 224–234.

[60]*Ustiuzhskii letopisnyi svod*, pp. 49–50.

[61]*P.S.R.L.*, X, pp. 182–186, s.a. 1319. Kuchkin, *Povesti o Mikhaile Tverskom*, pp. 134–152, presents a forced argument that the intent of the Nikon chronicle is to compromise Mikhail's Orthodoxy and present Uzbek as a model of an ideal sixteenth–century *tsar'* who renders a just verdict on the guilty Mikhail.

[62]John L. I. Fennell, "The Ideological Role of the Russian Church in the First Half of the Fourteenth Century," in *Gorski Vijenac. A Garland of Essays Offered to Professor Elizabeth Hill* (Cambridge, England, 1970), pp. 105–111, on the Tale of Mikhail of Tver', pp. 109–110, finds all early fourteenth–century Tverian texts "soft" on the Tatars, "cool and objective" in their attitude, deflecting moral censure from the Tatars onto other Russians, restrained in their language in never going beyond such standard and conventional nouns as "evil" (*zlo*), "harm" (*pakosti*), and "burden" (*tiagota*) or stock epithets for individuals such as "evil" (*liut, zol*). Fennell finds remarkable the presentation of the Tatars at times in a chivalrous light and of Tatar power as neutral or benevolent.

[63]Cherniavsky, "Khan or Basileus," *passim*, which is not cited by Fennell. Fennell does not distinguish between the portrayal of "the Tatars" and that of the khan/*tsar'* in the medieval Russian sources.

[64]Cherniavsky, *Tsar and People*, pp. 14–16.

[65]Kuchkin, *Povesti o Mikhaile Tverskom*, pp. 247–264, describes the political ideas of the Tale as "restrained" on the Tatar issue because Mongol power was still so strong that more explicit calls for liberation from the Tatar Yoke would have been imprudent. This argument translates medieval Russian allegorical and theological expression into modern political terms a bit too cleverly. Kuchkin still modernizes and fails to respect the apolitical stance of the Tale on Tatar sovereignty. See also V. A. Kuchkin, "Odin iz istochnikov Ellinskogo letopistsa vtorogo vida," *Vizantiiskii vremennik*, 27 (1967), pp. 319–324. His analysis also rests on the premise that the Mongols cared what was written about them in a Russian *vita*.

[66]*P.S.R.L.*, XV, s.a. 1326–1327, cols. 42–44.

[67]*Troitskaia letopis'*, s.a. 1327, pp. 358–359. Given the depiction of the consequences of Fedorchuk's campaign, it is not easy to explain this omission by a "pro–Tatar" attitude of the Trinity chronicler, although no other explanation has been offered.

[68]*P.S.R.L.*, IV, pp. 50–51.

[69]*Novgorodskaia pervaia letopis'*, s.a., 1327, p. 98.

[70]*Pskovskie letopisi*, tt. I–II (Moscow–Leningrad, 1941, 1955), ed., A. N. Nasonov, I, Pskov First Chronicle, pp. 16–17. It is indicative either of Pskovian provincialism or Tatar indifference that this is the first mention of the Tatars in the Pskov chronicle since the annal for 1240!

[71]*Russkaia zemlia* here is an anachronism.

[72]The Pskov chronicler's affection for and loyalty to Alexander Mikhailovich did not abate with his departure from the city; Alexander's death in the Horde is also recorded, s.a. 1339, *ibid.*, p. 18.

[73]On Shevkal's identity see Nasonov, *Mongoly i Rus'*, p. 91, no. 6.

[74]Both Cherepnin and Fennell describe Chol Khan as a *baskak*; see nos. 79, 81.

[75]Karamzin, IV, p. 129, observed aristocratically that the people (*narod*) would believe any slander against the Tatars, thought to be capable of any evil. Since the khans still protected the privileges of the Russian Orthodox Church, whoever invented the accusation knew he was lying. I am suspicious of the elitist implication that the naive and credulous masses could be so easily fooled.

[76]S. M. Soloviev, II, p. 230, who remembers that Uzbek's sister had converted to Orthodox Christianity to marry Yurii Daniilovich of Moscow, which would suggest that Uzbek was more flexible on religion when it came to politics.

[77]So writes G. A. Fedorov–Davydov, *Obshchestvennyi stroi Zolotoi Ordy* (Moscow, 1973), p. 137, an unfortunate slip for so trustworthy an orientalist.

[78]Presniakov, *Obrazovanie velikorusskago gosudarstva*, p. 137, sees Chol Khan's mission as to terrorize the Russian population, which relies too heavily upon the exaggerations of the chronicle. Presniakov is followed by Budovnits, *Obshchestvenno–politicheskaia mysl' drevnei Rusi*, pp. 377–378.

[79]This suggestion was made by B. A. Romanov in commentary in the 1948 edition of *Khozhenie za tri moria Afanasiia Nikitina*, p. 84. It is seriously developed in the works of Fennell. See John L. I. Fennell, "The Tver' Uprising of 1327: A Study of the Sources," *Jahrbücher für Geschichte Osteuropas*, XV (1967), pp. 161–179, and in his *The Emergence of Moscow*, pp. 105–110 *et passim*. Fennell wrote that no Soviet textological analysis of the 1327 tales existed, which would seem to slight Cherepnin's article (see no. 81).

[80]Fennell sees the events of 1339 which culminated in Alexander Mikhailovich's death as a replay of the provocation of 1327. Fennell, *The Emergence of Moscow*, pp. 157–169.

[81]Cherepnin speaks of the "preparation" for the uprising, which lends too much consciousness to the narrative, but his is the most sensitive appreciation of urban riot psychology concerning 1327. See L. V. Cherepnin, "Istochniki po istorii anti–mongol'skogo vosstaniia v Tveri v 1327 g.," *Arkheograficheskii ezhegodnik za 1958* (1960), pp. 37–53, and in his *Obrazovanie russkogo tsentralizovannogo gosudarstva*, pp. 475–496.

[82]This is Fennell's conclusion.

[83]See below, Chapter V, on the sources about the Muscovite civil war.

[84]For accusations of equal fantasy against Mamai, which most scholars also see as reflecting mid–fifteenth–century Russian opinion, see Chapter IV on the "chronicle tale" of 1380.

[85]O. Miller, "O drevnerusskoi literature po otnosheniiu k tatarskomu igu," p. 54, no. 6.
Presumably the theory that the Tatars followed Russian chronicle–writing rests upon the slim reed of a single reference to the presentation of Russian chronicles to the Horde in the dispute over dynastic succession in the Muscovite house in the middle of the fifteenth century (see Chapter V). I have never seen an explicit exposition of the theory that the Horde was informed of the contents and ideology of the medieval Russian written sources.

[86]Vodovozov, *Istoriia drevnei russkoi litertury*, pp. 134–137.
However, Ia. S. Lur'e pointed out to me that the surviving Tatars had been outside the city walls when the uprising took place, and might not have been informed of its nature.

[87]Fennell also describes the Trinity Chronicle narrative of the Fedorchiuk campaign as matter–of–fact and devoid of "emotional overtones" which might

arouse anti-Tatar hatred in the reader; I cannot agree.

[88]A case has been made that the 1327 uprising inspired several historical songs which reflect the "popular" (narodnyi) reaction to Chol Khan. However Chol Khan is credited with willingness to commit cannibalism against his own son in order to receive a grant of territories in Rus'. He also intends to execute any Russian who cannot or will not pay the tribute. Such fantastic narrative and other anachronistic errors make it difficult to extract a lucid, let alone contemporary, Russian political response to Chol Khan from the songs. For this theory see Budovnits, Obshchestvenno-politicheskaia mysl' drevnei Rusi, pp. 380–383; Cherepnin, Obrazovanie russkogo tsentralizovannogo gosudarstva, pp. 484–488; and Ia. S. Lur'e, "Rol' Tveri v sozdanii russkogo natsional'nogo gosudarstva," Uchenye zapiski L.G.U., #36, seriia ist. nauk, vyp. 3, 1939, pp. 102–104. A. A. Zimin, "Pesnia o Shchelkane i vozniknovenie zhanra istoricheskoi pesni," Istoriia SSSR, 1963, #3, pp. 98–110, attributes the songs to the sixteenth century, which would make it impossible to cite them as illustrations of fourteenth-century Russian public opinion.

[89]Istoriia russkoi literatury (1946), pp. 103–104, leaves the question of Chol Khan's motive or purpose open.

[90]P.S.R.L., X, pp. 194–195.

[91]Despite B.I. Dubentsov, "K voprosu o tak nazyvaevom 'Letopistse kniazheniia Tferskago,'" TODRL, XIII (1957), pp. 139–141.

[92]Nasonov, Mongoly i Rus', p. 4.

[93]For an uncritical and sometimes extravagant narrative of the anti-Tatar phase of Tverian politics see V. G. Kartsov, "Antiordynskaia politika Tverskogo kniazhestva," in Iz proshlogo Kalininskoi oblasti (Kalinin, 1974), pp. 58–81.

Chapter IV

[1]Soloviev, Istoriia Rossii s drenveishikh vremen, II, p. 287.

[2]N. Veselovskii, "Kulikovskaia bitva (po povodu ee piatisotletiia)," Drevniaia i Novaia Rossiia, XVIII, September, 1880, p. 5–23. Cf. the equally commemorative D. Ilovaiskii, Kulikovskaia pobeda Dmitriia Ivanovicha Donskago (Moscow, 1880), or the hortatory M. N. Tikhomirov, "Bor'ba russkogo naroda s mongolo-tatarskimi zavoevateliami. Dmitrii Donskoi," in his Drevniaia Rus' (Moscow, 1975), pp. 381–389, written in 1944. All three publications originated as speeches.

The six-hundredth anniversary of the battle of Kulikovo in 1980 inspired an extensive wave of new publications in the Soviet Union. Some selected titles include V. V. Kargalov, "Kulikovskaia bitva i ee mesto v otechestvennoi istorii," Prepodovanie istorii v shkole, 1979, #5, pp. 15–23, in anticipation of the coming anniversary; L. G. Beskrovnyi, ed., Kulikovskaia bitva. sbornik stat'ei (Moscow, 1980), the major collection of articles from the several 1980 conferences; and V. A. Kuchkin, "Pobeda na Kulikovom pole," Voprosy istorii, 1980, #8, pp. 3–21. Other literature will be cited below.

[3]Material in this chapter is taken from my "The Russian Land and the Russian Tsar," as published in the Forschungen zur osteuropaischen Geschichte, to which I shall make page references. While I have adjusted my summary of the textology of the texts to incorporate the latest, especially Soviet, research, my interpretations of the contents of the texts have not changed. I have tried to avoid repeating scholarly apparatus.

[4]The most convenient reference is Likhachev, *Kul'tura Rusi vremeni Andreia Rubleva i Epifaniia Premudrogo*. For a recent restatement of his appreciation of this period, see D. S. Likhachev, "Kulikovskaia bitva v istorii russkoi kul'tury. *Pamiatniki otechestva*, IV (Moscow, 1979), pp. 244–256.

Henrik Birnbaum, "Serbian models in the Literature and Literary Language of Medieval Russia," *Slavic and East European Journal*, 23:1 (Spring, 1979), pp. 1–13, criticizes the theories of Likhachev and others on fourteenth- and fifteenth–century Russian culture and advances yet another conceptualization.

[5]V. A. Plugin, "Nekotorye problemy izucheniia biografii i tvorchestva Andreia Rubleva," in *Drevnerusskoe iskusstvo. Khudozhestvennaia kul'tura Moskvy i prilezhashchikh k nei kniazhestv XIV-XVI vv.* (Moscow, 1970), pp. 73–86, and his *Mirovozrenie Andreia Rubleva (nekotorye problemy). Drevnerusskaia zhivopis' kak istoricheskii istochnik* (Moscow, 1974)), here especially pp. 30–46. Much of this monograph is art history, but Plugin's biography of Rublev (pp. 8–29) and appreciation of cultural context are impressive.

[6]For this interpretation see the numerous works of the prolific G. M. Prokhorov: "Etnicheskaia integratsiia v Vostochnoi Evrope v XIV v. (ot isikhastskikh sporov do Kulikovskoi bitvy)," *Doklady otdeleniia etnografii Geograficheskogo obshchestva*, vyp. 2 (Leningrad, 1966), pp. 81–110; "Povest' o Mitiae–Mikhaile i ee literaturnaia sreda." Dissertatsiia na soiskanii uchenoi stepeni kandidata filologicheskikh nauk (Leningrad, Institut russkoi literatury, 1968); "Isikhazm i obshchestvennaia mysl' v Vostochnoi Evrope v XIV v.," *TODRL*, XXIII (1968), pp. 86–108; *Povest' o Mitiae (Rus' i Vizantiia v epokhu Kulikovskoi bitvy)* (Leningrad, 1978) [see *Byzantine Studies*, 9:2 (1982), pp. 355–357]; "Kul'turnye svoeobrazie epokhi Kulikovskoi bitvy," *TODRL*, XXXIV (1979), pp. 3–17; and "Drevneishaia rukopis' s proizvedenniiami mitropolita Kipriana," *Pamiatniki kul'tury. Novye otkrytiia. Ezhegodnik 1978 g. Pis'mennost'. Iskusstvo. Arkheologiia* (Leningrad, 1979), pp. 17–30. Prokhorov's work on the Laurentian Chronicle's account of the invasion of Batu and on late fourteenth–century chronicle-writing is all of a piece.

Prokhorov's interpretation has exerted a major influence on John Meyendorff, *Byzantium and the Rise of Russia. A Study of Byzantine–Russian Relations in the Fourteenth Century* (Cambridge, England, 1981).

[7]Charles J. Halperin, "Kiev and Moscow: An Aspect of Early Muscovite Thought," *Russian History*, 7:3 (1980), pp. 312–321. Cf. N. S. Borisov, "Kulikovskaia bitva i nekotorye voprosy dukhovnoi zhizni Rusi XIV–XV vv.," *Vestnik Mosk. Univ.*, seriia, 8, Istoriia, 1980, #5, pp. 56–66.

[8]D. S. Likhachev, *Natsional'noe samosoznanie drevnei Rusi. Ocherki iz oblasti russkoi literatury XI-XVII vv* (Moscow–Leningrad, 1945), p. 71; Likhachev, *Russkie letopisi i ikh kul'turno–istoricheskoe znachenie*, pp. 292–305; Likhachev, *Kul'tura Rusi vremeni Andreia Rubleva i Epifaniia Premudrogo*, pp. 19–20; and in many other places.

[9]I. B. Grekov, "O pervonachal'nom variante 'Skazaniia o Mamaevom poboishche,'" *Sovetskoe slavianovedenie*, 1970, #6, pp. 27–36; I. B. Grekov, "Ideino–politicheskaia napravlennost' literaturnykh pamiatnikov feodal'noi Rusi kontsa XIV v.," in *Pol'sha i Rus'* (Moscow, 1974), pp. 378–421; I. B. Grekov, *Vostochnaia Evropa i upadok Zolotoi Ordy (na rubezhe XIV-XV vv.)* (Moscow, 1975), pp. 311–482 [see my review of this book in *American Historical Review*, 81:3 (June, 1976), pp. 626–627]; and "Kulikovskaia bitva—vazhnaia vekha v politicheskoi zhizni Vostochnoi Evropy vtoroi poloviny XIV v.," *Sovetskoe slavianovedenie*, 1980, #5, pp. 3–22.

While I share Grekov's approach, I disagree with his textual interpretations in ways too numerous to discuss.

[10] *Troitskaia letopis'*, pp. 415–416.   See Halperin, "The Russian Land and the Russian Tsar," p. 39.

[11] Cherepnin, *Obrazovanie russkogo tsentralizovannogo gosudarstva*, p. 595, draws a confused contrast between Mamai, *de facto* but not *de jure, tsar'*, and Donskoi, who is worthy to be a *tsar'* (but lacks the title?).   This misses the point of the Tale of the Battle on the river Vozha and obscures the logic of the so-called *vita* of Dmitrii Donskoi, which calls him *tsar'*. The victorious Russian army captured a priest, Ivan Vasil'evich, returning from the Horde with a supply of poison; he was sent to *Lache ozera* (*Troitskaia letopis'*, p. 417).   The Sofia First Chronicle likens his fate to that of Daniil *Zatochnik* (The Prisoner) (*P.S.R.L.*, V, s.a. 1379, p. 237).   The Nikon chronicler makes Ivan Vasil'evich a *tysiatskii* and member of the Vel'iaminov family (*P.S.R.L.*, XI, pp. 42–43).   The priest has been accused of intent to poison Dmitrii Donskoi or even the entire Russian army, or taken for a Tatar scout.   For a variety of views of his identification and activity see S. M. Soloviev, II, p. 294; Vodovozov, *Istoriia drevnei russkoi literatury*, p. 142; I. Grekov, *Ocherki po istorii mezhdunarodnykh otnoshenii Vostochnoi Evropy XIV–XVI vv.* (Moscow, 1963), p. 61, no. 238; Cherepnin, *Obrazovanie russkogo tsentralizovannogo gosudarstva*, pp. 595–596; Kuz'min, *Riazanskoe letopisanie*, p. 218; Poluboiarinova, pp. 20–21; and V. Zubkov, *Bitva na Vozhe* (Riazan', 1966), pp. 18–19.   Most serious scholars reject the interpolation of the Nikon chronicler and think the priest neither a member nor a servitor of the Vel'iaminov family; otherwise the sparse chronicle information on him makes it impossible to determine what he was doing in the steppe.

[12] *Troitskaia letopis*, pp. 419–421; *P.S.R.L.*, IV, pp. 75–83.   This discussion draws upon Halperin, "The Russian Land and the Russian Tsar," pp. 39–44.

[13] M. A. Salmina, "'Letopisnaia povest' o Kulikovskoi bitve' i 'Zadonshchina,'" in D. S. Likhachev and L. A. Dmitriev, eds., *Slovo o polku Igoreve i pamiatniki Kulikovskogo tsikla* (Moscow–Leningrad, 1966), pp. 344–384.

[14] This discussion is based upon Halperin, "The Russian Land and the Russian Tsar," pp. 58–68.

[15] Ia. S. Lur'e, "K probleme svoda 1448 g.," *TODRL*, XXIV (1969), pp. 142–146; "Troitskaia letopis' i moskovskoe letopisanie XIV v.," pp. 79–106; "Obshcherusskii svod—protograf Sofiiskoi I i Novgorodskoi IV letopisei," *TODRL*, XXVIII (1974), pp. 114–139; "Esche raz o svode 1448 g. i Novgorodskoi Karamzinskoi letopisi," *TODRL*, XXXII (1977), p. 199–218; *Obshcherusskie letopisi XIV–XV vv.*, pp. 36–121; and "Povest' o bitve na Lipitse 1216 g. v letopisanii XIV–XV vv.," pp. 96–115.

[16] S. N. Azbelev's response to the Salmina–Lur'e schema involves his ideosyncratic theory of the role of "oral historical songs" in the composition of the Kulikovo cycle and his insistence that Novgorodian troops participated in the battle.   Of his many articles on these themes see S. N. Azbelev: "Kulikovskaia bitva v slavianskom fol'klore," *Russkii fol'klor*, XI (1968), pp. 78–101; "Mladshie letopisi Novgoroda o Kulikovskoi bitvy," in *Problemy istorii feodal'noi Rossii. Sb. st. k 60–letiiu V. V. Mavrodina* (Moscow, 1971), pp. 110–117; "Skazanie o pomoshchi novgorodtsev Dmitriiu Donskomu," *Russkii fol'klor*, XIII (1972), pp. 77–102; "Povest' o Kulikovskoi bitvy v Novgorodskoi letopisi Dubrovskogo," *Letopisi i khroniki. Sb. st. 1973 g. posv. pamiati A. N. Nasonova* (Moscow, 1974), pp. 164–172; and "Ob ustnykh istochnikakh letopisnykh tekstov (po materialem Kulikovskogo tsikla)," *Letopisi i khroniki. M. N. Tikhomirov i letopisevedenie* (Moscow, 1976), pp. 78–101.

On Fedor Torusskii also see A. N. Kirpichnikov, *Kulikovskaia bitva* (Leningrad, 1980), pp. 8–9.

[17]I. B. Grekov, "Ideino-politicheskaia napravlennost' literaturnykh pamiatnikov feodal'noi Rusi kontsa XIV v.," pp. 386–389, 394–399; *Vostochnaia Evropa i upadok Zolotoi Ordy,* pp. 127–147, 314–318, 329–334, 443–455; and "Mesto Kulikovskoi bitvy v politicheskoi zhizni Vostochnoi Evropy kontsa XIV veka," in *Kulikovskaia bitva,* pp. 118–122.

Cf. W. Vodoff, "Quand a pu être composé le Panygirique du grand-prince Dmitrii Ivanovich, tsar' russe?" *Canadian-American Slavic Studies,* 13:1–2 (1979), pp. 86–87.

[18]M. A. Salmina, "Eshche raz o datirovke 'Letopisnoi povesti' o Kulikovskoi bitve," *TODRL,* XXIII (1977), pp. 3–39.

For a critique of Salmina's analysis and further discussion of the dating of the Chronicle Tale of 1380, see L. A. Dmitriev, "Kulikovskaia bitva 1380 goda v literaturnykh pamiatnikakh drevnei Rusi," *Russkaia literatura,* 1980, #3, pp. 15–19.

[19]V. A. Kuchkin, "Tverskoi istochnik Vladimirskogo polikhrona," *Letopisi i khroniki* (Moscow, 1976), pp. 102–112; G. M. Prokhorov, "Izbytochnye materialy Rogozhskogo letopistsa," *Vspomogatel'nye istoricheskie distsipliny,* VIII (1976), pp. 185–203; Prokhorov, "Kharakteristika Dionisiia Suzdal'skogo," in *Kul'turnoe nasledie drevnei Rusi. Istoki. Stanovlenie. Traditsii* (Moscow, 1976), pp. 86–88; Prokhorov, "Letopisets Velikii Russkii: Analiz ego upominaniia v Troitskoi letopisi," *Letopisi i khroniki* (Moscow, 1976), pp. 67–77; Prokhorov, "Letopisnye podborki rukopisi GPB, F.IV.603 i problema svodnogo obshcherusskogo letopisaniia," *TODRL,* XXXII (1977), pp. 165–198; Prokhorov, "Tsentral'norusskoe letopisanie vtoroi poloviny XIV v. (Analiz Rogozhskogo letopistsi i obshchie soobrazheniia)," *Vspomogatel'nye istoricheskie distsipliny,* X (1978), pp. 159–181; V. A. Plugin, "Nereshennye voprosy russkogo letopisaniia XIV–XV vekov (K vyvodu v svet knigi Ia. S. Lur'e, "Obshcherusskie letopisi XIV–XV vv.")," *Istoriia SSSR,* 1978, #4, pp. 73–93.

[20]For example, see the extensive review of Lur'e, *Obshcherusskie letopisi XIV–XV vv.,* by John L. I. Fennell in *Russia Mediaevalis,* IV (1979), pp. 71–78.

[21]Though medieval chronicle-writing may not have been so common-sensical, I retain my sympathy for this argument from 1973 and 1976. However, I am now more sensitive to the impossibility of proving it.

[22]Kuchkin, "Pobeda na Kulikovom pole," p. 8, argues that the *Friazi* are Venetians from Azov, not Genoese from Kaffa.

[23]Despite Kuz'min, *Riazanskoe letopisanie,* pp. 220–228.

[24]D. S. Likhachev, *Razvitie russkoi literatury X–XVII vekov. Etiudi i stili* (Leningrad, 1973), p. 102.

[25]Vodovozov, *Istoriia drevnei russkoi literatury,* p. 146, and *Ocherki istorii SSSR,* III, p. 228, notice this aspect of the exchange of envoys.

[26]*Troitskaia letopis',* p. 465.

[27]V. L. Egorov, "Zolotaia orda pered Kulikovskoi bitvy," in *Kulikovskaia bitva,* pp. 208–209, argues unconvincingly that Teliak was Mamai's name as khan, i.e., that Mamai actually usurped the imperial Chingisid title. This does not fit the language of the passage nor the evidence that Teliak was a separate person.

[28]For example, Soloviev, *Istoriia Rossii s drevneishikh vremen,* II, pp. 284, and *Istoriia russkoi literatury* (1946), p. 202, and many, many others.

[29]E.g., Tikhomirov, "Bor'ba russkogo naroda s mongolo-tatarskimi zavoevateliami. Dmitrii Donskoi," p. 385; *Povesti o Kulikovskoi bitvy,* p. 239, speculates that calling Mamai a *temnik* (from *t'ma* = tumen, ten thousand)

was a pun on the Russian word for darkness (*temno*), which seems gratuitous.

[30]Salmina contends that the main themes of the Expanded Redaction of the Chronicle Tale of 1380 are Russian princely unity and opposition to foreign enemies, particularly the Tatars. Certainly this has some merit. But in order to situate the text in the 1440s, Salmina creates a "subtext" in which each participant in the battle of Kulikovo is an allegorical stand-in for someone active in the 1440s: Dmitrii Donskoi is Vasilii II; Oleg of Riazan' is Dmitrii Shemiaka; and so on. Salmina concedes, however, that both Vasilii II and Shemiaka were vulnerable on the Tatar issue and provides no criteria for determining in whose interest the Expanded Redaction was composed.

Lur'e seems to argue in his publications that Vasilii II was the beneficiary of the Expanded Redaction, but in consultation he informed me that he believes that the bookmen responsible for composing the *svod* of 1448 did not care who won the Muscovite civil war, as long as unity was restored. These scribes worked in the chancellery of the metropolitan, although there was no metropolitan at the time. Lur'e asserts that the main theme of the new, expanded redactions of the chronicle tales associated with Dmitrii Donskoi, s.a. 1380, 1382, and 1389, was identical to the main theme of the "compilation" of 1448 as a whole. That theme was Russian liberation from the Tatar Yoke. Although Salmina does not employ this slogan, her discussion is consistent with Lur'e's position. According to Lur'e, reading the expanded redactions of these chronicle tales, compared to their earlier, shorter redactions (like reading the *svod* of 1448 compared to the earlier Trinity or Laurentian chronicles), exacerbated anti-Tatar emotion because of the more extensive descriptions of Tatar wrongdoing. This carefully formulated theory is reasonable, although it is difficult to extract it from Lur'e's published textological studies, which tend to be terse, laconic and compressed in the extreme. His attribution of the *svod* of 1448 to the metropolitan's chancellery rests upon a *cui bono* argument and *explication de texte*, and is presented without adducing any information about the metropolitan's chancellery or its scribes. He does not ask whether such a chronicle would be compiled in the absence of the guiding hand of a metropolitan. I believe Lur'e's theory also errs in minimizing the anti-Tatar thrust of the earlier redactions and chronicles.

Of course Lur'e is aware that the medieval Russian chronicles, including the *svod* of 1448, did not employ such modern language as "liberation from the Tatar Yoke," but this does not especially trouble him. To me the disparity between the medieval Russian lexicon and modern conceptual terms is central to any analysis of the theme of Russo-Tatar relations in the monuments of Old Russian literature.

[31]The accusation is repeated in *P.S.R.L.*, VI, p. 90; VIII, p. 34; XI, p. 46; XXIV, p. 143; XXV, p. 201; XXVII, pp. 72, 252, 331; XVI, p. 107.

[32]*P.S.R.L.*, XI, pp. 46–69.

[33]V. N. Tatishchev, *Istoriia Rossiiskaia*, 7 vv. (Moscow–Leningrad, 1962–1968), V, pp. 138–139, 141, contains a narrative which is not a literal quotation from sources, but seems to be a typically Tatishchevian composite, adulterated by modernized vocabulary (khan for *tsar'*, for example).

[34]See Halperin, "The Russian Land and the Russian Tsar," pp. 9–22 on the *Zadonshchina*.

[35]Azbelev has tried to establish the existence of a new genre of folklore, "oral heroic narratives" (*geroicheskye skazaniia*), of which the *Zadonshchina* would be a prime example. His views have met objections from Soviet folklorists and from Soviet *literaturovedy*, because Azbelev accepts the textological schema of the *Zadonshchina* favored by the "sceptics" about the authenticity of the Igor' Tale. For Azbelev's conception see (of those articles

accessible to me): S. N. Azbelev, "Ustnye geroicheskie skazaniia o Kulikovskoi bitve," in *Sovremennye problemy fol'klora* (Vologa, 1971), pp. 35–48; "Izobrazitel'nye sredstva geroicheskikh skazanii (k problematike izucheniia)," *Russkii fol'klor*, XIV (1974), pp. 144–165; and "Tekstologicheskie priemy izucheniia povestvovatel'nykh istochnikov o Kulikovskoi bitve s sviazi s fol'klornoi traditsiei," *Istochnikovedenie otechestvennoi istorii. sb. st. 1975 g.* (Moscow, 1976), pp. 163–190.

See the rejoinder by Likhachev: D. S. Likhachev, "'Takticheskie umolchaniia' v spore o vzaimootnoshenii 'Slova o polku Igoreve' i 'Zadonshchiny,'" *Russkaia literatura*, 1977, #1, pp. 88–93.

Soviet responses to the opinions of Czech, American and Italian Slavists about the *Zadonshchina* include: D. S. Likhachev, "Vzaimootnosheniia spiskov i redaktsii 'Zadonshchiny' (Issledovanie Andzhelo Danti)," *TODRL*, XXXI (1976), pp. 165–176 and R. P. Dmitrieva, "Nekotorye itogi izucheniia tekstologii 'Zadonshchiny' (s sviazi s voprosom o podlinnosti 'Slova o polku Igoreve')," *Russkaia literatura*, 1976, #2, pp. 87–91. The interpretation of I. Grekov seems to confuse the two *izvody* (sub-redactions) of the *Zadonshchina* with two *redaktsii*, in that he assigns different ideological tendencies to the Synodal and Undol'skii branches of the schema. (See Likhachev, *Tekstologiia*, pp. 116–127, on these technical terms of textology.) I. Grekov, "Ideino-politicheskaia napravlennost' literaturnykh pamiatnikov feodal'noi Rusi kontsa XIV v.," pp. 391–394, 407–412 and *Vostochnaia Evropa i upadok Zolotoi Ordy*, pp. 320–322, 401–418. Grekov's contrast of the ideologies of the two *izvody* is imaginative but forced.

For a purely literary discussion of the *Zadonshchina* as an autonomous Russian work of the late fourteenth century not based upon the Igor' Tale, see John Fennell in Fennell and Stokes, *Early Russian Literature*, pp. 97–107.

[36] R. P. Dmitrieva, "Byl li Sofonii riazanets avtora Zadonshchiny?" *TODRL*, XXXIV (1979), pp. 18–25.

[37] In addition to previous publications, see Likhachev, *Poetika drevnerusskoi literatury*, pp. 191–207, and *Velikoe nasledie*, pp. 239–253.

[38] Text of *Zadonshchina* in *Povesti o Kulikovskoi bitvy*, pp. 9–16; publication of all manuscripts in *Slovo o polku Igoreve i pamiatniki Kulikovskogo tsikla*, pp. 535–566.

[39] The only additional ethnonym in the text for pastoral nomads is "*khinove*," usually translated as Huns. Whatever its meaning, the author of the *Zadonshchina* found the term in the Igor' Tale.

[40] This is an allusion to the *Mat' syra zemlia*, Moist Mother Earth, of Slavic paganism, which Muslim Tatars would not invoke.

[41] Is the conception of *Rus'* as the *Zalesskaia orda*, the Horde beyond the Forest, a *translatio* to Russia of the Inner Asian socio-political identity of a Horde?

[42] This is, it will be recalled, Batu's achievement in the *vita* of Alexander Nevskii as well.

[43] In 1973 and 1976 I did not fully appreciate the significance of this passage.

[44] Rzhiga in *Povesti o Kulikovskoi bitvy*, p. 390; Adrianova-Peretts in *Voinskie povesti drevnei Rusi*, p. 161.

[45] Pereverzev insists this passage is unsuccessful because it was unnatural for fleeing Tatars to panic; he also concludes that the *Zadonshchina* as a whole is an artistic failure except when it imitates the Igor' Tale. See Pereverzev, *Drevniaia russkaia literatura*, pp. 162–168, on the Tatar lament, p. 166.

[46] D. S. Likhachev, *Chelovek v literature drevnei Rusi* (2nd ed., Moscow, 1970), p. 81. Epic prose is usually terse and laconic.

[47] Budovnits, *Obshchestvenno-politicheskaia mysl' drevnei Rusi*, pp. 454–455.

[48] *Istoriia russkoi literatury* (1946), pp. 211–212.

[49] G. N. Moiseeva, "K voprosu o datirovke Zadonshchiny (Nabliudeniia nad prazhskim spiskom Skazaniia o Mamaevom poboishche)," *TODRL*, XXXIV (1979), pp. 220–239, tries to verify Tikhomirov's dating of the *Zadonshchina* to 1384 on the basis of its list of the cities to which the news of victory spread (as found as an interpolation in a manuscript of the *Skazanie o Mamaevom poboishche*). The argument seems inconclusive.

[50] Vodovozov, *Istoriia drevnei russkoi literatury*, p. 153.

[51] See Likhachev, *Tekstologiia*, pp. 265–266. Dmitriev, pp. 4–15, tries to date the *Zadonshchina* to the 1380s or 1390s on textological grounds, arguing that the author of the Short Redaction of the Chronicle Tale of 1380 in the *Troitskaia letopis'* of 1408 used the epic as a source. This contention is not demonstrated adequately.

[52] The seventeenth-century Synodal manuscript of the *Zadonshchina* changes a sentence which refers to "*zemli svoei*" (his land) to "*Zolotoi Orde*" (The Golden Horde), an anachronism taken from the sixteenth-century *Kazanskaia istoriia*. See *Slovo o polku Igoreve i pamiatniki Kulikovskogo tsikla*, p 555.

[53] Halperin, "The Russian Land and the Russian Tsar," pp. 23–27.

[54] Moiseeva, "K voprosu o datirovke Zadonshchiny (Nabliudeniia nad prazhskim spiskom Skazaniia o Mamaevom poboishche)," pp. 220–239; V. K. Ziborov, "Khronograficheskii vid Pechatnogo varianta Osnovnoi redaktsii Skazaniia o Mamaevom poboishche," *TODRL*, XXXIV (1979), pp. 240–242.

[55] L. A. Dmitriev, "'Kniga o poboishchi Mamaia, tsaria tatarskogo, ot kniazia vladimirskogo i moskovskogo Dimitriia,'" *TODRL*, XXXIV (1979), pp. 61–62. In this article, pp. 61–71, Dmitriev introduces two new manuscripts of the "West Russian" redaction of the *Skazanie*, which may provide the key to discovering the origin of the phrase "the Tatar Yoke."

[56] I share my belief in this dating with I. B. Grekov, "O pervonachal'nom variante 'Skazaniia o Mamaevom poboishche,'" pp. 27–36, "Ideino-politicheskaia napravlennost' literaturnykh pamiatnikov feodal'noi Rusi kontsa XIV v.," pp. 405–407, and *Vostochnaia Evropa i upadok Zolotoi ordy*, pp. 384–401, although except on the issue of Kiprian and the Olgerdovichi I do not find Grekov's interpretation persuasive.

[57] Even the dating of Dmitriev, the scholar whose works did the most to bring scholarly attention to the text, is too early for the consensus: Dmitriev favors c. 1410, but the preferred dating is the 1440s–1460s, e.g., Begunov, Salmina, Lur'e. Dmitriev has remained loyal to the dating he proposed in the 1950s; see Dmitriev, "Kulikovskaia bitva 1380 goda v literaturnykh pamiatnikakh drevnei Rusi," pp. 19–29.

[58] Only the late A. A. Zimin and his student V. S. Mingalev dated the *Skazanie* at the turn of the sixteenth century. For citations to works representing the views summarized here, see my discussion cited in no. 53.

[59] See Charles J. Halperin, "Some Observations on Interpolations in the *Skazanie o Mamaevom poboishche*," *International Journal of Slavic Linguistics and Poetics*, XXIII (1981), [1982] pp. 93–112.

[60] Pereverzev, *Drevniaia russkaia literatura*, pp. 168–179. The crusading ethos in the sixteenth-century *Kazanskaia istoriia* is a function of the literary

influence of the *Skazanie.* See Frank Kämpfer, "Die Eroberung von Kazan in 1552 als Gegenstand der zeitgenössischen russischen Historiographie," *Forschungen zur osteuropaischen Geschichte,* XIV (1969), pp. 7–161.

Recent research on Kiprian, in addition to the studies of Prokhorov, includes N. S. Borisov, "Sotsial'no–politicheskoe soderzhanie literaturnoi deiatel'nosti mitropolita Kipriana," *Vestnik Mosk. Gos. Univ.,* seriia IX, Istoriia, 1975, #6, pp. 58–72; Dimitri Obolensky, "A *Philorhomaios anthropōs:* Metropolitan Cyprian of Kiev and all Russia (1375–1406)," *Dumbarton Oaks Papers,* 32 (1979), pp. 79–98; and Meyendorff.

[61]Azbelev finds the influence of oral narratives even in the *Skazanie*; in order to corroborate Novgorodian participation in the battle of Kulikovo from folkloric sources he must disregard such obvious anachronisms as references to Don Cossacks and Holy *Rus'* in a *skazka.* See Azbelev, "Kulikovskaia bitva v slavianskom fol'klore," pp. 85–95; "Skazanie o pomoshchi novgorodtsev Dmitriiu Donskomu," pp. 77–102; and "Ob ustnykh istochnikakh letopisnykh tekstov (po materialem kulikovskogo tsikla)," pp. 95–101.

[62]Despite Vodovozov, *Istoriia drevnei russkoi literatury,* p. 166.

[63]Dmitriev has recently tried to confirm his division into redactions in *Istoki russkoi belletristiki,* p. 297, no. 64. See his other comments in this volume on the *Skazanie* on pp. 308–309, and those of Lur'e on p. 349.

[64]*Povesti o Kulikovskoi bitvy,* pp. 43–76.

[65]The image of Russia as the *tsarev ulus* will recur below in discussing the epistle of Edigei of 1408 in this chapter, and the debates at the Horde during the Muscovite civil war in Chapter V.

[66]Despite Tikhomirov in *Povesti of Kulikovskoi bitvy,* p. 368.

[67]I omit here discussion of the conclusion of this manuscript of the Basic Redaction of the *Skazanie* because it is adulterated by interpolations from the *Zadonshchina* and the Expanded Redaction of the Chronicle Tale.

[68]*P.S.R.L.,* XXVI, pp. 125–145.

[69]*P.S.R.L.,* XI, pp. 46–69.

[70]*Povesti o Kulikovskoi bitvy,* pp. 111–158.

[71]Dmitriev in *Povesti o Kulikovskoi bitvy,* pp. 412–414, on the dating of the Expanded Redaction.

[72]For example, the Zabelin Redaction is actually a late sub–redaction (*izvod*) of the Basic Redaction with only minor variants, not always understandable. Mamai claims to control a dozen hordes and three *tsarstva.* As in numerous late manuscripts of the *Skazanie,* Mamai's lament as he flees is confused with the lament of the fleeing Tatars in the *Zadonshchina.* Mamai declares: "Already, brothers, we will never be in our palaces (*dvory*) and our patrimony (*otchina i dedina*)," terms not usually applied to the Tatars. See *Povesti o Kulikovskoi bitvy,* pp. 165–206.

[73]V. V. Kolesov, "Stilisticheskaia funktsiia leksicheskikh variantov v Skazanii o Mamaevom poboishche," *TODRL,* XXXIV (1979), pp. 33–48. Kolesov follows (and cites only) Dmitriev's dating, and attributes the *Skazanie* to a clerical author who could use both Church Slavonic and Old Russian.

[74]A. A. Amosov, "Skazanie o Mamaevom poboishche v litsevom svode Ivana Groznogo (Zametki k probleme prochteniia miniatiur Svoda)," *TODRL,* XXXIV (1979), pp. 49–60.

[75]See Halperin, "The Russian Land and the Russian Tsar," pp. 44–48. In this publication I accepted the possibility that late fifteenth–century

chronicles such as the Ermolin could contain an alternative, primary redaction of the Tale of 1382, different from that of the Trinity Chronicle. I now understand the flaw in that argument: a chronicle which as a whole derives from the *svod* of 1448 is not likely to have an individual annal which antedates its major source. I have adjusted the textological schema upon which my analysis is based accordingly; my interpretive conclusions remain largely unaltered.

[76]In 1971–1972 Salmina had alrealy completed the research to establish this schema. Although she had not published her article, Lur'e relied upon it in his more general works (for example, in *Istoki russkoi belletristiki*, pp. 266–269, and his *Obshcherusskie svody XIV–XV vv., passim*). In reviewing Lur'e's monograph, Plugin particularly emphasized the 1382 annal, asserting that later chronicles, such as the Ermolin, contained information, especially about architectural and artistic monuments, which had to originate in the primary redaction. Plugin concluded that the Expanded Redaction was primary, had been included in the "*Letopisets velikii russkii*," excluded from the *Troitskaia letopis'*, and then revived in the 1448 *svod*. Plugin, "Nereshennye voprosy russkogo letopisaniia XIV–XV vekov," pp. 82–88. As a result, Salmina published her article refuting Plugin's objections. M. A. Salmina, "Povest' o nashestvii Tokhtamysha," *TODRL*, XXXIV (1979), pp. 134–151.

[77]Salmina has presented an identical schema for the so-called *vita* of Dmitrii Donskoi, discussed below. The three "chronicle tales" of Donskoi surely deserve to be investigated as a group.

[78]For this reason the imaginative views of I. Grekov are methodologically unsound. Like Salmina, he misconstrues the Tatar issue. See I. Grekov, *Vostochnaia Evropa i upadok Zolotoi Ordy*, pp. 147–177 on narrative, 334–339, 456–464 on the Tale itself.

[79]*Troitskaia letopis'*, pp. 422–425.

[80]There is no hint of irony or humor in this passage.

[81]Dmitrii Donskoi's wife, grand princess Evdokiia, was the daughter of grand prince Dmitrii Konstantinovich of Suzdal'.

[82]Kuz'min explains the Muscovite punitive expedition as the result of a border dispute. His intention is to exonerate Oleg of Riazan' of any role in aiding Tokhtamysh, such as showing him where to ford the Volga river. Kuz'min, *Riazanskoe letopisanie*, pp. 228–230.

[83]Budovnits wrote that the very fact that the Mongols had to resort to surprise attack and deceit in 1382 proves that the Tatar Yoke was over as a result of Kulikovo (Budovnits, *Obshchestvenno–politicheskaia mysl' drevnei Rusi*, p. 459). Vodovozov infers from the fact that Tokhtamysh sent an envoy to Donskoi after the sack that the political gains of 1380 had not been erased (Vodovozov, *Istoriia drevnei russkoi literatury*, p. 150).

[84]Grekov and Iakubovskii ascribe to Tokhtamysh the desire to transform the Russian Lands into a simple Horde *ulus* (Grekov and Iakubovskii, *Zolotaia orda i ee padenie*, p. 324). No evidence for this exists.

[85]This does not entail that the "Expanded Redaction" was not written until the 1440s, only that no earlier chronicle is extant which contains it.

[86]*P.S.R.L.*, IV, pp. 84–90.

[87]For example, Likhachev, *Kul'tura Rusi vremeni Andreia Rubleva i Epifaniia Premudrogo*, pp. 104–105, or the earlier *Istoriia russkoi literatury* (1946), p. 208. Gudzii, *Istoriia drevnei russkoi literatury*, p. 256, sees the Adam reference as an interpolation, and perhaps unreliable.

[88]Cherepnin, *Obrazovanie russkogo tsentralizovannogo gosudarstva*, pp. 631–632.

[89]Lur'e in *Istoki russkoi belletristiki*, p. 267; Salmina, "Povest' o nashestvii Tokhtamysha," p. 143, no. 56. Lur'e believes the "compilation" of 1448 to have been composed in the chancellery of the metropolitan, and is therefore disinclined to see merchant influence in the 1382 tale.

[90]Karamzin, *Istoriia gosudarstva Rossiisskago*, IV, p. 50, expressed the notion that Donskoi sent Ostei to the city, which I. Grekov has repeated. While this is an attractive explanation for Ostei's presence, it is only speculation.

[91]I still believe this redaction makes sense as an anti-Kiprian polemic from the 1380s, before Kiprian recovered his episcopal seat on Donskoi's death in 1389.

[92]*P.S.R.L.*, XXIII, pp. 127–128.

[93]Salmina finds a textological parallel in the *Troitskaia letopis'* between the sentence in which Dmitrii Donskoi did not raise his hand against Tokhtamysh and another entry of the same chronicle in which, s.a. 1389, Dmitrii Olgerdovich of Trubchevsk does not raise his hand against Jagailo of Lithuania. She cites other analogous expressions, too, but does not discuss the Chingisid issue.

[94]See Lur'e in *Istoki russkoi belletristiki*, pp. 266–269.

[95]The text does not explain how the language barrier was overcome. Karamzin, V, p. 50, transforms the Horde princes into Tatar "bureaucrats" (*chinovniki*) who spoke Russian.

[96]Salmina does not use the phrase "liberation from the Tatar Yoke"; Lur'e does.

[97]*P.S.R.L.*, XV, 1st edition, Rogozh chronicle, col. 442.

[98]Lur'e in *Istoki russkoi belletristiki*, pp. 426–427; *P.S.R.L.*, XXI, p. 399. Tikhomirov discovered a short seventeenth-century chronicle variant about 1382 with some unique historical details which do not pertain to the Tatar issue. See M. N. Tikhomirov, "Maloizvestnye letopisnye pamiatniki," *Istoricheskii arkhiv*, VIII (1951), pp. 207–217.

[99]See Halperin, "The Russian Land and the Russian Tsar," pp. 69–78. The text is not a *vita* in literary form, although it does present Dmitrii Donskoi as a saint.
Few historians or literary specialists have accepted A. V. Soloviev's attribution of the text to Epifanii "the Wise" (*Premudrii*), in part because the consensus follows Salmina and dates the text to the 1440s, after Epifanii's death. The exceptions are Vodovozov, *Istoriia drevnei russkoi literatury*, pp. 160–161, and I. Grekov, *Vostochnaia Evropa i upadok Zolotoi Ordy*, pp. 326–329.

[100]M. A. Salmina, "Slovo o zhitii i o prestavlenii velikogo kniazia Dmitriia Ivanovicha, tsar'ia rus'kago," *TODRL*, XXV (1970), pp. 81–104, accepted by Fennell in Fennell and Stokes, *Early Russian Literature*, pp. 121–139, and W. Vodoff, "Quand a pu être composé le Panegirique du grand-prince Dmitrii Ivanovich, tsar' russe?" pp. 82–101. Also relevant to his views is W. Vodoff, "Remarques sur la valeur du terme *tsar'* appliqué aux princes russes avant le milieux du XVe siècle," *Oxford Slavonic Papers*, XI (1978), pp. 1–41.

[101]*Troitskaia letopis'*, p. 434.

[102]L. V. Cherepnin, ed., *Dukhovnye i dogovornye gramoty velikikh udel'nykh kniazei XIV–XVI vv.* (Moscow–Leningrad, 1950), #12, p. 36.

[103]Atypical and never repeated is the phrase in the treaty between Donskoi and his cousin, Vladimir Andreevich of Serpukhov (in 1389, no more than two months earlier than the will) which reads: "And if God changes, emancipates from the Horde, then two parts [of the tribute] go to me, and a third to you" (*A ony bog izbavit, oslobodit ot Ordy, ino mne dva zhereb'ia, a tebe tret'*). *Dukhovnye i dogovornye gramoty*, #11, p. 31.

[104]*P.S.R.L.*, IV, Appendix, pp. 349–357, here pp. 350–351.

[105]Cherniavsky, *Tsar and People*, pp. 25–28.

[106]Salmina identifies the major theme of the *slovo* as internal Russian affairs in the Muscovite civil war, and strengthening the hand of Vasilii II as the grandson of Dmitrii Donskoi. Lur'e amalgamates this into his conception of the *svod* of 1448 espousing national unification and liberation from the Tatar Yoke. Neither discusses the text's use of imperial titulature.

Fennell (as above, no. 100) and Pereverzev, *Drevniaia russkaia literatura*, pp. 159–162, conclude that the text had no political significance at all. They discuss only its admitted literary qualities.

Vodoff's analysis of the imperial titulature differs from my own.

[107]Charles J. Halperin, "Tverian Political Thought in the Fifteenth Century," *Cahiers du monde russe et soviétique*, 18:3 (July–September, 1977), pp. 267–273.

[108]Michael Cherniavsky, "The Reception of the Council of Florence in Muscovy," *Church History*, XXIV (1955), pp. 347–359.

[109]Mamai also threatens to change the Russians into *"ropaty"* (?).

[110]Despite Budovnits, *Obshchestvenno–politicheskaia mysl' drevnei Rusi*, p. 448.

[111]Following Cherepnin, *Obrazovanie russkogo tsentralizovannogo gosudarstva*, pp. 657, 659.

[112]Vodoff noted this similarity.

[113]The unnamed false Christians who denounce Dmitrii Donskoi are probably, as Salmina suggests, Oleg of Riazan' and Jagailo (even if he were still a pagan in 1380?). I had been prepared to see the phrase *zemskie tsari* as a gentle irony at Mamai's concern for his *tsarstvo* when he is only a *kniaz'*, but Vodoff has identified this phrase as a cliche from Psalms, so my overinterpretation may be discarded.

[114]Discussion of the *vitae* of Sergei and Stefan is taken from Halperin, "The Russian Land and the Russian Tsar," p. 70.

The attempt of I. Grekov to integrate these two texts into his schema of early Muscovite ideology is superficial. On the *vita* of Stefan of Perm', see I. Grekov, "Ideino–politcheskaia napravlennost' literaturnykh pamiatnikov feodal'noi Rusi kontsa XIV v.," pp. 400–401, and on the *vita* of Sergei, I. Grekov, *Vostochnaia Evropa i upadok Zolotoi Ordy*, p. 481.

[115]Epifanii Premudrii, "Zhitie prepodobnogo i bogonosnogo ottsa nashego Sergiia Chudotvortsa ...," ed., archimandrite Leonid, *Pamiatniki drevnei pis'mennosti*, no. LVIII (1885), pp. 125–127. The *vita* also mentions Tatar depredations as one factor in Sergei's father's decision to migrate to Radonezh, *ibid.*, p. 33.

[116]It is unclear why in Epifanii Premudrii, *Zhitie Sviatago Stefana*, ed., V. G. Druzhinin (St. Petersburg, 1907), pp. 40, 47, the Permians should describe the khan as a "false Tsar" when the same text notes that Stefan invented the Permian alphabet in a year in which "in the Horde and in Sarai over the Tatars ruled (*tsarstvuet*) Mamai, who had not been crowned (*no ne venchuet*

abie)." This text also says that Stefan died in the "sixteenth year of the *tsarstvo* of Tokhtamysh *tsar'*, who possessed the Mamai Horde; a second *tsar'*, by the name of Temir Kutlui, held the Volga Horde" (*ibid.*, pp. 74, 85). The *vita* as a whole, although not much concerned with the Tatars, was both informed of Horde affairs and respectful of Chingisid ideology.

[117]Halperin, "The Russian Land and the Russian Tsar," pp. 48-52.

[118]Grebeniuk argued that the full Tale was written at the turn of the fifteenth century and was included in the *Troitskaia letopis'*. He tries to show that an autonomous, non-chronicle manuscript of the tale from the second half of the fifteenth century contains a redaction earlier than the earliest extant chronicle redaction, so the Tale must be older. Unfortunately Grebeniuk, to my knowledge, has never fully published his 1971 "candidate's dissertation" on the Tale of Temir-Aksak. The only article of his I have since located provides no data on the points which are relevant here: V. P. Grebeniuk, "Litsevoe 'Skazanie ob ikone Vladimirskoi bogomateri,'" in *Drevnerusskoe iskusstvo. Rukopisnaia kniga* [tom 1] (Moscow, 1972), pp. 338-363.

[119]*P.S.R.L.*, XV, cols. 447-456. Cf. *P.S.R.L.*, VI, p. 124.

[120]This is one of the rare points in I. Grekov's analysis with which I can agree: I. Grekov, *Vostochnaia Evropa i upadok Zolotoi Ordy*, pp. 382-384. I am now less convinced of the importance for the tale's literary history of its depiction of Kiprian.

[121]The list of Timur's conquests was the basis for a sixteenth-century list of Tatar "lands," which demonstrates continued Russian geographical expertise in the Near East, Central Asia, and adjacent countries. See N. A. Kazakova, "'Tatarskim zemliam imenam,'" *TODRL*, XXXIV (1979), pp. 253-256.

[122]Variations in the later chronicle versions of the Tale and the legendary biography of Timur are insignificant from the perspective of this study. For example, the Nikon chronicle, *P.S.R.L.*, XI, pp. 158-161, 243-254, apparently drops the reference to Tokhtamysh's *kochevishche*. It also states Timur "subjugated" (*pokoril*) rather than "plundered" (*plenil*) many lands, taking the verb used in the Nevskii *vita* to describe Batu's activities, a logical adaptation. Finally it interpolates the name the "Great Horde" (*Bol'shaia orda*) into the list of his conquests, an obvious anachronism.

[123]Halperin, "The Russian Land and the Russian Tsar," pp. 52-53.

[124]*Troitskaia letopis'*, pp. 450-451.

[125]*P.S.R.L.*, V, p. 251.

[126]*P.S.R.L.*, XI, pp. 172-174,

[127]Cherniavsky, "Khan or Basileus," pp. 469-470.

[128]Jaroslaw Pelenski, *Russia and Kazan: Conquest and Imperial Ideology (1438-1560s)* (The Hague-Paris, 1973), pp. 154-170, sees in this passage a projection on to Vitovt of the concept of *Weltherrschaft* of the Muscovite bookmen of the 1550s. However, in the 1550s one would expect Livonia on the list, and perhaps the territories of the Balkan Slavs or Constantinople, not Poland. Besides, the Nikon chronicle was composed in the 1530s, not the 1550s. See B. M. Kloss: "Deiatel'nost' mitropolich'ei Knigopisnoi masterskoi v 20-kh-30-kh godov XVI veka i proiskhozhdenie Nikonovskoi letopisi," in *Drevnerusskoe iskusstvo. Rukopisnaia kniga* [tom I] (Moscow, 1972), pp. 318-337; "Mitropolit Daniil i Nikonovskaia letopis'," *TODRL*, XXVIII (1974), pp. 188-201; "Novgorodskaia V letopis' i vopros ob istochnikakh Nikonovskogo svoda," *Letopisi i khroniki. sb. st. 1973 g.* (Moscow, 1974), pp. 252-270; "Nikonovskaia letopis' i Maksim Grek," *TODRL*, XXX (1976), pp. 124-131; and *Nikonovskii svod i russkie letopisi XVI-XVII vekov* (Moscow, 1980).

For an interpretation equally as extravagant as Pelenski's, see I. Grekov, *Vostochnaia Evropa i upadok Zolotoi Ordy*, pp. 223–236.

[129]Halperin, "The Russian Land and the Russian Tsar," pp. 53–57.

[130]*Troitskaia letopis'*, pp. 468–471.

[131]*P.S.R.L.*, XV, cols. 177–186.

[132]*P.S.R.L.*, IV, pp. 110–111.

[133]Disregarding these contradictions, the Nikon Chronicle simply repeats all three texts one right after the other. *P.S.R.L.*, XI, pp. 205–211.

[134]In 1973 and 1976 the significance of this passage and its origin escaped my attention.

[135]Cherepnin, *Obrazovanie russkogo tsentralizovannogo gosudarstva*, p. 724. He attributes this unconvincingly to the aftermath of Kulikovo.

[136]Nancy Shields Kollman, "Kinship and Politics: The Origin and Development of the Muscovite *Boyar* Elite in the Fifteenth Century," Ph.D. dissertation, Harvard, 1980, pp. 176–180, 192–194, p. 242, no. 135, and notes on pp. 245–248, 252–253. I am grateful to Professor Kollman for calling my attention to her evidence on Fedor Koshka and his clan.

[137]For some original discussion not germane to my analysis, see I. Grekov, *Vostochnaia Evropa i upadok Zolotoi ordy*, pp. 257–266 on events, pp. 466–477 on ideology.

Chapter V

[1]Of the various narratives of the Muscovite civil war, I have found most useful and followed most often Cherepnin, *Obrazovanie russkogo tsentralizovannogo gosudarstva*, pp. 748–767, 768–770, 779–784, 787–791, 801–805. For his inimitable views see I. Grekov, *Ocherki po istorii mezhdunarodnykh otnoshenii Vostochnoi Evropy XIV–XVI vv.*, pp. 118–151.

[2]Much of the pathbreaking research on the significance of these treaties for the history of the civil war and the formation of the Muscovite state in general was done by L. V. Cherepnin for his study *Russkie feodal'nye arkhivy XIV–XV vekov*, chs. I–II (Moscow-Leningrad, 1948–1951), for example, I: p. 100, 104–106, 123–124, 129–131, 135, 139. As far as Russo-Tatar relations are concerned, little is said except in formulaic proscriptions of who could "know" the Horde and who should convey "news" about the Horde to whom. I shall not analyze this material here. On Cherepnin see Joan Afferica, "Academician Lev Vladimirovich Cherepnin, 1905–1977: In Memorium," *Slavic Review*, 39:4 (December, 1980), pp. 633–668.

[3]*P.S.R.L.*, XVIII, p. 168 (which includes a more ornate title than usual, "grand prince of Vladimir and Novgorod and all *Rus'*").

[4]*Ibid.*, pp. 171–172. *P.S.R.L.*, VI, p. 148, records the decision but not the debate; *P.S.R.L.*, IV, p. 433, has even less information.

[5]S. V. Veselovskii, *Issledovaniia po istorii klassa sluzhilykh zemlevladel'tsev* (Moscow, 1969), pp. 343–344, discusses Vsevelozhskii's later switch in allegiance to Shemiaka and draws from it unwarranted conclusions about Horde influence.
Ia. S. Lur'e, "Rasskaz o boiarine I. D. Vsevolozhskom v Medovartsevskom letopistse," *Pamiatniki kul'tury. Novye otkrytiia. Ezhegodnik 1977 goda* (Moscow, 1977), pp. 7–11, discusses a "tale" about the debates in

the Horde of 1431–1432 in a sixteenth–century chronicle. He believes the tale was censored from the contemporary chronicles. Its primary importance to Lur'e is as an explanation for Vesvolozhskii's defection from Vasilii II's camp. The passage also contains an explicit application of the concept of *ulus* to the grand principality of Vladimir, which goes beyond descriptions of it as the *tsarev ulus* (*ulus* of the khan) in the standard annals. Vsevolozhskii declares to the khan: "The lord free tsar (*gosudar' volnyi tsar'*) granted the *ulus*, the grand principality, to our lord, grand prince Vasilii, and now the great *tsar'* granted our prince, Lord (*gospodin*) Yurii Dmitrov, and Dmitrov has always (*iznachala*) been part of the *ulus* of the grand principality. Is this justice, lord? False words do not issue from the mouth of the *tsar'* (*Tsarevo slovo lozhno ot ust ne iskhodit*)." Here the grand principality of Vladimir is described as its own, separate *ulus*.

[6]The Mongols conducted their census in Russia in the thirteenth century. As a state secret, the *devter'* would have been kept under utmost security in Sarai, and should have perished when Timur burned the city. Indeed, it has not come down to us. But Muscovite treaties of the mid–fifteenth century, like this chronicle entry, imply that the Muscovites had physical possession of the *devter'*. See *Dukhovnye i dogovornye gramoty*, e.g., #34, 1434, p. 88, #38, 1441–1442, p. 118 *et passim*, as a standard formula.

[7]*P.S.R.L.*, XVIII, pp. 188–190. On the events from 1437 to 1445, see Gustave Alef, "The Battle of Suzdal' in 1445. An Episode in the Muscovite War of Succession," *Forschungen zur osteuropaischen Geschichte*, 25 (1978), pp. 11–20.

[8]This is undoubtedly a different person than the Usein of 1432, who was a supporter of Taginia.

[9]*P.S.R.L.*, XXIII, pp. 149–150.

[10]*P.S.R.L.*, XVIII, pp. 193–195; *P.S.R.L.*, XXV, p. 263.

[11]See the remarks of Berthold Spuler, *Die Goldene Horde. Die Mongolen in Russland* (2nd exp. ed., Wiesbaden, 1965), pp. 165–166, and their refutation by Vernadsky, *The Mongols and Russia*, pp. 316–322. The most revisionist analysis is that of Edward L. Keenan, Jr., "Muscovy and Kazan: Some Introductory Remarks on the Patterns of Steppe Diplomacy," *Slavic Review*, 26:4 (December, 1967), pp. 554–555, who sees Ulu Muhammed's release of Vasilii II as a logical result of their mutual alliance since 1432. To do this he blames the 1437–1438 Belev battle on the desire of the appanage princes to wreck this friendship, minimizes the importance of the ransom and virtually denies there was a battle at Suzdal'. His interpretation cannot be reconciled with the sources.

[12]*P.S.R.L.*, XVIII, p. 196; *P.S.R.L.*, XXV, p. 263; *P.S.R.L.*, XXIII, pp. 51–52.
On the political affiliations of these chronicles (the Simeon, Moscow *svod* of 1479, and Ermolin), see Lur'e, *Obshcherusskie letopisi XIV–XV vv.*, pp. 122–209, 241–254.

[13]*P.S.R.L.*, IV, p. 125, which would be virtually contemporary with the *svod* of 1448. Cf. also *P.S.R.L.*, XVI, p. 189; *P.S.R.L.*, XIII, pp. 66–68, 72.

[14]Presniakov, *Obrazovanie velikorusskago gosudarstva*, pp. 398–399. Cf. Vernadsky, *The Mongols and Russia*, pp. 330–332.
The narrative of the events of the Muscovite civil war in the *Kazanskaia istoriia*, ed., G. N. Moiseeva (Moscow–Leningrad, 1954), pp. 49–54, is thoroughly unreliable, as V. V. Vel'iaminov–Zernov, *Issledovaniia o Kasimovskikh tsariakh i tsarevichakh* (4 vv., Trudy Vostochnago otdeleniia Russkago arkheologicheskago obshchestva, tt. 9, 10, 11, 12; St. Petersburg,

1863–1887), I, pp. 5–6, 11, observes, despite M. G. Safargaliev, *Raspad Zolotoi Ordy*, pp. 244–245.

[15]Safargaliev, pp. 255–257, sees the establishment of Kasimov as an onerous and humiliating additional condition of Vasilii II's release by Ulu Muhammed. Keenan interprets it as an expression of their friendship. Vernadsky equated it with Russian liberation from the Tatar Yoke. The chronicles are discreetly silent about the establishment of Kasimov and draw no conclusions about its significance.

[16]Vel'iaminov–Zernov, I, pp. 280–281.

[17]S. M. Soloviev, II, p. 404, which Vernadsky echoes.

Vernadsky, *The Mongols and Russia*, pp. 321–322, sees Vasilii II's nickname, *Temnyi* (the Dark), not as a reference to the fact that he was blinded, but rather as an allusion to a proposal of Ulu-Muhammed that he become a *temnik*. No other historian has accepted this speculation.

[18]There was no metropolitan at the time. The previous metropolitan, the Greek Isador, had fled Muscovy over opposition to the Council of Florence, and the Russian Church has not yet taken the formal steps toward autocephaly. The future, autocephalous Russian metropolitan, Iona, ally of Vasilii II, was present at the Synod.

[19]*Akty istoricheskie, sobrannye i izdannye Arkheograficheskoiu kommisieiu* (St. Petersburg, 1841), #40, 1447, December 29, Epistle of the Russian clergy to the Uglich prince Dmitrii Iur'evich, pp. 75–83. Dmitrii Shemiaka is accused of failure to assist in the defense of Moscow against Makhmet or to come to the aid of Vasilii II at Suzdal'; for not returning the *dogovory, iarlyki, defter'* or treasury of the grand prince; for spreading slander about Vasilii II and the Tatars; and (quite mysteriously) for treasonous communication with Kazan' and failure to recognize Sedi-Akhmat of the Horde. He was threatened with excommunication if he persisted in his disobedience to Vasilii II.

[20]*P.S.R.L.*, XXIII, p. 153.

[21]*P.S.R.L.*, XXV, p. 265.

Chapter VI

[1]See, for example, Soloviev, II, pp. 77–82, and I. Grekov, *Ocherki po istorii mezhdunarodnykh otnoshenii Vostochnoi Evropy XIV–XVI vv.*, pp. 185–194, for narratives which pay rather little attention to 1480. George Vernadsky, *Russia at the Dawn of the Modern Age* (= A History of Russia, v., IV; New Haven, 1959), pp. 71–77, also minimizes the importance of 1480, since he believes the "Tatar Yoke" was terminated with the establishment of the Kasimov khanate. John L. I. Fennell, *Ivan the Great of Moscow* (London, 1961), p. 87, writes that the Stand on the Ugra meant the end of Russian vassaldom to the Horde and the beginning of national consciousness; the latter conclusion is quite dubious. For other traditional statements see G. E. Orchard, "The Stand on the Ugra," *New Review*, V:1 (March, 1965), pp. 34–43; Spuler, *Die Goldene Horde*, pp. 196–197; and V. D. Nazarov, "Konets zolotoordynskogo iga," *Voprosy istorii*, 1980, #10, pp. 104–120. A detailed narrative of events in the steppe is contained in M. G. Safargaliev, "Razgrom Zolotoi Ordy (k voprosu ob osvobozhdenii Rusi ot tatarskogo iga)," *Zapiski nauchno-issledovatel'skogo instituta pri Sovete Ministrov Mordovskogo ASSR*, 11, Istoriia i arkheologiia (Saransk, 1949), pp. 87–96. V. V. Kargalov, *Konets ordynskogo iga* (Moscow, 1980), is derivative.

Cherepnin, *Russkie feodal'nye arkhivy*, II, pp. 256–259, successfully disputes the contention that the *Sudebnik* of 1497 was compiled because of the liquidation of Tatar rule in 1480.

[2]K. V. Bazilevich, *Vneshniaia politika russkogo tsentralizovannogo gosudarstva vtoroi poloviny XV veka* (Moscow, 1952), pp. 118–119.

[3]*P.S.R.L.*, XXV, pp. 308–309, s.a. 1476. From this Fennell, *Ivan the Great of Moscow*, p. 72, infers that tribute-payment ceased.

[4]Sigismund von Herberstein, *Notes upon Russia*, tr. R. H. Major (Hakluyt Society, vv. 10, 12, London, 1851), I, p. 24; cf. Bazilevich, *Vneshniaia politika russkogo tsentralizovannogo gosudarstva*, pp. 120–121.

[5]A. E. Presniakov, "Ivan III na Ugre," in *Sbornik v chest' S. F. Platonova* (St. Petersburg, 1911), pp. 280–298; Presniakov, *Obrazovanie velikorusskago gosudarstva*, p. 450; Grekov and Iakubovskii, *Zolotaia orda i ee padenie*, pp. 427–428; Bazilevich, *Vneshniaia politika russkogo tsentralizovannogo gosudarstva*, pp. 134–147; I. M. Kudriavtsev, "'Ugorshchina' v pamiatnikakh drevnerusskoi literatury (Letopisnye povesti o nashestvii Akhmata i ikh literaturnaia istoriia)," in *Issledovaniia i materialy po drevnerusskoi literatury*, I (Moscow, 1961), pp. 23–67; Cherepnin, *Obrazovanie russkogo tsentralizovannogo gosudarstva*, pp. 874–882; Ia. S. Lur'e, "Iz istorii russkogo letopisaniia kontsa XV veka," *TODRL*, XI (1955), pp. 156–186; Ia. S. Lur'e, "Novonaidennyi rasskaz o 'stoianii na Ugre,'" *TODRL*, XVIII (1962), pp. 289–292; Fennell, *Ivan the Great of Moscow*, pp. 78–86.

[6]Events s.a. 1480–1481: *P.S.R.L.*, VI, pp. 20–21; XXV, pp. 327–328; XVIII, pp. 267–268; IV, p. 154; XXIII, pp. 180–182; XXIV, pp. 199–201; XXVII, pp. 282–284; *Ioasafovskaia letopis'*, ed., A. A. Zimin (Moscow, 1957), pp. 120–122.

[7]The *Tipografskaia letopis'* (*P.S.R.L.*, XXIV, pp. 199–201) reads that the Nogais "took" (*vzia*) Sarai (although they did not hold it). Compare in the same chronicle s.a. 1465 that *tsar'* Azigirei (of the Crimea and a Muscovite ally) "took" (*vzia*) the Horde while Akhmat was on the Don moving against *Rus'* (*ibid.*, p. 186). (The Crimeans did not retain the Horde then either.)

[8]*P.S.R.L.*, XXII, pp. 500–502; VIII, pp. 205–207; XXVIII, pp. 149–151.

[9]See *P.S.R.L.*, XXIII, s.a. 1472, p. 161: the Tatars ask the *boyare* of Ivan III if the grand prince can really stand up to the *tsar'*.

[10]See discussions in *Istoriia russkoi literatury* (1946), pp. 302–304; I. M. Kudriavtsev, "'Poslanie na Ugru' Vassiana Rylo kak pamiatnik publitsistiki XV v.," *TODRL*, VIII (1951), pp. 158–186; Vodovozov, *Istoriia drevnei russkoi literatury*, pp. 200–202; and Bazilevich, pp. 155–163.

[11]*P.S.R.L.*, XX, pp. 338–346; VI, pp. 235–238; VIII, pp. 205–213; XII, right column, pp. 198–212; and other citations below.

[12]N. P. Pavlov, "Deistvitel'naia rol' arkhiepiskopa Vassiana v sobytiiakh 1480 g.," *Uchenye zapiski Krasnoiarskogo gos. ped. instituta*, IV, 1 (1955), pp. 196–212, exercises considerable intellectual dexterity in portraying Vassian's actions in 1480 as unpatriotic. This article has been all but ignored in Soviet scholarship, and is virtually unknown in Western scholarship.

[13]Cherniavsky, "Khan or Basileus," pp. 474–473. I have deleted a footnote.

[14]*P.S.R.L.*, XXVI, pp. 262–274. Note that in the same chronicle, s.a. 1472, p. 250, God also "saves" (*izbavi*) the Christian clan (*rod*) from a campaign (*nakhozhdenie*) of the godless Hagarenes. It is as if there were no difference between the significance of the Tatar attacks of 1472 and 1480.

[15] *Ustiuzhskii letopisnyi svod*, pp. 93–94.

[16] Lur'e, "Novonaidennyi rasskaz o 'stoianii na Ugre,'" pp. 292–293.

[17] *P.S.R.L.*, XXI, pp. 555–565.

[18] D. P. Golokhvastov and archimandrite Leonid, "Blagoveshchenskii ierei Sil'vestr' i ego poslaniia," *Chteniia v Imperatorskom Obshchestve istorii i drevnostei Rossiisskikh pri Moskovskom universitete*, #88, 1874, kniga 1 (January–March), pp. 69–87 (quotes pp. 69, 70–72). See Ihor Ševčenko, "Muscovy's View of Kazan: Two Views Reconciled," *Slavic Review*, XXVI:4 (December, 1967), pp. 545–546, and Pelenski, *Russia and Kazan*, pp. 254–256.

[19] See the polemic between Edward L. Keenan, Jr., "Coming to Grips with the *Kazanskaya istoriya*: Some Observations on Old Answers and New Questions," *Annals of the Ukrainian Academy of Arts and Sciences in the United States*, vols. 31–32 (1967), pp. 143–183, and Pelenski, *Russia and Kazan*, pp. 27–52.

[20] *Kazanskaia istoriia* (Moiseeva), pp. 45, 55–57; *P.S.R.L.*, XIX, cols. 4–8 (the Kuntsevich edition). There are minor differences between the two texts which do not affect my analysis.

[21] See V. A. Kuchkin, "Iz istorii genealogicheskikh i politicheskikh sviazei moskovskogo kniazheskogo doma v XIV v.," *Istoricheskie zapiski*, 94 (1974), pp. 377–378.

[22] Tatishchev, VI, pp. 66, 69. Scepticism has been expressed ever since Karamzin, VI, pp. 91–103.

[23] Fennell, *Ivan the Great of Moscow*, pp. 78–86.

[24] Vernadsky speculated that the reference was to a *paiza* (patent of imperial authority), although Muscovites would surely have recognized a *paiza*, which bore a seal or emblem, not a physical likeness of the khan.

[25] *P.S.R.L.*, XXXII, the "Lithuanian" chronicle, s.a. 1486, p. 92, reads that Ivan III had been in a "subordinate condition" (literally: unfreedom, *nevolia*) and "subordination" (*poddanstvo*) to the Tatars, but he refused to greet a mounted Tatar envoy on foot, to touch his head to the ground before the envoy, or to accept a drink of kumiss. In this way, one infers, he signified the termination of his "subordination." The annal does not record the Tale of the Stand on the Ugra river, and of course the chronology is wrong.

[26] The text is published by Keenan and Bazilevich as cited below.

[27] Keenan, "The Yarlik of Axmed-khan to Ivan III," pp. 33–47.

I suspect Keenan's use of the concept of "forgery" is not in conformity with the definition in Likhachev, *Tekstologiia*, pp. 328–339.

[28] Bazilevich, pp. 163–167, taken from his "Iarlyk Akhmeda-khana Ivanu III," *Vestnik Mosk. Gos. Univ.*, 1948, #1, pp. 29–46.

[29] Safargaliev, *Raspad Zolotoi Ordy*, pp. 270–271; I. Grekov, *Ocherki po istorii mezhdunarodnykh otnoshenii Vostochnoi Evropy XIV–XVI vv.*, p. 153.

[30] M. A. Usmanov, "Ofitsial'nye akty khanstv Vostochnoi Evropy XIV–XVI vv. i ikh izuchenie," *Arkheograficheskii ezhegodnik za 1974* (1975), p. 131.

[31] A. P. Grigor'ev, *Mongol'skaia diplomatika*, p. 28.

[32] This was one of the factors which produced a different ideological response to 1480, not in the written sources but in the coinage. Substitution of Ivan III's name in Arabic for that of the Khan's on Muscovite coinage suggested that a new, Muscovite dynasty had replaced the Chingisids. Cherniavsky, "Khan or Basileus," p. 475.

Chapter VII

[1] *P.S.R.L.*, I, cols. 465–466.

[2] *Novgorodskaia pervaia letopis'*, pp. 298–303.

[3] *Troitskaia letopis'*, pp. 438–439.

[4] *P.S.R.L.*, XXVIII, p. 144.

[5] Lur'e, *Ovshcherusskie letopisi XIV–XV vv.*, p. 164.

[6] *P.S.R.L.*, V, s.a. 1319, p. 205.

[7] *P.S.R.L.*, XXV, pp. 194–195.

[8] E.g., *P.S.R.L.*, VIII, p. 27, XXIV, p. 136. Cf. Kliuchevskii, *Drevnerusskiia zhitiia sviatykh kak istoricheskii istochnik*, p. 136, no. 1.

[9] *P.S.R.L.*, X, p. 154.

[10] David B. Miller, "The *Velikie Minei Cheti* and the *Stepennaia kniga* of the Metropolitan Makarii and the Origins of Russian National Consciousness," *Forschungen zur osteuropaischen Geschichte*, 26 (1979), pp. 263–382.

"National consciousness" is probably a misnomer for sixteenth-century Muscovy: cf. Michael Cherniavsky, Chapter V, "Russia," in Orest Ranum, ed., *National Consciousness, History and Political Culture in Early Modern Europe* (Baltimore, 1975), pp. 118–143.

[11] David B. Miller, "The Coronation of Ivan IV of Moscow," *Jahrbücher für Geschichte Osteuropas*, XV (1967), pp. 559–574; David B. Miller, "Legends of the Icon of Our Lady of Vladimir: A Study in the Development of Muscovite National Consciousness," *Speculum*, XLIII:4 (October, 1968), pp. 657–670; Jaroslaw Pelenski, "Muscovite Imperial Claims to the Kazan Khanate," *Slavic Review*, XXVI:4 (December, 1967), pp. 559–576; and Pelenski, *Russia and Kazan*, passim.

Bibliography

Afferica, Joan, "Academician Lev Vladimirovich Cherepnin, 1905–1977: In Memorium," *Slavic Review*, XXXIX:4 (December, 1980), pp. 633–668.

Akty istoricheskie, sobrannye i izdannye Arkheograficheskoiu Kommissieiu, I, St. Petersburg, 1841.

Alef, Gustave, "The Battle of Suzdal' in 1445. An Episode in the Muscovite War of Succession," *Forschungen zur osteuropaischen Geschichte*, 25 (1978), pp. 11–20.

_____, "The Origin and Development of the Muscovite Postal Service," *Jahrbücher für Geschichte Osteuropas*, XV (1967), pp. 1–15.

Alexander, Alex E., "The Death of the Epic Hero in the *Kamskoye Poboishche Bylina*," *Slavonic and East European Review*, L:118 (January, 1972), pp. 1–9.

Allsen, Thomas T., "Mongol Census-Taking in Rus', 1245–1275," *Harvard Ukrainian Studies*, V:1 (March, 1981), pp. 32–53.

_____, "The Mongols and the Eastern Qipchaks," paper, American Association for the Advancement of Slavic Studies Convention, Philadelphia, Nov. 5, 1980.

Amosov, A. A., "Skazanie o Mamaevom poboishche v Litsevom svode Ivana Groznogo (Zametki k probleme prochteniia miniatiur Svoda)," *Trudy otdela drevnerusskoi literatury*, XXXIV (1979), pp. 49–60.

Anderson, Perry, *Passages from Antiquity to Feudalism*. London, 1974.

Anninskii, S. A., "Izvestiia vengerskikh missionerov XIII veka o tatarakh i Vostochnoi Evropy," *Istoricheskii arkhiv*, 3 (1940), pp. 71–112.

Azbelev, S. N., "Izobrazitel'nye sredstva geroicheskikh skazanii (k problematike izucheniia)," *Russkii fol'klor*, XIV (1974), pp. 144–165.

_____, "Kulikovskaia bitva v slavianskom fol'klore," *Russkii fol'klor*, XI (1968), pp. 78–101.

_____, "Mladshie letopisi Novgoroda o Kulikovskoi bitve," in *Problemy istorii feodal'noi Rossii. sb. st. k 60-l. V. V. Mavrodina* (Leningrad, 1971), pp. 110–117.

_____, "Ob ustynkh istochnikakh letopisnykh tekstov (po materialem Kulikovskogo tsikla)," *Letopisi i khroniki* (1976), pp. 78–101.

_____, "Povest' o Kulikovskoi bitve v Novgorodskoi letopisi Dubrovskogo," *Letopisi i khroniki* (1974), pp. 164–172.

_____, "Skazanie o pomoshchi novgorodtsev Dmitriiu Donskomu," *Russkii fol'klor*, XIII (1972), pp. 77–102.

_____, "Tekstologicheskie priemy izucheniia povestvovatel'nykh istochnikov o Kulikovskoi bitve s sviazi s fol'klornoi traditsiei," *Istochnikovedenie otechestvennoi istorii* (Moscow, 1976), pp. 163–190.

_____, "Tekstologiia kak vspomogatel'naia istoricheskaia distsiplina," *Istoriia SSSR*, 1966, #4, pp. 81–106.

_____, "Ustnye geroicheskie skazaniia o Kulikovskoi bitve," in *Sovremennye problemy fol'klora* (Vologda, 1971), pp. 35–48.

Bazilevich, K. V., "Iarlyk Akhmeda-khana Ivanu III," *Vestnik Mosk. Gos. Univ.*, 1948, #1, pp. 29–46.

_____, *Vneshniaia politika russkogo tsentralizovannogo gosudarstva vtoroi poloviny XV veka*, Moscow, 1952.

Begunov, Iu. K., "Kogda zhitie Aleksandra Nevskogo voshlo v sostav

_____, Lavrent'evskoi letopisi?" *Welt der Slaven*, XVI (1971), pp. 111–120.

_____, *Pamiatnik russkoi literatury XIII v. "Slovo o pogibeli russkoi zemli,"* Moscow–Leningrad, 1965.

_____, "Die Vita des Fürsten Aleksandr Nevskij in der Novgoroder Literatur des 15 Jahrhunderts," tr. W. Förster, *Zeitschrift für Slavistik*, XVI (1971), pp. 88–109.

_____, "Zhitie Aleksandra Nevskogo v sbornike iz sobranii N. P. Likhacheva," *Trudy otdela drevnerusskoi literatury*, XXX (1976), pp. 60–72.

Beskrovnyi, L. G., *et al.*, *Kulikovskaia bitva. sbornik stat'ei*, Moscow, 1980.

Bezzola, Gian Andri, *Die Mongolen in abenländischen Sicht (1220–1270), Ein Beitrag zur Frage der Völkerbegegnung*, Bern, 1974.

Birnbaum, Henrik, "Serbian Models in the Literature and Literary Language of Medieval Russia," *Slavic and East European Journal*, 23:1 (Spring, 1979), pp. 1–13.

Borisov, N. S., "Kulikovskaia bitva i nekotorye voprosy dukhovnoi zhizni Rusi XIV–XV vv.," *Vestnik Mosk. Univ.*, seriia 8, Istoriia, 1980, #5, pp. 56–66.

_____, "Sotsial'no–politicheskoe soderzhanie literaturnoi deiatel'nosti mitropolita Kipriana," *Vestnik Mosk. Gos. Univ.*, seriia IX, Istoriia, 1975, #6, pp. 58–72.

Böss, Otto, *Die Lehre der Eurasier. Ein Beitrag zur russischen Ideengeschichte des 20 J*, Veröffentlichungen des Osteuropa–Instituts München, Band, XV. Wiesbaden, 1961.

Boyle, John Andrew, tr., *Juwaini, The History of the World Conqueror*, 2 vv., Manchester and Cambridge, Mass., 1958.

Budovnits, I. U., "Ideinaia osnova rannykh narodnykh skazanii o tatarskom ige," *Trudy otdela drevnerusskoi literatury*, XIV (1958), pp. 169–175.

_____, *Obshchestvenno–politicheskaia mysl' drevnei Rusi (XI–XIV vv)*, Moscow, 1960.

Buganov, V. I., *Otechestvennaia istoriografiia russkogo letopisaniia, Obzor sovetskoi literatury*, Moscow, 1975.

_____, "Russkoe letopisanie v sovetskoi istoriografii," *Voprosy istorii*, 1966, #12, pp. 143–155.

Burns, Robert Ignatius, S.J., *Islam under the Crusaders: Colonial Survival in the Thirteenth–Century Kingdom of Valencia*, Princeton, 1973.

_____, "Spanish Islam in Transition: Acculturative Survival and its Price in the Christian Kingdom of Valencia," in Speros Vryonis, Jr., ed., *Islam and Cultural Change in the Middle Ages* (Wiesbaden, 1975), pp. 87–105.

Ch'en, Paul Heng–chao, *Chinese Legal Tradition under the Mongols. The Code of 1291 as Reconstructed*, Princeton, 1979.

Cherepnin, L. V., "Istochniki po istorii anti–mongol'skogo vosstaniia v Tveri v 1327 g.," *Arkheograficheskii ezhegodnik za 1958* (1960), pp. 37–53.

_____, "Letopisets Daniila Galitskogo," *Istoricheskie zapiski*, 12 (1945), pp. 228–253.

_____, *Obrazovanie russkogo tsentralizovannogo gosudarstva v XIV–XV vv.: Ocherki sotsial'no–ekonomicheskoi i politicheskoi istorii Rusi*, Moscow, 1960.

_____, *Russkie feodal'nye arkhivy XIV–XV vekov*, chs. I–II, Moscow–Leningrad, 1948–1951.

Cherniavsky, Michael, "Khan or Basileus: An Aspect of Russian Medieval Political Theory," *Journal of the History of Ideas*, XX (1959), pp.

459–476. Reprinted in Michael Cherniavsky, ed., *The Structure of Russian History* (New York, 1970), pp. 65–79.

_____, "The Reception of the Council of Florence in Muscovy," *Church History*, XXIV (1955), pp. 347–359.

_____, Chapter V, "Russia," in Orest Ranum, ed., *National Consciousness, History and Political Culture in Early Modern Europe* (Baltimore, 1975), pp. 118–143.

_____, *Tsar and People: Studies in Russian Myths*, New Haven, 1961, 1970.

Cleaves, Francis Woodman, "A Chancellery Practice of the Mongols in the Thirteenth and Fourteenth Centuries," *Harvard Journal of Asiatic Studies*, 14 (1951), pp. 493–526.

Dawson, Christopher, ed., *Mission to Asia. Narratives and Letters of the Franciscan Missionaries in Mongolia and China in the Thirteenth and Fourteenth Centuries*, (previous title: *The Mongol Mission*, [1955]), New York, 1966.

Dimnik, Martin, C.S.B., "Kamenec," *Russia Mediaevalis*, IV (1979), pp. 25–34.

_____, *Mikhail, Prince of Chernigov and Grand Prince of Kiev, 1224–1246*, Toronto, 1981.

_____, "Russian Princes and their Identities in the First Half of the Thirteenth Century," *Mediaeval Studies*, XL (1978), pp. 157–198.

_____, "The Siege of Chernigov in 1235," *Mediaeval Studies*, XLI (1979), pp. 387–403.

_____, "The Struggle for Control over Kiev in 1235 and 1236," *Canadian Slavonic Papers*, 21 (1979), pp. 28–44.

Dmitriev, L. A., "Kniga o poboishchi Mamaia, tsaria tatarskogo, ot kniazia vladimirskogo i moskovskogo Dimitriia," *Trudy otdela drevnerusskoi literatury*, XXXIV (1979), pp. 61–71.

_____, "Kulikovskaia bitva 1380 goda v literaturnykh pamiatnikakh drevnei Rusi," *Russkaia literatura*, 1980, #3, pp. 3–29.

Dmitrieva, R. P., "Byl li Sofonii riazanets avtorom Zadonshchiny?" *Trudy otdela drevnerusskoi literatury*, XXXIV (1979), pp. 13–25.

_____, "Nekotorye itogi izucheniia tekstologii 'Zadonshchiny' (s sviazi s voprosom o podlinnosti 'Slova o polku Igoreve')," *Russkaia literatura*, 1976, #2, pp. 87–91.

Dubentsov, B. I., "K voprosu o tak nazyvaevom 'Letopistse kniazheniia Tferskago,'" *Trudy otdela drevnerusskoi literatury*, XIII (1957), pp. 118–157.

Dukhovnye i dogovornye gramoty velikikh i udel'nykh kniazei XIV–XVI vv., ed., L. V. Cherepnin, Moscow-Leningrad, 1950.

Emmauskii, A. V., "Letopisnye izvestie o pervom nashestvii mongolo-tatar na Vostochnuiu Evropu," *Uchenye zapiski Kirovsk. gos. ped. inst. imeni V. I. Lenina*, vyp. 17, fakul'tet istoriko-filologicheskii, t. 3, 1958, pp. 59–109.

Epifanii, Premudrii, "Zhitie prepodognogo i bogonosnogo ottsa nashego Sergiia Chudotvortsa...," ed. archimandrite Leonid, *Pamiatniki drevnei pis'mennosti*, LVIII, St. Petersburg, 1885.

_____, *Zhitie Sviatago Stefana*, ed., V. G. Druzhinin, St. Petersburg, 1907.

Eremin, I. P., "Volynskaia letopis' 1289–1290 gg.," *Trudy otdela drevnerusskoi literatury*, XIII (1957), pp. 102–117.

Fedorov-Davydov, G. A., *Obshchestvennyi stroi Zolotoi Ordy*, Moscow, 1973.

Fennell, John L. I., *The Emergence of Moscow 1304-1359*, Berkeley and Los Angeles, 1968.

_____, "The Ideological Role of the Russian Church in the First Half of the Fourteenth Century," in *Gorski Vijenac. A Garland of Essays Offered to Professor Elizabeth Hill* (Cambridge, England, 1970), pp. 105-111.

_____, *Ivan the Great of Moscow*, London, 1961.

_____, "The Tale of the Death of Vasil'ko Konstantinovič: A Study of the Sources," in Hans Lemberg, Peter Nitsche, and Erwin Oberländer, eds., *Osteuropa in Geschichte und Gegenwart. Festschrift für Gunther Stökl zum 60 Geburtstag* (Köln, 1977), pp. 34-46.

_____, "The Tale of Baty's Invasion of North-east Rus' and its Reflexion in the Chronicles of the Thirteenth-Fifteenth Centuries," *Russia Mediaevalis*, III (1977), pp. 41-78.

_____, "The Tatar Invasion of 1223: Source Problems," *Forschungen zur osteuropaischen Geschichte*, 27 (1980), pp. 18-31.

_____, "The Tver Uprising of 1327: A Study of the Sources," *Jahrbücher für Geschichte Osteuropas*, XV (1967), pp. 161-179.

_____, Review of Ia. S. Lur'e, *Obshcherusskie letopisi XIV-XV vv.*, in *Russia Mediaevalis*, IV (1979), pp. 71-78.

Fisher, Alan W., "Muscovite-Ottoman Relations in the Sixteenth and Seventeenth Centuries," *Humaniora Islamica*, I (1973), pp. 207-217.

Fuhrmann, Joseph T., "Metropolitan Cyril II (1242-1281) and the Politics of Accommodation," *Jahrbücher für Geschichte Osteuropas*, XXIV (1976), pp. 161-172.

Golokhvastov, D. P. and Leonid, archimandrite, "Blagoveshchenskii ierei Sil'vestr' i ego poslaniia," *Chteniia v Imperatorskom Obshchestve istorii i drevnostei Rossiiskikh pri Moskovskom universitete*, #88, 1874, kniga 1 (January-March), pp. 69-87.

Golubinskii, Evgenii, *Istoriia russkoi tserkvy*, t. II, ch. 1, St. Petersburg, 1900.

Gorlin, Michel, "Serapion de Wladimir, prédicateur de Kiev," *Revue des études slaves*, 24 (1948), pp. 21-28.

Gramoty Velikogo Novgoroda i Pskova, ed., S. N. Valk, Moscow-Leningrad, 1949.

Grebeniuk, V. P., "Litsevoe 'Skazanie ob ikone Vladimirskoi bogomateri,'" in *Drevnerusskoe iskusstvo. Rukopisnaia kniga* [t. I] (Moscow, 1972), pp. 338-363.

Grekov, B. D. and Iakubovskii, A. Iu., *Zolotaia orda i ee padenie*, Moscow-Leningrad, 1950.

Grekov, I. B., "Ideino-politicheskaia napravlennost' literaturnykh pamiatnikov feodal'noi Rusi kontsa XIV v.," in *Pol'sha i Rus'* (Moscow, 1974), pp. 378-421.

_____, "Kulikovskaia bitva—vazhnaia vekha v politicheskoi zhizny Vostochnoi Evropy vtoroi poloviny XIV v.," *Sovetskoe slavianovedenie*, 1980, #5, pp. 3-22.

_____, "O pervonachal'nom variante 'Skazanii o Mamaevom poboishche,'" *Sovetskoe slavianovedenie*, 1970, #6, pp. 27-36.

_____, *Ocherki po istorii mezhdunarodnykh otnoshenii Vostochnoi Evropy XIV-XVI vv.*, Moscow, 1963.

_____, *Vostochnaia Evropa i upadok Zolotoi Ordy (na rubezhe XIV-XV vv.)*, Moscow, 1975.

Grigor'ev, A. P., *Mongol'skaia diplomatika XIII-XV vv. (Chingizidskie zhalovannye gramoty*), Leningrad, 1978.

Grushevskii (Hrushevsky), M., *Ocherki istorii Kievskoi zemli ot smerti Iaroslava do kontsa XIV stoletiia*, Kiev, 1891.

Gudzii, N. K., "Gde i kogda protekali literaturnaia deiatel'nost' Serapiona Vladimirskogo?" *Izvestiia otdeleniia literatury i iazyka Akademii Nauk SSSR*, XI, vyp. 5, Moscow, 1952, pp. 450–456.

_____, *Istoriia drevnei russkoi literatury*, 7th ed., Moscow, 1966.

Halecki, Oscar, *The Limits and Divisions of European History*, New York, 1950.

Halperin, Charles J., "Bulgars and Slavs in the First Bulgarian Empire: A Reconsideration of the Historiography," *Archivum Eurasiae Medii Aevi*, III (1983), pp. 183–200.

_____, "A Chingisid Saint of the Russian Orthodox Church: 'The Life of Peter, *tsarevich* of the Horde,'" *Canadian–American Slavic Studies*, 9:3 (Fall, 1975), pp. 324–335.

_____, "The Concept of the *ruskaia zemlia* and Medieval National Consciousness," *Nationalities Papers*, VIII:1 (Spring, 1980), pp. 75–86.

_____, "The Concept of the Russian Land from the Ninth to the Fourteenth Centuries," *Russian History*, II:1 (1975), pp. 29–38.

_____, "The Defeat and Death of Batu," *Russian History*, 10:1 (1983), pp. 50–65.

_____, "George Vernadsky, Eurasianism, the Mongols and Russia," *Slavic Review*, 41:3 (Fall, 1982), pp. 477–493.

_____, "The Ideology of Silence: Prejudice and Pragmatism on the Medieval Religious Frontier," *Comparative Studies in Society and History*, 26:3 (July, 1984), pp. 442–466.

_____, "Kiev and Moscow: An Aspect of Early Muscovite Thought," *Russian History*, 7:3 (1980), pp. 312–321.

_____, "Know Thy Enemy: Medieval Russian Familiarity with the Mongols of the Golden Horde," *Jahrbücher für Geschichte Osteuropas*, 30 (1982), pp. 161–175.

_____, "Medieval Myopia and the Mongol Period of Russian History," *Russian History*, 5:2 (1978), pp. 188–191.

_____, *Russia and the Golden Horde: The Mongol Impact on Medieval Russian History*, Bloomington, Indiana, in press.

_____, "Russia and the Steppe: George Vernadsky and Eurasianism," *Forschungen zur osteuropaischen Geschichte*, 36 (1985), pp. 55–194.

_____, "Russia and the 'Tatar Yoke': Concepts of Conquest, Liberation and the Chingisid Idea," *Archivum Eurasiae Medii Aevi*, II (1982), pp. 99–107.

_____, "The Russian Land and the Russian Tsar: The Emergence of Muscovite Ideology, 1380–1408," *Forschungen zur osteuropaischen Geschichte*, 23 (1976), pp. 7–103.

_____, "Sixteenth–Century Foreign Travel Accounts to Muscovy: A Methodological Excursus," *The Sixteenth Century Journal*, VI:2 (October, 1975), pp. 89–111.

_____, "Some Observations on Interpolations in the *Skazanie o Mamaevom poboishche*," *International Journal of Slavic Linguistics and Poetics*, XXIII (1981) [1982], pp. 93–112.

_____, "Soviet Historiography on Russia and the Mongols," *Russian Review*, 41:3 (July, 1982), pp. 306–322.

_____, "The Tatar Yoke and Tatar Oppression," *Russia Mediaevalis*, 5:1 (1984), pp. 20–39.

_____, "*Tsarev ulus*: Russia in the Golden Horde," *Cahiers du monde russe et soviétique*, 23:2 (April–June, 1982), pp. 257–263.

_____, "Tverian Political Thought in the Fifteenth Century," *Cahiers du monde russe et soviétique*, XVIII:3 (July–September, 1977), 267–273.

Herberstein, Baron Sigismund von, *Notes upon Russia*, tr. R. H. Major, 2 vv. Hakluyt Society, vv. 10, 12, London, 1851.

Ilovaiskii, D., *Kulikovskaia pobeda Dmitriia Ivanovicha Donskago*, Moscow, 1880.

Ioasafovskaia letopis', ed., A. A. Zimin, Moscow, 1957.

Istoki russkoi belletristiki. Vozniknovenie zhanrov siuzhetnogo povestvovaniia v drevnerusskoi literature, ed., Ia. S. Lur'e, Leningrad, 1970.

Istoriia russkoi literatury, t. II, ch. 1, Moscow–Leningrad, 1946.

Iugov, A., "Daniil Galitskii i Aleksandr Nevskii," *Voprosy istorii*, 1945, #3–4, pp. 99–107.

Ivanov, A. I., and Veselovskii, N. I., *Pokhody mongolov na Rossiiu po ofitsial'noi kitaiskoi istorii Iuan'shi*, from Zapiski Razriada voennoi arkheologii i arkheografii Imp. Rus. Voenno–Ist. Obshchestva, St. Petersburg, 1914.

Kämpfer, Frank, "Die Eroberung von Kazan 1552 als Gegenstand der zeitgenössischen russischen Historiographie," *Forschungen zur osteuropaischen Geschichte*, XIV (1969), pp. 7–161.

Karamzin, N. M., *Istoriia gosudarstva Rossiiskago*, 12, vv., St. Petersburg, 1892.

Kargalov, V. V., "Baskaki," *Voprosy istorii*, 1972, #5, pp. 212–216.

_____, *Konets ordynskogo iga*, Moscow, 1980.

_____, "Kulikovskaia bitva i ee mesto v otechestvennoi istorii," *Prepodovanie istorii v shkole*, 1979, #5, pp. 15–23.

_____, "Osvoboditel'naia bor'ba Rusi protiv mongolo–tatarskogo iga," *Voprosy istorii*, 1969, #2, pp. 145–157; #3, pp. 105–118; #4, pp. 121–137.

_____, *Vneshnepoliticheskie faktory razvitiia feodal'noi Rusi: Feodal'naia Rus' i kochevniki*, Moscow, 1967.

Kartsov, V. G., "Antiordynskaia politika Tverskogo kniazhestva," in *Iz proshlogo Kalininskoi oblasti* (Kalinin, 1974), pp. 58–81.

Kataev, I. M., "Tatary i poraboshchenie imi Rusi," in M. V. Dovnar–Zapol'skii, ed., *Russkaia istoriia v ocherkakh i stat'iakh* (Moscow, 1909), pp. 564–575.

Kazakova, N. A., "'Tatarskim zemliam imenam,'" *Trudy otdela drevnerusskoi literatury*, XXXIV (1979), pp. 253–256.

Keenan, Edward L., Jr., "Coming to Grips with the *Kazanskaya istoriya*: Some Observations on Old Answers and New Questions," *Annals of the Ukrainian Academy of Arts and Sciences in the United States*, 31–32 (1967), pp. 143–183.

_____, "Muscovy and Kazan: Some Introductory Remarks on the Patterns of Steppe Diplomacy," *Slavic Review*, XXVI:4 (December, 1967), pp. 548–558.

_____, "The *Yarlik* of Axmed–Khan to Ivan III: A New Reading—A Study in Literal *Diplomatica* and Literary *Turcica*," *International Journal of Slavic Linguistics and Poetics*, 11 (1967), pp. 33–47.

Khozhenie za tri moria Afanasiia Nikitina 1466–1472 gg., ed., V. P. Adrianova–Peretts, 1st ed., Moscow, 1948; 2nd ed., Moscow, 1958.

Kirpichnikov, A. N., *Kulikovskaia bitva*, Leningrad, 1980.

Kliuchevskii, V. O., *Drevnerusskiia zhitiia sviatykh kak istoricheskii istochnik*, Moscow, 1871.

Kloss, B. M., "Deiatel'nost' mitropolich'ei Knigopisnoi masterskoi v 20-kh-30-kh godakh XVI veka i proiskhozhdenie Nikonovskoi letopisi," in *Drevnerusskoe iskusstvo. Rukopisnaia kniga*, [t. I] (Moscow, 1972), pp. 318-337.

_____, "Mitropolit Daniil i Nikonovskaia letopis'," *Trudy otdela drevnerusskoi literatury*, XXVIII (1974), pp. 188-201.

_____, "Nikonovskaia letopis' i Maksim Grek," *Trudy otdela drevnerusskoi literatury*, XXX (1976), pp. 252-270.

_____, *Nikonovskii svod i russkie letopisi XVI-XVII vekov*, Moscow, 1980.

_____, "Novgorodskaia V letopis' i vopros ob istochnikakh Nikonovskogo svoda," *Letopisi i khroniki* (1974), pp. 252-270.

Kolesov, V. V., "Stilisticheskaia funktsiia leksicheskikh variantov v Skazanii o Mamaevom poboishche," *Trudy otdela drevnerusskoi literatury*, XXXIV (1979), pp. 33-48.

Kollman, Nancy Shields, "Kinship and Politics: The Origin and Evolution of the Muscovite *Boyar* Elite in the Fifteenth Century," Ph.D. dissertation, Harvard University, 1980.

Kolobanov, V. A. "K voprosu ob uchastii Serapiona Vladimirskogo v sobornykh 'deianiiakh' 1274 g.," *Trudy otdela drevnerusskoi literatury*, XVI (1960), pp. 442-445.

_____, "O Serapione Vladimirskom kak vozmozhnom avtore 'Poucheniia k popom,'" *Trudy otdela drevnerusskoi literatury*, XIV (1958), pp. 159-162.

_____, "Oblichenie kniazheskikh mezhdousobii v poucheniiakh Serapiona Vladimirskogo," *Trudy otdela drevnerusskoi literatury*, XVI (1961), pp. 329-333.

Komarovich, V. L., "Iz nabliudenii nad Lavrent'evskoi letopisi," *Trudy otdela drevnerusskoi literatury*, XXX (1976), pp. 27-59.

_____, "K literaturnoi istorii povesti o Nikole Zaraiskom," *Trudy otdela drevnerusskoi literatury*, V (1947), pp. 57-72.

Kuchkin, V. A., "Iz istorii genealogicheskikh i politicheskikh sviazei moskovskogo kniazheskogo doma v XIV v.," *Istoricheskie zapiski*, 94 (1974), pp. 365-384.

_____, "Nizhnyi Novgorod i Nizhegorodskoe kniazhestvo v XIII-XIV vv.," in *Pol'sha i Rus'* (Moscow, 1974), pp. 234-260.

_____, "Odin iz istochnikov Ellinskogo letopistsa vtorogo vida," *Vizantiiskii vremennik*, 27 (1967), pp. 319-324.

_____, "Pobeda na Kulikovom pole," *Voprosy istorii*, 1980, #8, pp. 3-21.

_____, *Povesti o Mikhaile Tverskom. Istoriko-tekstologicheskoe issledovanie*, Moscow, 1974.

_____, "Tverskoi istochnik Vladimirskogo polikhrona," *Letopisi i khroniki* (1976), pp. 102-112.

Kudriavtsev, I. M., "'Poslanie na Ugru' Vassiana Rylo kak pamiatnik publitsistiki XV v.," *Trudy otdela drevnerusskoi literatury*, VIII (1951), pp. 158-186.

_____, "'Ugorshchina' v pamiatnikakh drevnerusskoi literatury (Letopisnye povesti o nashestvii Akhmata i ikh literaturnaia istoriia)," *Issledovaniia i materialy po drevnerusskoi literatury*, I (Moscow, 1961), pp. 23-69.

Kuz'min, A. G., "Letopisnye izvestiia o razorenii Riazani Batyem," *Vestnik Moskovskogo Universiteta*, seriia IX, Istoriia, 1963, #2, pp. 55–70.

_____, *Nachal'nye etapy drevnerusskogo letopisaniia*, Moscow, 1977.

_____, *Riazanskoe letopisanie: Svedeniia letopisei o Riazani i Murome do serediny XVI veka*, Moscow, 1965.

_____, "Spornye voprosy metologii izucheniia russkikh letopisei," *Voprosy istorii*, 1973, #2, pp. 32–53.

Lattimore, Owen, *Inner Asian Frontiers of China*, 1940; Boston, 1962.

_____, *Studies in Frontier History. Collected Papers 1928–1958*, London, 1962.

Leitsch, Walter, "Einige Beobachtungen zur politischen Weltbild Aleksandr Nevskijs," *Forschungen zur osteuropaischen Geschichte*, 25 (1978), pp. 202–216.

Lenhoff, Gail, "Beyond Three Seas: Afanasij Nikitin's Journey from Orthodoxy to Apostasy," *East European Quarterly*, XIII:4 (1971), pp. 431–447.

Likhachev, D. S., *Chelovek v literature drevnei Rusi*, 2nd ed., Moscow, 1970.

_____, "Galits kak literaturnaia traditsiia v zhitii Aleksandra Nevskogo," *Trudy otdela drevnerusskoi literatury*, V (1947), pp. 36–56.

_____, "K istorii slozheniia Povesti o razorenii Riazani Batyem," *Arkheograficheskii ezhegodnik za 1962* (1963), pp. 48–51.

_____, "Kulikovskaia bitva v istorii russkoi kul'tury," *Pamiatniki otechestva*, kn. IV (Moscow, 1979), pp. 244–256.

_____, *Kul'tura Rusi vremeni Andreia Rubleva i Epifaniia Premudrogo (konets XIV–nachalo XV v.)*, Moscow–Leningrad, 1962.

_____, "Literaturnyi etiket drevnei Rusi (k probleme izucheniia)," *Trudy otdela drevnerusskoi literatury*, XVII (1961), pp. 5–16.

_____, *Natsional'noe samosoznanie drevnei Rusi. Ocherki iz oblasti russkoi literatury XI–XVII vv*, Moscow–Leningrad, 1945.

_____, "Po povodu stat'i S. N. Azbeleva, 'Tekstologiia kak vspomogatel'naia istoricheskaia distsiplina,'" *Istoriia SSSR*, 1967, #2, pp. 230–235.

_____, *Poetika drevnerusskoi literatury*, Leningrad, 1967.

_____, "Povesti o Nikolae Zarazskom," *Trudy otdela drevnerusskoi literatury*, VII (1949), pp. 257–406.

_____, *Razvitie russkoi literatury X–XVII vekov. Epokhi i stili*, Leningrad, 1973.

_____, *Russkie letopisi i ikh kul'turno–istoricheskoe znachenie*, Moscow–Leningrad, 1947.

_____, "A. A. Shakhmatov kak issledovatel' russkogo letopisaniia," in *A. A. Shakhmatov. Sbornik statei i materialov*, ed. akad. S. P. Obnorskii (Moscow–Leningrad, 1947), pp. 253–293.

_____, "'Takticheskie umolchaniia' v spore o vzaimootnoshenii 'Slova o polku Igoreve' i 'Zadonshchiny,'" *Russkaia literatura*, 1977, #1, pp. 88–93.

_____, *Tekstologiia. na materiale russkoi literatury X–XVII vv.*, Moscow–Leningrad, 1962.

_____, *Velikoe nasledie: Klassicheskie proizvedeniia literatury drevnei Rusi*, Moscow, 1975.

_____, "Vzaimootnosheniia spiskov i redaktsii 'Zadonshchiny' (Issledovanie Andzhelo Danti)," *Trudy otdela drevnerusskoi literatury*, XXXI (1976), pp. 165–175.

_____, Ianin, V. L. and Lur'e, Ia. S., "Podlinnye i mnimye voprosy metologii izucheniia russkikh letopisei," *Voprosy istorii*, 1973, #8, pp. 194–203.

Lo, Jung-pang, "The Controversy over Grain Conveyance during the Reign of Qubilai Qaqun, 1260–1294," *Far Eastern Quarterly*, 13 (1954), pp. 262–285.

Lur'e, Ia. S., "Eshche raz o svode 1448 g. i Novgorodskoi Karamzinskoi letopisi," *Trudy otdela drevnerusskoi literatury*, XXXII (1977), pp. 199–218.

_____, "Iz istorii russkogo letopisaniia kontsa XV veka," *Trudy otdela drevnerusskoi literatury*, XI (1955), pp. 156–186.

_____, "Izuchenie russkogo letopisaniia," *Vspomogatel'nye istoricheskie distsipliny*, I (1968), pp. 4–32.

_____, "K izucheniiu letopisnogo zhanra," *Trudy otdela drevnerusskoi literatury*, XXVII (1972), pp. 76–93.

_____, "K probleme svoda 1448 goda," *Trudy otdela drevnerusskoi literatury*, XXIV (1969), pp. 142–146.

_____, "Lavrent'evskaia letopis'—svod nachala XIV v.," *Trudy otdela drevnerusskoi literatury*, XXIX (1974), pp. 50–67.

_____, "Novonaidennyi rasskaz o 'stoianii na Ugre,'" *Trudy otdela drevnerusskoi literatury*, XVIII (1962), pp. 289–293.

_____, "O nekotorykh printsipakh kritiki istochnikov," *Istochnikovedenie otechestvennoi istorii*, I (1973), pp. 78–100.

_____, "O shakhmatovskoi metodike issledovaniia letopisnykh svodov," *Istochnikovedenie otechestvennoi istorii* [II] *sb. st. 1975 g.* (Moscow, 1976), pp. 86–107.

_____, *Obshcherusskie letopisi XIV–XV vv.*, Leningrad, 1976.

_____, "Obshcherusskii svod—protograf Sofiiskoi I i Novgorodskoi IV letopisei," *Trudy otdela drevnerusskoi literatury*, XXVIII (1974), pp. 114–139.

_____, "Podvig Afanasiia Nikitina (k 500–letiiu nachala ego puteshestviia)," *Izvestiia Vsesoiuznogo Geograficheskogo obshchestva*, t. 99, 1967, #5, pp. 435–442.

_____, "Povest' o bitve na Lipitse 1216 g. v letopisanii XIV–XVI vv.," *Trudy otdela drevnerusskoi literatury*, XXXIV (1979), pp. 96–115.

_____, "Problema rekonstruktsii nedoshedshikh svodov pri issledovanii letopisei," in *Tekstologiia slavianskikh literatur* (Leningrad, 1973), pp. 137–144.

_____, "Problemy izucheniia russkogo letopisaniia," in *Puty izucheniia drevenerusskoi literatury i pis'mennosti* (Leningrad, 1970), pp. 43–48.

_____, "Rasskaz o boiarine I. D. Vsevolozhskom v Medovartsevskom letopistse," *Pamiatniki kul'tury. Novye otkrytiia. Ezhegodnik 1977 g.* (Moscow, 1977), pp. 7–11.

_____, "Rol' Tveri v sozdanii russkogo natsional'nogo gosudarstva," *Uchenye zapiski Leningradskogo gosudarstvennogo universiteta*, #36, seriia istoricheskikh nauk, vyp. 3, 1939, pp. 85–109.

_____, "Troitskaia letopis' i moskovskoe letopisanie XIV v.," *Vspomogatel'nye istoricheskie distsipliny*, VI (1974), pp. 79–106.

Mansikka, V., *Zhitie Aleksandra Nevskogo. Razbor redaktsii i teksty*, Pamiatniki drevnei pis'mennosti i iskusstva, t. CLXXX, St. Petersburg, 1913.

Martin, Janet, "The land of darkness and the Golden Horde. The fur trade under the Mongols. XIII–XIV centuries," *Cahiers du monde russe et soviétique*, XIX:4 (1978), pp. 405–422.

Mavrodin, V. V., "Levoberezhnaia Ukraina pod vlast'iu tataro-mongolov," *Uchenye zapiski Leningradskogo gosudarstvennogo universiteta*, #32, vyp. 2, 1939, pp. 39–65.

Meyendorff, John, *Byzantium and the Rise of Russia. A Study of Byzantine-Russian Relations in the Fourteenth Century*, Cambridge, England, 1981.

Miller, David B., "The Coronation of Ivan IV of Moscow," *Jahrbücher für Geschichte Osteuropas*, XV (1967), pp. 559–574.

———, "Legends of the Icon of Our Lady of Vladimir: A Study in the Development of Muscovite National Consciousness," *Speculum*, XLIII:4 (October, 1968), pp. 657–670.

———, "The *Velikie Minei Cheti* and the *Stepennaia kniga* of Metropolitan Makarii and the Origins of Russian National Consciousness," *Forschungen zur osteuropaischen Geschichte*, 26 (1979), pp. 263–382.

Miller, O., "O drevnerusskoi literature po otnosheniiu k tatarskomu igu," *Drevniaia i Novaia Rossiia*, tom II, #5 (1876), pp. 49–60.

Moiseeva, G. M., "K voprosu o datirovke Zadonshchiny (Nabliudeniia nad prazhskom spiskom Skazaniia o Mamaevom poboishche)," *Trudy otdela drevnerusskoi literatury*, XXXIV (1979), pp. 220–239.

———, ed., *Kazanskaia istoriia*, Moscow–Leningrad, 1954.

Mote, F. W., "Confucian Eremitism in the Yüan Period," in A. F. Wright, ed., *The Confucian Persuasion* (Stanford, 1960), pp. 202–240, 348–353.

Nasonov, A. N., *Istoriia russkogo letopisaniia XI–nachala XVIII veka. Ocherki i issledovaniia*, Moscow, 1969.

———, "Lavrent'evskaia letopis' i Vladimirskoe velikokniazheskoe letopisanie pervoi poloviny XIII v.," *Problemy istochnikovedeniia*, XI (1963), pp. 429–480.

Nazarov, V. D., "Konets zolotoordynskogo iga," *Voprosy istorii*, 1980, #10, pp. 104–120.

Noonan, Thomas S., "Medieval Russia, the Mongols, and the West: Novgorod's Relations with the Baltic, 1100–1350," *Medieval Studies*, 37 (1975), pp. 316–339.

Novgorodskaia pervaia letopis' starshego i mladshego izvodov, ed., A. N. Nasonov, Moscow–Leningrad, 1950.

Obolensky, Dimitri, "A *Philorhomaios anthropōs*: Metropolitan Cyprian of Kiev and all Russia," *Dumbarton Oaks Papers*, XXXII (1979), pp. 79–98.

Ocherki istorii SSSR, vv. II–III, Moscow, 1953.

Olbricht, Peter, *Das Postwesen in China unter der Mongolenherrschaft im 13. und 14 Jh.*, Göttinger Asiatische Forschungen, 1, Wiesbaden, 1954.

Orchard, G. Edward, "The Eurasian School of Russian Historiography," *Laurentian University Review*, X:1 (November, 1977), pp. 97–106.

———, "The Stand on the Ugra," *New Review*, V:1 (March, 1965), pp. 34–43.

Orlov, A. S., "O Galitsko-Volynskom letopisanii," *Trudy otdela drevnerusskoi literatury*, V (1947), pp. 15–35.

Ostrowski, Donald G., Review of Ia. S. Lur'e, *Obshcherusskie letopisi XIV–XV vv.* and A. G. Kuz'min, *Nachal'nye etapi drevnerusskogo letopisaniia* in *Kritika*, XVI:1 (Winter, 1980), pp. 5–23.

Pashuto, V. T., "Galitsko-Volynskoe kniazhestvo vremen Daniila Romanovicha," *Uchenye zapiski Leningradskogo Gosudarstvennogo Universiteta*, seriia ist. nauk, #67, vyp. 7, 1941, pp. 25–82.

_____, "Kievskaia letopis' 1238 g.," *Istoricheskie zapiski*, 26 (1948), pp. 273–305.

_____, "Nekotorye obshchie voprosy letopisnogo istochnikovedeniia," *Istochnikovedenie otechestvennoi istorii*, I (1973), pp. 64–77.

_____, *Obrazovanie litovskogo gosudarstva*, Moscow, 1959.

_____, *Ocherki po istorii Galitsko-Volynskoi Rusi*, Moscow–Leningrad, 1950.

_____, "A. A. Shakhmatov—burzhuaznyi istochnikoved," *Voprosy istorii*, 1952, #2, pp. 47–73.

Pavlov, N. P., "Deistvitel'naia rol' arkhiepiskopa Vassiana v sobytiiakh 1480 goda," *Uchenye zapiski Krasnoiarskogo gos. ped. inst.*, IV, 1, 1955, pp. 196–212.

Pelenski, Jaroslaw, "Muscovite Imperial Claims to the Kazan Khanate," *Slavic Review*, XXVI:4 (December, 1967), pp. 559–576.

_____, *Russia and Kazan: Conquest and Imperial Ideology (1438–1560s)*, The Hague–Paris, 1973.

Pereverzev, V. F., *Literatura Drevnei Rusi*, Moscow, 1971.

Perfecky, George A., "Studies on the Galician–Volynian (Volhynian) Chronicle," *Annals of the Ukrainian Academy of Arts and Sciences in the United States*, 12:1-2 (33–34) (1972), pp. 62–112.

_____, ed. & tr., *The Hypatian Codex. Part II. The Galician-Volynian Chronicle. An Annotated Translation*, Munich, 1973.

Petukhov, E. V., *Serapion Vladimirskii, russkii propovednik XIII v.*, Zapiski istoriko–filologicheskago fakul'teta St. Peterburgskago universiteta, ch. XVII, St. Petersburg, 1888.

Philipp, Werner, "Heiligkeit und Herrschaft in der Vita Aleksandr Nevskijs," *Forschungen zur osteuropäischen Geschichte*, 18 (1973), pp. 55–72.

Picchio, Riccardo, "Models and Patterns in the Literary Tradition of Medieval Orthodox Slavdom," in V. Terras, ed., *American Contributions to the Seventh International Congress of Slavists, Warsaw, August 21-27, 1973*, v. II, *Literature and Folklore* (The Hague, 1973), pp. 439–467.

_____, "On Russian Humanism: The Philological Revival," *Slavia*, 44:2 (1975), pp. 161–171.

Plugin, V. A., *Mirovozrenie Andreia Rubleva (nekotorye problemy). Drevnerusskaia zhivopis' kak istoricheskii istochnik*, Moscow, 1974.

_____, "Nekotorye problemy izucheniia biografii i tvorchestva A. Rubleva," in *Drevnerusskoe iskusstvo. Khudozhestvennaia kul'tura Moskvy i prilezhashchikh k nei kniazhestv XIV–XVI vv.* (Moscow, 1970), pp. 73–86.

_____, "Nereshenye voprosy russkogo letopisaniia XIV–XV vekov (K vykhodu v svet knigi Ia. S. Lur'e, 'Obshcherusskie letopisi XIV–XV vv.')," *Istoriia SSSR*, 1978, #4, pp. 73–93.

Polnoe sobranie russkikh letopisei, 35 vv. to date.   Moscow–St. Petersburg–Leningrad, 1841–1980.

Poluboiarinova, M. D., *Russkie liudi v Zolotoi Orde*, Moscow, 1972.

Povesti o Kulikovskoi bitvy, ed. M. N. Tikhomirov, V. F. Rzhiga, and L. A. Dmitriev, Moscow, 1959.

Prawer, Joshua, *The Latin Kingdom of Jerusalem: European Colonialism in the Middle Ages*, London, 1973.

Presniakov, A. E., "Ivan III na Ugre," in *Sbornik v chest' S. F. Platonova* (St. Petersburg, 1911), pp. 280–298.

_____, *Obrazovanie velikorusskogo gosudarstva: Ocherki po istorii XIII–XIV* stoletiia, Petrograd, 1918.

Priselkov, M. D., "Istoriia rukopisi Lavrent'evskoi letopisi i ee izdanie," *Uchenye zapiski Leningradskogo gos. ped. inst. im. A. Gertsena*, t. XIX, 1939, pp. 175–197.

_____, *Istoriia russkogo letopisaniia XI–XV vv.*, Leningrad, 1940.

_____, "Lavrent'evskaia letopis' (istoriia teksta)," *Uchenye zapiski Leningradskogo Gosudarstvennogo Universiteta*, t. 32, seriia ist. nauk, vyp. 2, 1939, pp. 76–142.

Prokhorov, G. M., "Drevneishaia rukopis' s proizvedeniiami mitropolita Kipriana," *Pamiatniki kul'tury. Novye otkrytiia. Ezhegodnik 1978 g. Pis'mennost'. Iskusstvo. Arkheologiia* (Leningrad, 1979), pp. 17–30.

_____, "Etnicheskaia integratsiia v Vostochnoi Evrope v XIV v. (ot isikhastskikh sporov do Kulikovskoi bitvy)," *Doklady otdeleniia etnografii Geograficheskogo Obshchestva SSSR*, 2 (1966), pp. 81–110.

_____, "Isikhazm i obshchestvennaia mysl' v Vostochnoi Evrope v XIV v.," *Trudy otdela drevnerusskoi literatury*, XXIII (1968), pp. 86–108.

_____, "Izbytochnye materialy Rogozhskogo letopistsa," *Vspomogatel'nye istoricheskie distsipliny*, 8 (1976), pp. 185–203.

_____, "Kharakteristika Dionisiia Suzdal'skogo," in *Kul'turnoe nasledie drevnei Rusi. Istoki. Stanovlenie. Traditsii* (Moscow, 1976), pp. 86–88.

_____, "Kodikologicheskii analiz Lavrent'evskoi letopisi," *Vspomogatel'nye istoricheskie distsipliny*, 4 (1973), pp. 77–104.

_____, "Kul'turnoe svoeobrazie epokhi Kulikovskoi bitvy," *Trudy otdela drevnerusskoi literatury*, XXXIV (1979), pp. 3–17.

_____, "Letopisnye podborki rukopisi GPB F.IV.603 i problema svodnogo obshcherusskogo letopisaniia," *Trudy otdela drevnerusskoi literatury*, XXXII (1977), pp. 165–198.

_____, "Letopisets Velikii Russkii: Analiz ego upominaniia v Troitskoi letopisi," *Letopisi i khroniki* (1976), pp. 67–77.

_____, "Povest' o Batyevom nashestvii v Lavrent'evskoi letopisi," *Trudy otdela drevnerusskoi literatury* (1974), pp. 77–98.

_____, "Povest' o Mitiae–Mikhaile i ee literaturnaia sreda," Dissertatsiia na soiskanii uchenoi stepeni kandidata filologicheskikh nauk. Institut russkoi literatury. Leningrad, 1968.

_____, *Povest' o Mitiae (Rus' i Vizantiia v epokhu Kulikovskoi bitvy)*, Leningrad, 1978.

_____, "Tsentral'norusskoe letopisanie vtoroi poloviny XIV v (Analiz rogozhskogo letopistsa i obshchie soobrazheniia)," *Vspomogatel'nye istoricheskie distsipliny*, 10 (1978), pp. 159–181.

Pskovskie letopisi, I–II, ed. A. N. Nasonov, Moscow–Leningrad, 1941–1955.

Putilov, B. N., "K voprosu o sostave Riazanskogo pesennogo tsikla," *Trudy otdela drevnerusskoi literatury*, XVI (1960), pp. 230–244.

_____, "Pesnia o Evpatii Kolovrate," *Trudy otdela drevnerusskoi literatury*, XI (1955), pp. 118–139.

_____, "Pesnia ob Avdot'e Riazanochke (k istorii Riazanskogo pesennogo tsikla)," *Trudy otdela drevnerusskoi literatury*, XIV (1958), pp. 163–168.

Riasanovsky, Nicholas V., "The Emergence of Eurasianism," *California Slavic Studies*, IV (1967), pp. 39–72.

_____, "Prince N. S. Trubetskoy's 'Europe and Mankind,'" *Jahrbücher für Geschichte Osteuropas*, XIII (1964), pp. 207–220.

Roublev, Michel, *The Scourge of God*, unpublished monograph.

_____, "Le tribut aux Mongoles d'après les Testaments et Accords des Princes Russes," *Cahiers du monde russe et soviétique*, VII (1966), pp. 487–530, tr. and rpt., "The Mongol Tribute according to the Wills and Agreements of the Russian Princes," in Michael Cherniavsky, ed., *The Structure of Russian History* (New York, 1970), pp. 29–64.

Russkaia istoricheskaia biblioteka, t. VI, 2nd ed., St. Petersburg, 1908.

Safargaliev, M. G., "Razgrom Zolotoi Ordy (k voprosu ob osvobozhdenii Rusi ot tatarskogo iga)," *Zapiski nauchno-issledovatel'skogo instituta pri Sovete Ministrov Mordovskogo ASSR*, 11, Istoriia i arkheologiia (Saransk, 1949), pp. 78–96.

_____, *Raspad Zolotoi Ordy*, Saransk, 1960.

Salmina, M. A., "Esche raz o datirovke 'Letopisnoi povesti' o Kulikovskoi bitve," *Trudy otdela drevnerusskoi literatury*, XXXII (1977), pp. 3–39.

_____, "'Letopisnaia povest' o Kulikovskoi bitve i 'Zadonshchina,'" in D. S. Likhachev and L. A. Dmitriev, ed., *Slovo o polku Igoreve i pamiatniki Kulikovskogo tsikla* (Moscow–Leningrad, 1966), pp. 344–384.

_____, "Povest' o nashestvii Tokhtamysha," *Trudy otdela drevnerusskoi literatury*, XXXIV (1979), pp. 134–151.

_____, "Slovo o zhitii i o prestavlenii velikogo kniazia Dmitriia Ivanovicha, tsaria Rus'skago," *Trudy otdela drevnerusskoi literatury*, XXV (1970), pp. 81–104.

Saunders, John Joseph, *The History of the Mongol Conquests*, New York, 1971.

Schurmann, Herbert Franz, *Economic Structure of the Yüan Dynasty: Translation of Chapters 93 and 94 of the Yüan Shih*, Harvard–Yenching Institute Studies, XVI, Cambridge, Mass., 1956.

Serebrianskii, N., *Drevnerusskie kniazheskie zhitiia (obzor redaktsii i teksty)*. St. Petersburg, 1915.

Ševčenko, Ihor, "The Decline of Byzantium Seen Through the Eyes of its Intellectuals," *Dumbarton Oaks Papers*, XV (1961), pp. 167–186.

_____, "Muscovy's View of Kazan: Two Views Reconciled," *Slavic Review*, XXVI:4 (December, 1967), pp. 541–547.

Shakhmatov, M. V., "Otnoshenie drevne–russkikh knizhnikov k tataram," *Trudy IV S″ezd Russkikh Akademicheskikh Organizatsii za granitsi v Belgrade 16–23 Sent. 1928*, ch. I (Belgrade, 1929), pp. 165–173.

Shapiro, A. L., *Russkaia istoriografiia perioda imperializma. Kurs lektsii*, Leningrad, 1962.

Sinor, Denis, "The Barbarians," *Diogenes*, 18 (1957), pp. 47–60.

Soloviev, S. M., *Istoriia Rossii s drevneishikh vremen*, 15 vv. Moscow, 1963.

Spuler, Berthold, *Die Goldene Horde. Die Mongolen in Russland*, 2nd exp. ed., Wiesbaden, 1965.

Stökl, Gunther, "Kanzler und Mitropolit," *Studien zur Geschichte Osteuropas*, Teil III (Wiener Archiv für Geschichte des Slaventums und Osteuropas. Graz–Cologne, 1966), pp. 150–175.

Sverdlov, M. B., "K voprosu o letopisnykh istochnikakh 'Povesti o bitve na Kalke,'" *Vestnik Leningradskogo Universiteta*, #2, seriia istorii, iazyka i literatury, vyp. I (1963), pp. 139–144.

Szamuely, Tibor, *The Russian Tradition*, New York, 1975.

Szczesniak, B., "A Note on the Character of the Tartar Impact upon the Russian State and Church," *Études Slaves et Est-Européens*, 17 (1972), pp.

230 BIBLIOGRAPHY

92-98.

Tatishchev, V. N., *Istoriia Rossiiskaia*, 7 vv., Moscow-Leningrad, 1962-1968.

Tikhomirov, M. N., gl. 20, "Bor'ba 'menskikh' i 'viatshikh' liudei v Novgorode serediny XIII v.," in his *Krest'ianskie i gorodskie vosstaniia na Rusi XI-XIII vv.* (Moscow, 1955), pp. 265-274.

———, "Bor'ba russkogo naroda s mongolo-tatarskimi zavoevateliami. Dmitrii Donskoi," in his *Drevniaia Rus'* (Moscow, 1975), pp. 381-389.

———, "Maloizvestnye letopisnye pamiatniki," *Istoricheskii arkhiv*, VII (1951), pp. 207-253.

———, "Vossozdanie russkoi pis'mennoi traditsii v pervye desiatiletiia Tatarskogo iga," *Vestnik istorii mirovoi kul'tury*, 1957, #3, pp. 3-13.

Troitskaia letopis'. Rekonstruktsiia teksta, ed. M. D. Priselkov, Moscow-Leningrad, 1950.

Usmanov, A. A., "Ofitsial'nye akty khanstv Vostochnoi Evropy XIV-XVI vv. i ikh izuchenie," *Arkheograficheskii ezhegodnik za 1974* (1975), pp. 117-135.

Ustiuzhskii letopisnyi svod (Arkhangelogorodskii letopisets), ed. K. N. Serbina, Moscow-Leningrad, 1950.

Vel'iaminov-Zernov, V. V., *Issledovaniia o Kasimovskikh tsariakh i tsarevichakh*, 4 vv., Trudy Vostochnago otdeleniia Russkago arkheologicheskago obshchestva, 9-12, St. Petersburg, 1863-1887.

Vernadskii, Georgii, "Dva podviga sv. Aleksandra Nevskogo," *Evraziiskii vremennik*, IV (1925), pp. 318-337.

———, "K voprosu o veroispovedaniiakh mongol'skikh poslov 1223 g.," *Seminarium Kondakovianum*, 3 (1929), pp. 145-148.

(Vernadsky, George), *The Mongols and Russia* (= v. 3, A History of Russia), New Haven, 1959.

Veselovskii, N. I., "Khan iz temnikov Zolotoi Ordy Nogai i ego vremia," *Zapiski Rossiiskoi Akademii Nauk, po otdeleniiu istoricheskikh nauk i filologii*, seriia VIII, t. XIII, #6 (Petrograd, 1922), pp. 1-58.

———, "Kulilovskaia bitva (po povodu ee piatisotletiia)," *Drevniaia i Novaia Rossiia*, XVIII (sentiabr', 1880), pp. 5-23.

———, "O religii tatar po russkim letopisiam," *Zhurnal Ministerstva Narodnago Prosveshcheniia*, t. 64 (1916), pp. 81-101.

———, "Tatarskoe vliianie na posol'skii tseremonial v moskovskii period russkoi istorii," *Otchet Sv. Peterburgskago Universiteta za 1910*, pp. 1-19, and separate publication, St. Petersburg, 1911.

Veselovskii, S. V., *Issledovaniia po istorii klassa sluzhilykh zemlevladel'tsev*, Moscow, 1969.

Vodoff, W., "Quand a put être composé le Panygirique du grand-prince Dmitrii Ivanovich, tsar' russe?" *Canadian-American Slavic Studies*, 13:1-2 (1979), pp. 82-101.

———, "Remarques sur la valeur de terme tsar' appliqué aux princes russes avant le mileux du XVe siecle," *Oxford Slavonic Papers*, 11 (1978), pp. 1-41.

Vodovozov, N. V., *Istoriia drevnei russkoi literatury*, Moscow, 1962.

———, "Povest' o bitve na reke Kalke," *Uchenye zapiski Mosk. gorod. ped. inst. im. V. P. Potemkina*, t. 67, kafedra rus. lit., vyp. 6, 1957, pp. 3-17.

———, "Povest' o razorenii Riazani Batyem," *Uchenye zapiski Mosk. gorod. ped. inst. im. V. P. Potemkina*, t. 67, kafedra rus. lit., vyp. 6, 1957, pp. 21-45.

Voegelin, E., "The Mongol Orders of Submission to European Powers, 1245–1255," *Byzantion*, 15 (1941), 378–413.

Voinskie povesti drevnei Rusi, ed. V. P. Adrianova–Peretts, Moscow–Leningrad, 1949.

Vryonis, Speros, Jr., "The Byzantine Legacy and Ottoman Forms," *Dumbarton Oaks Papers*, 23–24 (1969–1970), pp. 253–308.

_____, "Byzantium and Islam, Seventh–Seventeenth Centuries," *East European Quarterly*, II (1968), pp. 205–240.

Wittogel, Karl A., *Oriental Despotism. A Comparative Study of Total Power*, New Haven, 1957.

_____, "Russia and the East: A Comparison and Contrast," and "Reply," *Slavic Review*, XXIII:4 (December, 1963), pp. 627–643, 656–662.

Zakirov, Salikh, *Diplomaticheskie otnosheniia Zolotoi Ordy s Egiptom (XIII–XIV vv.)*, Moscow, 1966.

Zatko, James, "The Union of Suzdal, 1222–1252," *Journal of Ecclesiastical History*, 8 (1957), pp. 33–52.

Ziborov, V. K., "Khronograficheskii vid Pechatnogo varianta Osnovnoi redaktsii Skazaniia o Mamaevom poboishche," *Trudy otdela drevnerusskoi literatury*, XXXIV (1979), pp. 240–242.

Zimin, A. A., "Pesnia o Shchelkane i vozniknovenie zhanra istoricheskoi pesni," *Istoriia SSSR*, 1963, #3, pp. 98–110.

_____, "Trudyne voprosy metodiki istochnikovedeniia Drevnei Rusi," in *Istochnikovedenie. Teoreticheskie i metodicheskie problemy* (Moscow, 1969), pp. 427–449.

Zubkov, V., *Bitva na Vozhe*, Riazan', 1966.

OTHER SLAVICA BOOKS

American Contributions to the Eighth International Congress of Slavists (Zagreb and Ljubljana, Sept. 3-9, 1978), *Vol 1: Linguistics and Poetics,* ed. by Henrik Birnbaum, 1978; *Vol. 2: Literature,* ed. by Victor Terras, 1978

American Contributions to the Ninth International Congress of Slavists (Kiev 1983) *Vol. 1: Linguistics,* ed. by Michael S. Flier, 1983; *Vol. 2: Literature, Poetics, History,* ed. by Paul Debreczeny, 1983

Patricia M. Arant: *Russian for Reading,* 1981

Howard I. Aronson: *Georgian: A Reading Grammar,* 1982

James E. Augerot and Florin D. Popescu: *Modern Romanian,* 1983

John D. Basil: *The Mensheviks in the Revolution of 1917,* 1984

Henrik Birnbaum: *Lord Novgorod the Great   Essays in the History and Culture of a Medieval City-State   Part One: The Historical Background,* 1981

Henrik Birnbaum & Thomas Eekman, eds.: *Fiction and Drama in Eastern and Southeastern Europe: Evolution and Experiment in the Postwar Period,* 1980

Henrik Birnbaum and Peter T. Merrill: *Recent Advances in the Reconstruction of Common Slavic (1971-1982),* 1985

Karen L. Black, ed.: *A Biobibliographical Handbook of Bulgarian Authors,* 1982

Marianna Bogojavlensky: *Russian Review Grammar,* 1982

Rodica C. Boţoman, Donald E. Corbin, E. Garrison Walters: *Îmi Place Limba Română/A Romanian Reader,* 1982

Gary L. Browning: *Workbook to Russian Root List,* 1985

Catherine V. Chvany and Richard D. Brecht, eds.: *Morphosyntax in Slavic,* 1980

Jozef Cíger-Hronský: *Jozef Mak* (a novel), translated from Slovak by Andrew Cincura, Afterword by Peter Petro, 1985

Frederick Columbus: *Introductory Workbook in Historical Phonology,* 1974

Gary Cox: *Tyrant and Victim in Dostoevsky,* 1984

R. G. A. de Bray: *Guide to the South Slavonic Languages (Guide to the Slavonic Languages, Third Edition, Revised and Expanded, Part 1),* 1980

R. G. A. de Bray: *Guide to the West Slavonic Languages (Guide to the Slavonic Languages, Third Edition, Revised and Expanded, Part 2),* 1980

OTHER SLAVICA BOOKS

R. G. A. de Bray: *Guide to the East Slavonic Languages (Guide to the Slavonic Languages, Third Edition, Revised and Expanded, Part 3)*, 1980

Bruce L. Derwing and Tom M. S. Priestly: *Reading Rules for Russian: A Systematic Approach to Russian Spelling and Pronunciation, with Notes on Dialectal and Stylistic Variation*, 1980

Dorothy Disterheft: *The Syntactic Development of the Infinitive in Indo-European*, 1980

Thomas Eekman and Dean S. Worth, eds.: *Russian Poetics* Proceedings of the International Coloquium at UCLA, September 22-26, 1975, 1983

James Elliott: *Russian for Trade Negotiations with the USSR*, 1981

Michael S. Flier and Richard D. Brecht, eds.: *Issues in Russian Morphosyntax*, 1985

Michael S. Flier and Alan Timberlake, eds.: *The Scope of Slavic Aspect*, 1986

John M. Foley, ed.: *Oral Traditional Literature A Festschrift for Albert Bates Lord*, 1981

Diana Greene: *Insidious Intent: An Interpretation of Fedor Sologub's The Petty Demon*, 1986

Charles E. Gribble, ed.: *Medieval Slavic Texts, Vol. 1, Old and Middle Russian Texts*, 1973

Charles E. Gribble: *Russian Root List with a Sketch of Word Formation, Second Edition*, 1982

Charles E. Gribble: *A Short Dictionary of 18th-Century Russian/Словарик Русского Языка 18-го Века*, 1976

Charles E. Gribble, ed.: *Studies Presented to Professor Roman Jakobson by His Students*, 1968

George J. Gutsche and Lauren G. Leighton, eds.: *New Perspectives on Nineteenth-Century Russian Prose*, 1982

Morris Halle, ed.: *Roman Jakobson: What He Taught Us*, 1983

William S. Hamilton: *Introduction to Russian Phonology and Word Structure*, 1980

Pierre R. Hart: *G. R. Derzhavin: A Poet's Progress*, 1978

Michael Heim: *Contemporary Czech*, 1982

Michael Heim, Zlata Meyerstein, and Dean Worth: *Readings in Czech*, 1985

M. Hubenova & others: *A Course in Modern Bulgarian, Vols. 1 and 2*, 1983

Martin E. Huld: *Basic Albanian Etymologies*, 1984

OTHER SLAVICA BOOKS

Roman Jakobson, with the assistance of Kathy Santilli: *Brain and Language Cerebral Hemispheres and Linguistic Structure in Mutual Light*, 1980

Donald K. Jarvis and Elena D. Lifshitz: *Viewpoints: A Listening and Conversation Course in Russian, Third Edition*, 1985; plus *Instructor's Manual*

Leslie A. Johnson: *The Experience of Time in Crime and Punishment*, 1985

Raina Katzarova-Kukudova and Kiril Djenev: *Bulgarian Folk Dances*, 1976

Emily R. Klenin: *Animacy in Russian: A New Interpretation*, 1983

Andrej Kodjak, Krystyna Pomorska, and Kiril Taranovsky, eds.: *Alexander Puškin Symposium II*, 1980

Andrej Kodjak, Krystyna Pomorska, Stephen Rudy, eds.: *Myth in Literature*, 1985

Andrej Kodjak: *Pushkin's I. P. Belkin*, 1979

Andrej Kodjak, Michael J. Connolly, Krystyna Pomorska, eds.: *Structural Analysis of Narrative Texts (Conference Papers)*, 1980

Demetrius J. Koubourlis, ed.: *Topics in Slavic Phonology*, 1974

Richard L. Leed, Alexander D. Nakhimovsky, and Alice S. Nakhimovsky: *Beginning Russian, Vol. 1*, 1981; *Vol. 2*, 1982; plus a Teacher's Manual

Edgar H. Lehrman: *A Handbook to Eighty-Six of Chekhov's Stories in Russian*, 1985

Lauren Leighton, ed.: *Studies in Honor of Xenia Gąsiorowska*, 1983

Rado L. Lencek: *The Structure and History of the Slovene Language*, 1982

Jules F. Levin and Peter D. Haikalis, with Anatole A. Forostenko: *Reading Modern Russian*, 1979

Maurice I. Levin: *Russian Declension and Conjugation: A Structural Description with Exercises*, 1978

Alexander Lipson: *A Russian Course, Parts 1, 2, and 3*, 1981; *Teacher's Manual* by Stephen J. Molinsky, 1981

Yvonne R. Lockwood: *Text and Context Folksong in a Bosnian Muslim Village*, 1983

Sophia Lubensky & Donald K. Jarvis, eds.: *Teaching, Learning, Acquiring Russian*, 1984

Horace G. Lunt: *Fundamentals of Russian*, 1982

Paul Macura: *Russian-English Botanical Dictionary*, 1982

Thomas G. Magner, ed.: *Slavic Linguistics and Language Teaching*, 1976

OTHER SLAVICA BOOKS

Vladimir Markov and Dean S. Worth, eds.: *From Los Angeles to Kiev Papers on the Occasion of the Ninth International Congress of Slavists*, 1983

Mateja Matejić and Dragan Milivojević: *An Anthology of Medieval Serbian Literature in English*, 1978

Peter J. Mayo: *The Morphology of Aspect in Seventeenth-Century Russian (Based on Texts of the Smutnoe Vremja)*, 1985

Vasa D. Mihailovich and Mateja Matejic: *A Comprehensive Bibliography of Yugoslav Literature in English, 1593-1980*, 1984

Edward Możejko: *Yordan Yovkov*, 1984

Alexander D. Nakhimovsky and Richard L. Leed: *Advanced Russian*, 1980

The Comprehensive Russian Grammar of A. A. Barsov/ Обстоятельная грамматика А. А. Барсова, Critical Edition by Lawrence W. Newman, 1980

Felix J. Oinas: *Essays on Russian Folklore and Mythology*, 1985

Hongor Oulanoff: *The Prose Fiction of Veniamin Kaverin*, 1976

Slava Paperno, Alexander D. Nakhimovsky, Alice S. Nakhimovsky, and Richard L. Leed: *Intermediate Russian: The Twelve Chairs*, 1985

Papers for the V. Congress of Southeast European Studies (Belgrade, September 1984), ed. by Kot K. Shangriladze, 1984

Ruth L. Pearce: *Russian For Expository Prose, Vol. 1 Introductory Course*, 1983; *Vol. 2 Advanced Course*, 1983

Gerald Pirog: *Aleksandr Blok's* Итальянские Стихи *Confrontation and Disillusionment*, 1983

Stanley J. Rabinowitz: *Sologub's Literary Children: Keys to a Symbolist's Prose*, 1980

Gilbert C. Rappaport: *Grammatical Function and Syntactic Structure: The Adverbial Participle of Russian*, 1984

Lester A. Rice: *Hungarian Morphological Irregularities*, 1970

David F. Robinson: *Lithuanian Reverse Dictionary*, 1976

Robert A. Rothstein and Halina Rothstein: *Polish Scholarly Prose A Humanities and Social Sciences Reader*, 1981

Don K. Rowney & G. Edward Orchard, eds.: *Russian and Slavic History*, 1977

Catherine Rudin: *Aspects of Bulgarian Syntax: Complementizers and WH Constructions, 1986*

Ernest A. Scatton: *Bulgarian Phonology*, 1975 (reprint: 1983)

Ernest A. Scatton: *A Reference Grammar of Modern Bulgarian*, 1984

OTHER SLAVICA BOOKS

William R. Schmalstieg: *Introduction to Old Church Slavic, second edition, revised and expanded,* 1983

R. D. Schupbach: *Lexical Specialization in Russian,* 1984

Peter Seyffert: *Soviet Literary Structuralism: Background Debate Issues,* 1985

Michael Shapiro: *Aspects of Russian Morphology, A Semiotic Investigation,* 1969

J. Thomas Shaw: *Pushkin A Concordance to the Poetry,* 1985

Theofanis G. Stavrou and Peter R. Weisensel: *Russian Travelers to the Christian East from the Twelfth to the Twentieth Century,* 1985

Gerald Stone and Dean S. Worth, eds.: *The Formation of the Slavonic Literary Languages, Proceedings of a Conference Held in Memory of Robert Auty and Anne Pennington at Oxford 6-11 July 1981,* 1985

Roland Sussex and J. C. Eade, eds.: *Culture and Nationalism in Nineteenth-Century Eastern Europe,* 1985

Oscar E. Swan: *First Year Polish, second edition, revised and expanded,* 1983

Charles E. Townsend: *Continuing With Russian,* 1981

Charles E. Townsend: *Czech Through Russian,* 1981

Charles E. Townsend: *The Memoirs of Princess Natal'ja Borisovna Dolgorukaja,* 1977

Charles E. Townsend: *Russian Word Formation, corrected reprint,* 1975 (1980)

Walter N. Vickery, ed.: *Aleksandr Blok Centennial Conference,* 1984

Daniel C. Waugh, ed. *Essays in Honor of A. A. Zimin,* 1985

Daniel C. Waugh: *The Great Turkes Defiance On the History of the Apocryphal Correspondence of the Ottoman Sultan in its Muscovite and Russian Variants,* 1978

Susan Wobst: *Russian Readings and Grammatical Terminology,* 1978

James B. Woodward: *The Symbolic Art of Gogol: Essays on His Short Fiction,* 1982

Dean S. Worth: *Origins of Russian Grammar Notes on the state of Russian philology before the advent of printed grammars,* 1983

JOURNALS:

Folia Slavica
International Journal of Slavic Linguistics and Poetics
Oral Tradition